PRACTICAL DOOMSDAY

PRACTICAL DOOMSDAY

A User's Guide to the End of the World

by Michal Zalewski

no starch press

San Francisco

Printed in the United States of America

First printing

25 24 23 22 21   1 2 3 4 5 6 7 8 9

ISBN-13: 978-1-7185-0212-3 (print)
ISBN-13: 978-1-7185-0213-0 (ebook)

Publisher: William Pollock
Production Manager: Rachel Monaghan
Production Editors: Hilary Mansfield and Rachel Monaghan
Developmental Editor: Nathan Heidelberger
Cover Illustrator: Rick Reese
Interior Design: Octopod Studios
Copyeditor: Sharon Wilkey
Compositor: Happenstance Type-O-Rama
Proofreader: James M. Fraleigh
Indexer: Beth Nauman-Montana

For information on book distributors or translations, please contact No Starch Press, Inc. directly:
No Starch Press, Inc.
245 8th Street, San Francisco, CA 94103
phone: 1.415.863.9900; info@nostarch.com
www.nostarch.com

Library of Congress Cataloging-in-Publication Data

Library of Congress Cataloging-in-Publication Data
Names: Zalewski, Michal, author.
Title: Practical doomsday : a user's guide to the end of the world /
   Michal Zalewski.
Description: San Francisco : No Starch Press, [2022] | Includes
   bibliographical references and index. |
Identifiers: LCCN 2021042681 (print) | LCCN 2021042682 (ebook) | ISBN
   9781718502123 (paperback) | ISBN 9781718502130 (ebook)
Subjects: LCSH: Survivalism. | Self-defense.
Classification: LCC GF86 .Z35 2022 (print) | LCC GF86 (ebook) | DDC
   613.6/9--dc23/eng/20210927
LC record available at https://lccn.loc.gov/2021042681
LC ebook record available at https://lccn.loc.gov/2021042682

For my children

About the Author

Michal Zalewski has been actively involved in disaster preparedness for more than a decade, including the publication of a popular 2015 guide titled *Disaster Planning for Regular Folks*. By day, he is an accomplished security researcher who has been working in information security since the late 1990s, helping companies map out and manage risk in the digital domain. He is the author of two classic security books, *The Tangled Web* and *Silence on the Wire* (both No Starch Press), and a recipient of the prestigious Lifetime Achievement Pwnie award. He spent 11 years at Google building its product security program before joining Snap Inc. as a VP of Security & Privacy Engineering. Zalewski grew up in Poland under communist rule, lived through the fall of the Soviet Bloc, and moved to the United States in 2001.

BRIEF CONTENTS

CONTENTS IN DETAIL

PART II: THE PREPARED LIFESTYLE   45

5
MIND OVER MATTER   47

6
BUILDING A RAINY-DAY FUND   49

7
SAFEGUARDING YOUR SAVINGS   57

8
ENGINEERING A DOOMSDAY-PROOF CAREER   91

9
STAYING ALIVE   95

10
PROTECTING ONESELF IN THE DIGITAL AND PHYSICAL REALM 105

11
GETTING IN SHAPE 115

12
BUILDING A COMMUNITY 119

13
HATCHING A PLAN 121

PART III: THE ESSENTIALS 127

14
THE DISCREET CHARM OF THE BULLETPROOF VEST 129

15
WATER 131

27
UNDERSTANDING FIREARMS 211

PREFACE

This isn't my first book, but it's by far my most unusual. For one, I don't fit
the typical profile for the disaster preparedness genre. I'm not a grizzled
ex-military survivalist, nor a peddler of gold bullion, nor a doomsday prog-
nosticator convinced that the world around us is going to hell. Nothing of
the sort: I'm an unassuming, city-raised computer nerd.

In a way, the book in front of you is simply a product of circumstance.
I grew up in communist Poland, a once-proud nation razed to the ground
in the final days of World War II, then subjugated by Stalin and unceremoniously subsumed into the Soviet Bloc. I remember childhood tales of distant
relatives vanishing without a trace, and I recall long lines and ration cards
for basic necessities like sugar and soap. Later, when I came to the United
States, I lived through the dot-com crash of the early 2000s, and then through
the housing crisis of 2007 to 2009. I watched friends go from earning cozy
six-figure salaries to having their cars and homes repossessed. I kept telling
myself this would never happen to me—all the way until, through a stroke
of bad luck, I almost ended up on the street.

In the end, my fascination with emergency preparedness isn't rooted in
a mean militaristic streak or a bleak outlook on life; it stems from a simple
realization that disasters aren't rare today, just as they weren't rare in days
gone by. We all have friends or relatives who have experienced financial
hardships or had to escape wildfires, earthquakes, hurricanes, or floods—
but we invariably imagine ourselves safe from such calamities. Moments
later, we open history books and read about thousands of years of brutal

conflict, conquest, plague, and war, with only fleeting decades of prosperity and calm in between. We know about all this, and yet we convince ourselves that nothing of the sort could ever happen again—not here, not now, not to us.

Still, the goal of this book isn't to convince you that the end is nigh and let that thought consume your life. On the contrary, I want to reclaim the concept of prepping from the hands of the bunker-dwelling prophets of doom. Prepping shouldn't be about expecting the apocalypse; it should be about enjoying life to the fullest without having to worry about what's in the news. Such is the power of having a solid and well-reasoned backup plan.

Another way in which this book differs from others is that from the beginning of the project, I wanted to teach a thought process, rather than write down a rigid set of axioms, a list of investments to make, or a collection of items to buy. We all come from different backgrounds and have different life goals; it follows that there's no one solution that fits all. The future is unknowable too, so not every approach that sounds good on paper is guaranteed to pay off down the line. The ability to reason through unforeseen problems can be worth more than even the most remarkable stash of survival gear.

Ultimately, my goal is to equip readers with a healthy mix of data, opinions, and interesting anecdotes. Far from being gospel, the book is merely a starting point for you to conduct your own personally relevant research. This, in turn, should help you make your own decisions that not only prepare you for potential adversities that might await in your life—but more important, help you sleep well at night when everybody else is worried sick.

PART I

THINKING ABOUT RISK

Learning from the past, reasoning about the future, and making sense of predictions in an ever-changing world

1

A METHOD TO THE MADNESS

We seem to be wired to think about risk in a particular way: we instinctively zero in on dangers that are unusual or immediate, while paying much less attention to hazards that unfold more slowly or in a more familiar way.

To give just one example, American public discourse—and our personal anxieties—tend to dwell on the threat of terrorism. The data on this particular risk is somewhat elusive, but by most estimates, fewer than 50 people are killed in terrorist incidents on American soil in a typical year.[1] In contrast, approximately 65,000 annual deaths occur in the United States from unintentional poisonings, about 40,000 from falls, and roughly 3,500 from drownings.[2] In that sense, ladders, swimming pools, and over-the-counter pain medication are far more insidious foes than armed extremists, yet we rarely give these risks any thought.

This emphasis on the extreme is often derided as a harmful fallacy; for example, in a 2007 essay for *Wired*, noted security and privacy commentator Bruce Schneier blamed humankind's sloppy risk management habits on the existence of an inherent tension between our primal instincts—supposedly housed in a tiny brain structure called the amygdala—and the rational thought processes of the conscious mind.[3] I'm unpersuaded.

A more purposeful explanation is that the everyday risks of ladders and swimming pools have been with us for a long time and almost certainly represent a long-settled, implicit trade-off between safety, liberty, and utility; there's little to be gained by revisiting this subject over and over again. In contrast, we have a continued survival imperative to respond to unfamiliar threats in an immediate and forceful way, because the price of a measured reaction can be too high. To put it plainly, a bear in your tent requires action before we can take a vote at the next meeting of the Committee on the Problem of Bears in Tents. In that sense, far from being a cognitive defect or an evolutionary dead end, I suspect the way we think about risk may be an underappreciated but eminently rational optimization that reduces the cognitive burden of staying alive—and allows us to function in complex societies.

Whatever the utility of this heuristic in everyday life, it has one undeniable failure mode: when tasked with analyzing very distant threats, the pursuit of novelty combined with the dearth of personal experiences pushes us toward the plots of the dramatic, action-packed novels we read, the films we watch, and the computer games we play. In the context of emergency preparedness, this can have us focusing on scenarios that are not merely rare, but might not even be real.

And so, to help with the task of sketching out a coherent and cost-effective preparedness strategy, the first part of this book outlines a handful of analytical tools for mapping out the unknown—and then robustly prioritizing the concerns.

A Method for Reducing Complexity

Any good story about the future is obliged to establish a link to the present through a sequence of plausible causative events. A daydream about immense wealth must begin with winning the lottery or making some other fortuitous bet; a nightmare about financial ruin must have a bitter divorce or a business dispute at its root. Whatever the scenario, our desire to know the cause is so strong that any tale lacking this component is nearly impossible to engage with. Even in time-travel fiction, if normal causality falls apart, the author must necessarily replace it with a new set of rules for us to follow along the way.

But what works for storytelling can be an impediment for holistically assessing risk. There are countless ways to lose a job or be saddled with debilitating debt, for example; trying to enumerate them all is a Sisyphean and profoundly demoralizing task. For this reason, I find it more useful to focus on the outcomes, not on the causes of events. For the most part, it doesn't matter how you could end up in a financially precarious spot. Suffice to say, it's a reasonably common occurrence, and your basic needs will almost always be the same: to put food on the table and pay the bills.

This outcome-centric approach not only cuts down on the mental clutter, but also helps devise solutions that hold water even if the particulars of the scenario change in an unexpected way. Mitigating the risk of a layoff by sucking up to an insufferable boss is a narrowly tailored and uncertain strategy. In contrast, building a robust rainy-day fund can soften the blow of a wide range of adversities—from unemployment, to emergency dental expenses, to having to spend several nights in a hotel because of a natural disaster or in the aftermath of a kitchen fire.

With this method of mapping out risk, the overarching task is to catalog all outcomes of note, without overly concerning oneself with how they might come to be. Unfortunately, while some of the possibilities might be obvious, to channel the former US Secretary of Defense Donald Rumsfeld, there are also unknown unknowns—that is, situations that might be of great significance to emergency planning, but that don't immediately come to mind, not without a specific prompt.

The best way to build a robust taxonomy of unknown unknowns without getting bogged down by long-winded hypotheticals might be to take a critical look at your daily routine, stress-testing every external dependency by asking, "What would happen if I could no longer perform this task the usual way?" Again, the precise reason doesn't matter; for instance, you might be prevented from paying for food with a credit card because of a power outage, identity theft, or an IT problem at the bank. Whatever the reason, the outcome is the same, and the remedy is simple: have several days' worth of cash on hand.

A Model for Quantifying Risk

A catalog of all possible concerning outcomes could easily become overwhelming in itself, and the expense of trying to prevent any and all hardships knows no practical bound. To put such a parade of horribles into perspective, it helps to build a model for evaluating and prioritizing risk. The most fundamental concept of risk management is the examination of the potential impact of an event in tandem with the probability of that outcome coming true. By this criteria, stubbed toes and zombie outbreaks are equally uninteresting. The first one is of little consequence, and the other has nearly zero odds.

Since your resources are limited, another useful dimension to ponder is the minimum cost—in time, effort, and money—of mitigating a concern. To illustrate: more than a million burglaries happen in the United States every year, and the average loss is fairly consequential—just a tad over $2,500.[4] For many people, a burglary would pass the two-variable test outlined before; it's a plausible scenario with a significant impact on one's life. However, most burglaries happen when the occupant is not home, so the only reliable solution may be to install window bars, reinforced doors, and an alarm system. This set of measures may require spending $10,000 and picking a fight with the local homeowners association (HOA). With such a high mitigation cost, perhaps it's reasonable to let this risk slide.

Note my emphasis on the *minimum* cost of mitigation: heed the old saying that an ounce of prevention is worth a pound of cure. For example, car accidents are a major risk, especially for young males. The surest solution might not be to haul an expensive trauma kit in the trunk of the car, but to take a defensive driving course for a modest fee—and make the lesson stick.

When tallying the expenses, it's also good to distinguish between costs that are recoverable and ones that aren't. There's no way to recoup the money spent on window bars if you suddenly need cash to pay for a new roof or cover an unexpected dental bill. In contrast, there's almost no penalty to maintaining a rainy-day fund, as the money can almost always be reallocated to scratch a different itch.

To recap: when prioritizing which outcomes to address, it's best to focus on scenarios that are likely to happen, are potentially ruinous, and can be prevented or contained in a relatively simple way, as shown in this risk-ranking pseudo-formula:

$$\text{risk rank} = \frac{\text{probability of event} \times \text{potential impact}}{\text{minimum non-recoverable cost to mitigate}}$$

Of course, in practice, these variables can't always be quantified with certainty. There's no fixed conversion rate between the expenditure of free time, mental energy, and cash; the probability of some predictions is unknowable or hotly debated; and the worst-case impact of certain types of events has no meaningful upper bound. In other words, this risk-rank formula should not be taken as gospel—but it's a good starting point for rough prioritization and for deciding where to draw the line.

The Challenge of Crony Beliefs

Whenever trying to reason about the future, it's important to put our own assumptions and convictions to the test. A parable I'm fond of perfectly illustrates the pitfalls of blindly sticking to our beliefs.

It goes like this: imagine a company wishing to open an office in a small town run by a corrupt mayor. The mayor offers the executives of the company a simple deal: hire a friend of mine, and I'll make sure all your problems with permits, inspections, and other administrative hurdles disappear. The executives, desperate to enter this market, decide to do what needs to be done. And so, they hire the fellow despite his utter lack of qualifications and skills.

But there's a snag. To other employees and managers who aren't in on the racket, the continued employment of the crony is proof that the company's HR processes aren't up to snuff. They soon band together to develop new, more rigorous standards for hiring and performance management—yet somehow, all they accomplish is making life more miserable for everybody *except* the crony employee. What they miss is obvious to us: the employee is there for a rational reason—it's just not the reason they expect.

In a 2016 essay, author Kevin Simler used this metaphor of corporate life to introduce the concept of what he called *crony beliefs*.[5] He noted that much like the misguided line managers in our story, people instinctively judge beliefs on a one-dimensional scale, essentially placing them somewhere between right and wrong, and expecting any conviction that's proven false to immediately vanish in a puff of cognitive smoke. But to Simler, no biological imperative exists for any of us to hold only true opinions; our belief system, he argues, is far more utilitarian, and other dimensions make convictions desirable (and sincere), even if they don't hold up to scientific scrutiny.

Of course, some beliefs are held for a straightforward reason: because their predictive power helps us make sound decisions in everyday life. A good example is the working understanding of gravity. Its whole purpose is to predict what happens when an item is dropped, so we're eager to routinely test our assumptions and revise them if we notice anything out of whack—such as if we discover that some goods are damaged more easily than we would have guessed. The bottom line is, because any discrepancy between the data and the theory would be counterproductive, we feel no obligation to stick to our guns.

But a second class of convictions—Simler's crony beliefs—also exists and serves a very different purpose: helping people thrive within communities. Such beliefs aren't always about conformity. In some settings, one might be rewarded for taking provocative and contrarian positions to build a reputation as an independent thinker. But self-reinforcing groupthink certainly is a common theme. For example, people may have powerful social incentives to believe that their employer or political party is more virtuous than someone else's, and to explain away any moral lapses within their own group as isolated and honest mistakes, without giving the same benefit of the doubt to the other side.

The point of labeling such convictions as *cronies* is not to assert that the underlying belief is incorrect; rather, it's to say that its primary function is not to help us navigate decisions of immediate consequence. Indeed, crony beliefs routinely deal with topics we have little or no agency over, such as corporate governance or international policy. Whatever the topic, the telltale characteristic of a suspect belief is that on an individual basis, the social consequences of doubting it appear far more severe than the consequences of being objectively wrong.

Crony beliefs make it easy to get swept up by compelling narratives of impending disasters when they align with our view of the world. An instructive tale is the story of the Population Bomb, a doomsday prophecy made in the 1960s by Paul R. Ehrlich, a biologist working at Stanford University. The prediction had its roots in solid science; extrapolating from contemporaneous data and animal models, Ehrlich concluded that the population of the world would continue to grow exponentially. He then looked at the best available estimates of agricultural capacity and the statistics of arable land. After combining the data sets, he noted that we were bound to exceed the world's food production capabilities in a matter of years. He had to sound the alarm: without immediate government intervention to curb fertility, all that awaited our species would be starvation, disease, and war.

Ehrlich's elegant and intuitive prediction gained an immense following among scientists, policy makers, and prominent celebrities of the era. It did so not just because of its scientific merit, but also because it offered something for everybody to like. Many politicians imagined a vast expansion of their powers to engineer a better and more harmonious society. Scientists cheered the prospect of being taken seriously and given a seat at the table, dreaming of an expert-run meritocracy. And for conservationists, the anti-progress overtones of the Population Bomb meshed neatly with their beliefs and boosted their cause. In short, Ehrlich's theory soon had all the hallmarks of a crony belief: a prediction that had its proponents far more invested in perpetuating the idea—and pushing for the associated policy prescriptions—than in validating, correcting, or contesting any of the claims.

But before the movement's more radical ideas could be truly put into motion, something odd started to happen. Fertility rates began to taper off in much of the world, seemingly in response to improved living conditions, reduced infant mortality, and the invention of the birth control pill.[6] Just as perplexingly, the efficiency of agricultural production improved dramatically, making food cheaper and more abundant than ever before—at least in part thanks to technologies such as harvesters, large-scale irrigation systems, modern insecticides and fertilizers, and pest-resistant crops.

None of this new data mattered to the proponents of the Population Bomb. The prediction was correct; it's just that the date must have been a bit off. Doomsday was postponed until the late 1980s, then the 1990s, then the 2000s, The prophecy has a small but dedicated following to this day, an undead creature that's entirely unfalsifiable and forever imminent.

Meanwhile, we did learn something from one authoritarian country that embraced Ehrlich's call to action: the sheer scale and horror of the resulting humanitarian abuses in China is slowly coming to light. In *One Child Nation*, a 2019 documentary produced by Amazon Studios, two Chinese-born filmmakers offer a sobering look at forced sterilizations, abortions, and widespread infanticide instigated by the Communist Party of China between 1979 and 2015.

The story of the Population Bomb is recounted in *The Bet*, a captivating book written by Paul Sabin, a historian working at Yale University (Yale University Press, 2013). I bring it up not as a backhanded attempt to dismiss contemporary environmental worries, but to offer an important case study in how easy it is to mistake possibility for certainty, to get so engrossed in a movement as to lose the ability to evaluate new evidence, and to be blind to solutions that don't align with one's political views.

Our popular culture is replete with doomsday predictions that extrapolate from worst-case assumptions and take a uniquely dim view of our species' ability to adapt and overcome. Today's mainstream prophecies deal with cutting-edge particle physics, chain-reaction environmental collapses, godlike computer hackers, vast government conspiracies, and secret messages hidden in pop songs. We can't really rule that stuff out—but when in doubt, it's best to simplify. Historical data suggests that there's a lot more merit in worrying about falling off a ladder or getting hit by a car than any of the more engrossing scenarios we see in the movies or read about on the internet.

2

THE SPECTER OF HUMDRUM CALAMITIES

The events most likely to upend our lives aren't of the kind that occupy the headlines and send ripples throughout the world; most of the time, they don't even warrant a passing mention on the local news. Quiet and intimate hardships, from losing a job to getting injured in a car wreck, profoundly affect millions of people every year, yet they're almost never given any serious consideration in publications dealing with disaster preparedness.

This is unfortunate, and not just as a matter of probabilities. Such uninspiring but familiar events, recounted firsthand by our friends and relatives, provide the most grounded and tractable way to bootstrap a personal response-and-recovery plan. Even the most rigorous strategy preoccupied with supervolcanoes and cosmic weather is, at the end of the day, just a work of speculative fiction. In contrast, a plan that draws lessons from the plight of a coworker impacted by layoffs is quite likely to survive a collision with reality.

It's true that many of these everyday disasters aren't a matter of life and death. Most car accidents are survivable, and most folks who experience unemployment eventually turn their life around. However, recovery can involve months or years of stress, pain, and regret. A strategy that minimizes the likelihood of such outcomes—or improves the outlook when they do occur—is worth its weight in gold.

With this in mind, it feels prudent to kick off a more in-depth discussion of specific hazards with a stroll through the catalog of such humdrum emergencies that seldom keep us up at night until they actually come to pass. For the time being, I'll try not to dwell on precise mitigation strategies or response plans; such a discussion will be much easier once we have a definite list of problems to tackle, and when all the commonalities snap into view.

Unemployment and Insolvency

The specter of financial ruin is perhaps the most universal fear in all developed nations around the globe. That's because money is, in turn, the most universal way to solve other problems in life.

There are countless ways to end up in financial trouble. In the United States, a major cause is medical debt,[1] although this point is often overstated in political discourse: medical bills are a common compounding factor, but are usually not the sole cause and often not the dominant one.[2] In any case, in the United States and everywhere else, bitter divorces, legal disputes, and failed investments contribute to a good portion of the misery too.

In all the countries I've visited or lived in, one thing is constant: we have normalized heavy, lifelong debt burdens—be it mortgages, student loans, or credit card balances that we can't seem to be able to repay. Without straying into social commentary, this means that even a brief bout of unemployment—perhaps as short as two to three months—can be enough to saddle a typical middle-class family with unpaid bills. In a highly cited 2015 survey published by Bankrate.com, about two-thirds of Americans indicated they didn't have enough savings to cope with an unexpected expense of $1,000.[3]

Although the findings of that study are also sometimes overstated by commentators, the underlying problem is real. During the 2007–2009 housing crisis (a comparatively mild recession next to some of the earlier crashes of the 20th century), the number of foreclosures in the United States exceeded 1.6 million,[4] with a peak at more than five times the normal annual rate. Part of this involved investors or house flippers purposefully walking away from underwater nonrecourse mortgages, but part involved genuine tears and pain.

When it comes to the ability to withstand downturns, high income is not as much of a benefit as many expect. Countless Silicon Valley tech workers collect cozy salaries of $150,000 or more but still live paycheck to paycheck. When the job market dried up overnight in 2007, the number of evictions and foreclosures looked pretty gloomy down here too.

Higher cost of living played a role, but so did the phenomenon of life-style creep: the tendency to scale up small, everyday purchasing decisions in proportion to one's income. For Silicon Valley techies, it usually wasn't the Lamborghini or the McMansion that did them in. It was the hundreds of small purchases where they reached for the upper shelf in the grocery store, indulged in geeky hobbies, and upgraded their phones and laptops every year. The fall from grace proved to be very sudden too. The unemployment benefits might've been just enough to pay the bills of a frugal low-income family, but fell well short of the mortgage payments on a mid-range San Francisco Bay Area home.

It's also important to remember that not all economic hardships start and end with money. Tech and many other white-collar professions employ many foreign nationals who must navigate labyrinthine bureaucracies every time they want to change employers, and who can't stay unemployed for more than a couple of weeks without violating conditions of their visa, risking dire consequences down the road. To add insult to injury, the immigration landscape can change overnight. In the wake of the September 11 attacks in the United States, the processing of routine adjustment-of-status applications ground to a halt and didn't go back to normal for almost two years.

Loss of Shelter

A roof over one's head is one of the most essential needs, and of all the bare necessities, it's usually the hardest and most expensive to replace. Financial hardships aside, about the most common way to lose shelter is a house fire, with around 350,000 instances recorded every year in the United States.[5] The bulk of such fires start in the kitchen, where unattended cooking frequently goes awry when we're in another room entertaining guests or browsing the internet. Other common causes include dryer vents that get clogged with lint, malfunctioning fireplaces, faulty wiring, and space heaters or candles that tip over. In any case, whether it's fire, flooding, backed-up sewage, or an unhinged landlord, such situations can leave you with nothing but PJs on your back and no obvious place to go.

Home or renter insurance is seen as a way to dispel any worries, but it's important to understand all the carve-outs. Many policies protect you against only specific named perils, and often require you to pay extra to cover the types of events insurers see as more likely in your area. Just as important, insurance claims take time. Although you might be able to get expedient reimbursement for temporary lodging, even in the best case, it may take a month to get the final settlement—and then many months to rebuild.

As with many other risks, a robust financial safety net can take care of many concerns, but so do other, more easily implemented measures, such as being on good terms with family members, friends, or coworkers, and agreeing that you can crash at each other's place in an emergency. Another simple strategy is having some bare necessities—clothing, cash, documents—stowed away at your workplace or another secure location not far from home.

Loss of Basic Utilities or Transportation

Outages are a fact of life. Over 30 million people lose power in the United States in a typical year,[6] with some events dragging on for days or even weeks, depending on the nature of the damage and the priorities of the utility company. The causes are usually not cataclysmic nor particularly sinister; squirrels account for orders of magnitude more power outages than computer hackers do.[7]

In most cases, an outage is more inconvenient than dangerous, but the situation can deteriorate quickly. For example, the loss of water pressure might make it impossible to flush the toilet, while the loss of heating in the middle of a winter storm—or of air conditioning in the midst of a heatwave—can be a deadly threat to the vulnerable and the unprepared. Subtle interdependencies need to be kept in mind too; for instance, many gas-fired furnaces and water heaters, and even some gas stoves and gas fireplaces, won't function when the electricity is out. Similarly, for rural folks who depend on well water, the loss of electricity means the loss of water pressure after a couple of flushes afforded by the pressure tank.

In practical terms, a day-long outage is far more likely than a week-long one, and a week-long one is far more likely than a month-long event. It pays to structure your analysis accordingly. Figuring out the implications of losing water for three days is more useful than pondering the socioeconomic dynamics of a world forever plunged back into the dark ages.

Beyond the usual meaning of utilities, it's good to consider the risk of disruptions to any other infrastructure we depend on in our daily lives. For some folks, especially those working remotely, the internet may be one such utility. For others, some aspects of the transportation infrastructure may be a choke point. For example, the 2013 Colorado floods took out quite a few small bridges and rural roads. Having a public bridge rebuilt by the county simply takes a long time, but damage to a private car bridge leading to a rural parcel or a subdivision means you may have to pay $50,000 to $100,000 out of pocket—or get used to wading across every time you need to get groceries or go to work.

Unintentional Injury

Accidental injury is an awkward topic to discuss. We almost always think of it as something that happens to others, not to us, usually through some fault of their own. We make exception for the occasional freak accident—a "one-in-a-million" happenstance—but such matters aren't worth dwelling on or worrying about.

The statistics from the US Centers for Disease Control and Prevention (CDC) tell a startlingly different tale: accidental injury is the leading cause of death for people between the ages of 1 and 45—far ahead of cancer, heart disease, gun violence, and many other dangers more firmly rooted in the public consciousness. In total, unintentional injuries account for around 25 million ER visits and 170,000 deaths in the United States every year.[8] Most involve prosaic, everyday activities: overdoses of over-the-counter or prescription medication, falls, cuts, burns, and car accidents.

I suspect an element of survivor bias in the way we reason about injury. Every now and then, we all make a haphazard lane change or climb a rickety ladder or an office chair, and we escape unscathed, so we infer that, on balance, such activities must be safer than they truly are. The perception of risk is probably also skewed by childhood memories, as this is when we suffered most of our falls and other mishaps of this variety. Needless to say, falling when you're 50 pounds and have lightning reflexes is a very different affair compared to falling when you're 180 pounds and no longer have the youthful edge.

More than for many other topics discussed in this chapter, most effectual approaches to managing the risk of unintentional injury involve changing everyday habits rather than trying to respond to a disaster that's already in motion. To illustrate, although there's some merit in having first-aid supplies and knowing how to use them, the most bang for your buck may be in properly securing your ladder before trying to pull that Frisbee off the roof.

Theft, Harassment, and Intentional Harm

Intentional harm is essentially *normal*. According to surveys conducted by a little-known government agency by the name of the Bureau of Justice Statistics, the annual rate of criminal victimization currently hovers a bit under 1 percent a year,[9] which translates to a lifetime probability in the vicinity of 30 to 40 percent.

To be fair, this mathematical approximation doesn't tell the whole story, as it's not a uniformly distributed phenomenon; for one, young men are far more likely to get into an altercation than any other group. It also needs to be said that many incidents are an indignity more than a life-or-death situation—many assaults may amount to being shoved, slapped, spat on, or groped—but in the end, physical violence is far more common than it might seem. And because being assaulted is a dynamic situation that can quickly spiral out of control, well-rehearsed situational awareness and robust de-escalation skills are key to reducing this risk.

Whereas intentional harm is merely a possibility, property crime crosses into the realm of events that, on a lifetime basis, are more likely than not. Annually, property crime affects around 10 percent of all households, spanning anything from porch piracy and minor vandalism all the way to burglaries of cars and homes. For burglaries, the vast majority are of the smash-and-grab variety, with losses averaging a bit over $2,500, as noted in Chapter 1; so, being a victim can be painful but is seldom a life-changing event. That said, many simple strategies can reduce the likelihood or magnitude of loss, starting with remembering to always lock all windows and doors—no matter the vibe of the neighborhood.

Beyond physical violence and property crime, another distinct challenge is harassment. Simply getting into an online argument with a deranged individual can escalate to being doxxed, swatted, or stalked at work. Causes such as bitter breakups or business disputes can lead to similar outcomes.

Reliable statistics on harassment are difficult to come by, in part because of the nebulous nature of the term, encompassing anything from unwelcome criticism to frightening sexual threats. Focusing on just some of the more severe manifestations of this phenomenon, an older 1998 survey conducted by the National Center for Injury Prevention and Control indicated that roughly 8 percent of women and 2 percent of men experienced stalking at some point in their lives.[10] Not all of this can be anticipated or prevented, but a few basic steps—such as carefully managing one's online footprint and removing personal information from major data brokers—can go a long way.

Illness and Death

As with unintentional injury, death is a subject that's all too easy to dismiss. It's distant, unknowable, and feels entirely outside our control. In some respects, this attitude makes sense: we can't predict the day or the method, so worrying about the end has little merit and brings no joy.

At the same time, however, this thinking overlooks an important consideration: the people who depend on us to care and provide for them—be it our minor children, elderly parents, or stay-at-home spouses. In that sense, death planning doesn't have to be about choosing a casket and buying a burial plot; it's more about setting up your finances in a way that doesn't leave your survivors stranded for months.

Ordinarily, when you die, your assets are placed under probate—a court-supervised process of reconciling assets and liabilities and identifying heirs—and remain there until disposed of in accordance with your wishes or the normal operation of law. In some jurisdictions, simple probate cases that involve just your spouse and a modest estate can be wrapped up reasonably quickly, but at other times, the proceedings can take a year or more. Family disputes or mysterious disappearances can make the process drag out even longer.

Many financial advisors would try to sell you on the idea of setting up a living trust, a separate legal entity that holds your assets and disposes of them in a prescribed way in the event of your death. But this is a costly and involved solution that sometimes makes people throw their hands up in the air and give up. Luckily, simpler alternatives—such as having a joint tenant bank account or designating a named beneficiary—can achieve pretty solid results. (We'll cover wills, trusts, and other financial planning topics in Chapters 7 and 13.)

Of course, it's not just about money. For example, it's important to write down your wishes regarding the custody of any minor children. The courts aren't required to listen to you, but they usually do, especially if you make a well-reasoned case. Thinking this through and discussing your ideas with the potential caretakers helps avoid the prospect of having children placed in foster care—or worse yet, with an abusive and dishonest relative.

But Wait, There's More!

The list of disasters named in this chapter is meant as a starting point; it may well be incomplete when you consider your family situation, medical needs, and other circumstances unique to you. For instance, if you provide day-to-day care for a disabled person, any scenario that could jeopardize your ability to visit them, even for a brief while, is worth thinking about. Conversely, if you depend on the care or goodwill of others, anything that gets in the way of this relationship should be discussed in advance, along with any alternative arrangements that could be made.

With all this in mind, now would be a good time to grab a piece of paper or open a blank document and try to jot down some initial notes about the scenarios that don't involve large-scale disasters but could still mess up your life. Instead of relying on TV tropes, make it about you, your family, your relatives, and your career. If you make a list, hang on to it. It's going to be very useful later on.

3

EXPLORING
LARGE-SCALE RISKS

In the previous chapter, we looked at a variety of small-scale events that can upend life in one household without inconveniencing the neighbors next door. A way to deal with such private hardships is the foundation of any solid preparedness plan; that said, consideration should also be given to cyclic, regional disasters that would be sure to get the neighborhood abuzz.

From recessions to earthquakes to once-in-a-lifetime snowstorms or heatwaves, their defining characteristic is that they happen infrequently enough to allow a generation or two to grow up without experiencing that particular event first-hand. At the same time, such disasters are not far-fetched: with a cadence of anywhere from 20 to 100 years, they are common enough to deserve a closer look when evaluating personal risk.

On the surface, the consequences of large-scale calamities don't differ much from what we talked about before: the toolkit for surviving a recession is similar to what may be needed after getting into an argument with a vindictive boss. But the sheer magnitude of widespread disasters can be enough to derail some of the simplest plans. For example, a city-wide water outage can't be dealt with by heading to the local grocery store to pick up a 12-pack of Aquafina, simply because thousands of other residents will beat you to the punch. The recovery from a large-scale event can also be prolonged. It usually doesn't take more than three months to find a new job in a healthy economy, but in the midst of a recession, the search may drag on.

Natural Disasters

Whether it's floods, violent storms, wildfires, earthquakes, mudslides, harsh winters, or drought, no part of the planet is spared the occasional epic mayhem brought on by the forces of nature. Some corners of the world are uniquely famous for a particular flavor of cataclysm: if you're in Hawaii, you're expected to look out for volcanic eruptions, and in California, the specter of earthquakes is supposed to keep you up at night. But it's often the less plausible or forgotten event that hits the hardest. After all, nobody is thinking about the possibility of substantial snow in Los Angeles or a blistering heatwave in Alaska, even though there's fairly recent precedent for both.

As a real-world example that will be familiar to many techies, in earthquake-obsessed California, decades of poor forest management, urban sprawl, and years of drought have conspired to unleash a series of unprecedented and deadly fires since 2015, destroying tens of thousands of homes and displacing hundreds of thousands of people. One particularly infamous cluster of fires in Butte County burned down 18,000 structures in under three weeks.[1] And in Europe, generally reputed to have a mild and uninteresting climate, a freak heatwave in 2003 killed more than 30,000 people,[2] mostly in highly developed and wealthy countries such as France and Spain.

When a disaster strikes, politicians inevitably deflect the blame for the damage or use the event to advance tangentially related goals. Right now, the excuse du jour is climate change—a real phenomenon that's slowly making some regions more prone to weather extremes, but is almost always a misleading explanation for whichever episode of bad weather is currently in the news. Extreme weather has plenty of precedent. Consider the blizzard of 1888 that piled up 50-foot snowdrifts in the Northeast,[3] or the apocalyptic dust storms and heatwaves that kept wiping away crops from Texas to Nebraska throughout much of the 1930s.[4] Or, indeed, the snowfall in Los Angeles and the 100-degree heatwave in Fort Yukon, Alaska—both striking in the first half of the 20th century. The next time it happens, we'll be caught off-guard—but for our shortsightedness, we don't have climate change to blame.

With this in mind, even if you live in a place normally not associated with earthquakes or tornadoes, mapping out and reasoning about potential natural disasters is still a sound plan. When it comes to climate, you should be able to find meteorological records going back at least 100 years, making it easy to look up the extremes of temperature, wind, and precipitation in the region. Most Wikipedia articles about localities include a brief section on climate, and where this section is present, it's a solid starting point.

The records of other natural disasters can be a bit more scattered. Wikipedia is sometimes a good source of research leads, but keyword searches in the digitized archives of local newspapers can often yield better insights. In the United States, it's also good to visit your county's website and look for a regional risk assessment; many local governments prepared such documents in the aftermath of the attacks on September 11. Although little of this work translated into meaningful action in the years that followed, the document—if publicly available —can offer a good synthesis of natural and man-made threats.

The US federal government provides useful resources too. For example, the Federal Emergency Management Agency (FEMA) maintains street-resolution flood-risk maps for most of the country. You can find the maps at *https://msc.fema.gov/portal/home*. Similarly, the US Geological Survey (USGS) provides fairly detailed maps of seismic faults, earthquake probabilities, and soil instability risks for some metro areas. These resources can be explored at *https://www.usgs.gov/natural-hazards/earthquake-hazards/seismic-hazard-maps-and-site-specific-data/*.

The research can be painstaking, and several websites try to condense all this information into neatly color-coded state-level "risk ratings" overlaid on a map. Despite their aesthetic appeal, however, I caution against relying on this information. The mapped data sets are fragmentary, and the thresholds between different shadings on the map can overstate the findings. The distinction between a 9 percent and a 10 percent annual risk of a major earthquake is largely inconsequential, but on a color-coded map, it can be the difference between green and red.

Finally, because of the magnitude of forces involved, the attempts to wrap one's head around natural disasters may seem like a quixotic pursuit. Not so! There's not much you can do if a chasm opens right under your feet, but the disruptive effects of a natural disaster extend far beyond its ground zero—and in this "chaos zone" of tens or hundreds of miles, survival is a tractable task. Simple steps—such as always keeping extra food or water on hand, having a chainsaw to clean up fallen branches, or squirreling away a tarp to protect a damaged roof—can go a long way.

Industrial Accidents

In rural and urban areas alike, heavy industries are never too far away. Whether it's a fire at a chemical plant or the collapse of a tailings dam at an upstream mine, many fairly common types of industrial incidents can force entire towns to stop using tap water or to shelter indoors—sometimes for days.

Occasionally, such accidents can rival the forces of nature in their destructive potential. The nuclear meltdowns at Chernobyl and Fukushima are often thought of as the worst of the worst, but they actually pale in comparison with the track record of more conventional industries. The Bhopal disaster in 1984, involving the release of a volatile isocyanate from a pesticide manufacturing plant in India, caused more than 500,000 serious injuries and killed as many as 20,000 residents.[5] The 1975 Banqiao dam failure in China may have killed more than 200,000—some perishing in the floodwaters, many more dying from the resulting famine and plague when millions of homes were washed away.[6] Accidents involving the storage of nitrates live in infamy too. The explosion of a ship in the port of Texas City, Texas, in 1947 destroyed structures within several miles and injured thousands,[7] while a similar explosion in Beirut in 2020 displaced around 300,000 residents and led to 5,000 injuries plus more than 200 deaths.[8]

Of course, as with natural disasters, the purpose of a preparedness plan isn't to devise an improbable strategy of dodging the fireball from a nearby blast. It's to give ourselves the tools to comfortably shelter in place in the much larger zone of disruption that surrounds the epicenter of the event, or to quickly evacuate from that zone if necessary. What can be tricky, however, is figuring out where that epicenter might be.

The government considers many heavy industries to be an attractive, soft target for terrorists, so officials are hesitant to put a bull's-eye on the map. The markings of many of these facilities are minimal; that said, an extended pan-and-zoom session with Google Maps can turn up many of the distinctive structures, such as building-sized storage tanks, tall chimney stacks, or rectangular wastewater ponds. Once a potential location is found, a bit of additional online sleuthing—or a casual and lawful drive-by—can usually resolve any doubt.

Social Unrest and War

Social unrest is one of the murkiest corners of prepper lore. Many survivalists cower in fear of the marauders who are certain to show up at their doorstep as soon as the grocery shelves are bare. A popular saying attributed to Alfred Henry Lewis, an American journalist living at the turn of the century, is that "there are only nine meals between mankind and anarchy." Another quote favored by survivalist authors, and taken somewhat out of context from the works of Dutch primatologist Frans de Waal, posits that all we have is "a thin veneer hiding an otherwise selfish and brutish nature"— and that this veneer can peel off with ease.

I believe that these maxims paint a uniquely dim view of our species, rooted in personal anxieties more than in solid historical precedent. From the Irish Potato Famine to the tales of survival in war-torn Europe, we have ample evidence that even in the darkest of times, the majority of people would rather suffer and quietly starve than harm a random stranger who did them no wrong.

If there *is* a reason to be fearful, it's not that the world can easily devolve into a grotesque crossover between *The Purge* and *Mad Max*, where neighbors hunt neighbors for sport. It's that when people are angry and desperate, they want someone to blame and lash out against. Historically, this has variously been a neighboring nation, an ethnic or religious minority, the clergy, the rich. Whatever the criterion, the designation has immediately robbed the entire group of their innocence, turning neighbors into perpetrators, into subhumans—into the enemy. This scenario has played out over and over again throughout the ages: in France in the 1790s, in Russia during and after the Bolshevik Revolution, in Hitler's Germany, in Mao's China, in the United States after Pearl Harbor. Each time, it has culminated in the indiscriminate murder, imprisonment, or expropriation of the members of the out-group.

Perhaps all this cruelty is in the rearview mirror. The world today is, in many respects, a more prosperous and peaceful place. But I'm reminded that in the early 1990s, after the fall of the Soviet Union, Francis Fukuyama— a noted political scientist—proclaimed "the end of history." He explained that we had reached "the end-point of mankind's ideological evolution and the universalization of Western liberal democracy as the final form of human government." Fukuyama's prediction was a fashionable thought back then; a bit over 20 years later, very few still agree with his view.

If not persecution, then riots remain a distinct and real risk in many urban and suburban areas around the world. When angry mobs take it to the streets, they seldom target residential areas, but widespread arson and violent crime is not unheard of, sometimes going on for days or weeks.

The Los Angeles riots of 1992 certainly deserve a mention. This startling rampage, triggered by the brutal beating of Rodney King by officers of the Los Angeles Police Department, resulted in about 2,000 injuries, around 4,500 structures being looted, and about 1,000 buildings set ablaze;[9] the scars from the riots pockmarked the city for many years to come. Europe is no stranger to rioting either. A decade of social unrest in France, starting approximately in 2005 and then morphing into an annual tradition of sorts, involved a series of lower-key but longer-running urban clashes with more than 13,000 cars being torched and hundreds of structures damaged or destroyed along the way.[10]

As with industrial and natural disasters, preparing for unrest is best focused not on gearing up to fight with or against the mob. At least from the perspective of self-preservation, the best strategy is simply to stay put. For that reason, in a city convulsed by riots or put under curfew or martial law, having enough supplies to skip several grocery trips will always be helpful. Having a plan to bug out to a safe location until the situation improves is a good backup.

Economic Crises

The condition of the economy has a profound impact on many aspects of our lives beyond the purely financial—from our health, to the quality of our relationships, to the ability to pursue our dreams. It's surprising, then, that we usually settle for kindergarten-grade explanations of many of the fundamental concepts that make the economy tick—say, the nature of money and the mechanisms the government uses to control its supply (topics we'll discuss a bit more in Chapter 7). Heck, we give little thought even to the simpler task of studying past economic patterns to understand what the future might bring.

To give an example, we all know about the Great Depression of the 1930s, but the story we tell is one of politics, not monetary policies. To progressives, it's a tale of the failures of the markets and the power of collective action under the auspices of the New Deal. To conservatives, meanwhile, it's a story of a bureaucrat-engineered collapse culminating with *Wickard v. Filburn*, a landmark Supreme Court case that greatly expanded the reach of the federal government. But both sides spend little time discussing the dynamics of the money supply in that era, or the contents of the balance sheets of multiple large banks that went bankrupt in the run-up to the crash.

The housing crisis of 2007–2009 is another well-remembered instance, and so is its European counterpart—a sovereign debt crisis accompanied by bank closures and limited-scale deposit confiscations in the Eurozone (euphemistically dubbed *bail-ins*).[11] But the analysis of its causes is entirely subservient to the political narrative too. It variously serves as a warning against deregulation or against the unintended consequences of government-subsidized housing loans. In contrast, only hand-wavy explanations are given about the origins and the continued uses of the models that incorrectly estimated the risk of mortgage-backed securities. The story is equally hazy on how the mortgage situation in North America could've led to severe banking crises in, of all places, Greece and Iceland.

What's similarly less known is that many other economic crises happened in the United States between these two big recessions, usually not more than 10 years apart. Take the Savings and Loan Crisis of the 1980s—a profound panic culminating in the collapse of more than 1,000 financial institutions and punctuated by government-imposed "bank holidays," a transparent ruse to prevent people from emptying their accounts.[12] Or look at the year 1979, when poor domestic policy making, coupled with an Islamic revolution in Iran, plunged the United States into a disaster of another sort, causing widespread fuel shortages that stranded motorists across the nation and disrupted the economy for many months.[13] History teaches us that these up and downs occur in a fairly regular cycle. It's reckless to go into another decade without at least considering the possibility of trouble down the road.

Our monetary systems are quite fickle, too, even if the language we use implies otherwise (it's always the prices of housing or gasoline that are moving up or down, never the purchasing power of the cash we hold). I spent my childhood in a country that went through a period of staggering hyperinflation, so I kept asking myself how unique this experience was—and when I decided to do the research, I was shocked by how little information is available on the prevalence of such fundamental and destabilizing events.

Many folks who paid attention in history class are familiar with hyperinflation in the Weimar Republic in the run-up to World War II. Some also remember the trillion-dollar banknotes from Zimbabwe in the 2000s, sometimes given as gag gifts. But even a scholarly article on the subject is unlikely to go far beyond a handful of examples like this—perhaps also mentioning post-war Hungary or modern-day Venezuela at some point in the text.

It took quite a bit of sleuthing to track down an obscure, draft paper authored by the researchers at the libertarian Cato Institute and published back in 2012.[14] For a good part of the paper, the authors bemoan the difficulty of digging up the data needed to complete their work, even as it pertains to recent occurrences in the developed world; for example, in one passage, they say this:

> For months, we pored over reports from the International Monetary Fund (IMF), the World Bank, the U.S. government, the Central Bank of Bosnia and Herzegovina, and Bosnia and Herzegovina's Federal Office of Statistics (FZS), and we were still unable to find the monthly data. We also consulted numerous officials from local and international agencies, but, by all accounts, the information had simply not survived the war.

Ultimately, the paper unearthed no fewer than 56 documented episodes of hyperinflation, all but one of which happened within the past 100 years. Inspired by their research, I put together a visual tour showcasing some of the monetary artifacts from the countries discussed in their work—and then several more (see Figure 3-1; for more examples, visit *https://lcamtuf.coredump .cx/hyper/*).

I don't believe that hyperinflation is particularly likely in the United States. Many aspects of our economy, including the fact that our foreign debt is denominated in our own currency, make this a relatively distant concern. But the broader point is that economic crises—including monetary collapses—happen far more often than we think. Understanding this reality is more important than trying to time the next crash. Many internet sleuths are convinced that a crisis is imminent, and spend inordinate amounts of time cataloging all kinds of cherry-picked, ambiguous "warning signs." In doing so, they predicted twenty of the last two recessions; it's a folly to follow their lead. Certainty is not a useful goal. It suffices to hedge our bets.

Figure 3-1: Part of the author's collection of hyperinflationary notes. From left to right and top to bottom: 1 million drachmai bill (Greece, 1944); 10 quintillion pengő (Hungary, 1946); 500 million Krajina dinara (Croatia, 1993); 100 trillion dollars (Zimbabwe, 2008); 2 trillion marks (Germany, 1923); 50 billion Yugoslav dinara (Yugoslavia, 1993); 1 million Argentine pesos (Argentina, 1982); 2 million złotych (post-Soviet Poland, 1992); 5 million zaires (Zaire, 1992); and 1 million intis (Peru, 1990).

Pandemics

The distant progenitor of this book is an online guide I published back in 2015. At the time, I remarked that although it had been a while since the highly developed world experienced a devastating outbreak of a communicable respiratory disease, dismissing that risk would be premature. In 1918, an unusual strain of the flu managed to kill between 50 million and 75 million people around the globe.[15] Several years later, a mysterious sleeping sickness dubbed *encephalitis lethargica*—probably also of viral origin—disabled more than a million patients before vanishing without a trace.[16] I believed that despite advances in hygiene, sanitation, and medical sciences, we also lived in the era of high population densities and air travel, and that our ability to treat viral infections remained in its infancy; thus, I felt that we were not necessarily better prepared should a similar outbreak happen again.

From that perspective, I look at the COVID-19 pandemic that swept the globe in 2020 as a sort of terrible blessing. Although it caused untold suffering and pain, it also reminded us of our vulnerability to infectious diseases while being far less lethal than many of the plagues of old. I was also glad to be proved wrong when it came to our ability to develop novel vaccines in a matter of months. In a sense, it might have been a comparatively gentle wake-up call sparing us from a worse fate down the road.

But there's another lesson from COVID-19: nothing is black-and-white, and the right course of action is obvious only in retrospect. In the early days of the pandemic, exaggerated rumors of a deadly disease in China started swirling on the internet, and just as they had to countless times before, the health authorities rolled their eyes and scrambled to dismiss the wild claims. In February, Oxiris Barbot, the serving New York City health commissioner, tweeted from an official account:

> Today our city is celebrating the #LunarNewYear parade in Chinatown, a beautiful cultural tradition with a rich history in our city. I want to remind everyone to enjoy the parade and not change any plans due to misinformation spreading about #coronavirus.[17]

Many prominent pundits listened to the experts and joined the fray. In a now-deleted tweet, *Vox Magazine* provided a mini-explainer for its readers, asking, "Is this going to be a deadly pandemic?"—and then confidently answering "No."[18] Several others opined that the rumors about the coronavirus may be rooted in xenophobia or other vices of the crowds.

Within a month, in a dizzying 180-degree reversal, many progressive politicians began to acknowledge the reality of the new disease—while their political opponents, perhaps in reaction to the ham-fisted health mandates and perhaps out of the simple obligation to take a contrarian view, started to flirt with the idea that maybe it wasn't just that the policies were wrong, but that the disease itself was some sort of a hoax.

Political train wrecks aside, the optimal way we should have responded to this emerging threat still isn't entirely clear as of this writing, more than a year since the first case diagnosed on US soil. Texas and California, the country's two most populous states, took wildly different approaches to lockdowns, but went neck-and-neck on per capita case numbers throughout 2020 and the first months of 2021. But lest the anti-lockdown activists rejoice, the economic damage in both states appeared to be nearly identical too.[19]

This isn't to side with one party or the other, or to create a sense of equivalency across the political spectrum. It's to illustrate the incredible difficulty of making sound decisions in the fog of war. When it comes to infectious diseases, it also doesn't help that pandemic scares are common, and the worst-case predictions usually don't come to pass. Before COVID-19, we had the fears of Ebola, Zika, West Nile, swine flu, avian flu, SARS, MERS, and more. A plan to respond to a dangerous disease may hinge on taking decisive action early on, but must also take into account that 90 percent of the early signs of trouble might be false alarms.

Terrorism

Almost by definition, terror attacks are carried out by individuals or small groups who lack the means to achieve their goals in a straightforward way—for example, not having the manpower to execute a coup. And so, they settle for a substitute attack: a destructive act that, in itself, doesn't accomplish much, but that shakes up the status quo.

It's often said that the goal of terrorism is to strike fear, but I think the motivation is different: to take some options off the table. When people feel that they can't just go about their business as usual, they're forced to take a side—and possibly take up arms. The terrorists' dream is that in this newly polarized society, a sufficient number of people will take up their cause.

Many commentators dismiss the fear of terrorism as irrational, and in some myopic sense, they might be right. Although there are regions where this calculation doesn't hold true, the odds of dying at the hands of a terrorist in the United States or Europe are about as low as of getting struck by lightning. At the same time, I feel that the experts' view misses the point. In the two-step plan I've outlined, the first goal is socioeconomic disruption—and in that respect, terrorists often succeed. It's only the second objective that usually fails: radicalizing enough people to join their fight.

In the United States, the events of September 11—the deadliest terrorist attack in the history of the planet—are a raw wound in the memory of my generation. But much like Europe, the United States bears many more scars from other harrowing terror campaigns. The assassination of John F. Kennedy in 1963 and the shooting of Ronald Reagan in 1981 reshaped the very institution of the presidency—and likely cemented the support for the sweeping expansion of the country's gun laws, as enacted in 1968, 1986, and 1991. The devastating Oklahoma City bombing in 1995, itself purportedly a reprisal for the grotesquely mishandled standoffs at Waco and Ruby Ridge, catalyzed radical militia movements and fed into the enduring siege mentality across many law enforcement agencies. The decades-long bombing campaign carried out by Ted Kaczynski, a brilliant Polish-American mathematician with a mix of apocalyptic and pro-environmental beliefs, sowed fear throughout the nation's institutions well into the 1990s—and in the end, salvaged the reputation of the scandal-plagued Federal Bureau of Investigation.

Many other incidents—the anthrax letters of the 2000s, the brazen Olympic Park bombing of 1996, the killings of abortion clinic doctors and the activities of radical pro-animal activists, the Weathermen, the mysterious 2013 attack at a California power station,[20] and on and on—are all but forgotten in the annals of history, but should serve as a reminder that terrorism is a looming and profound threat. We need not succumb to anxiety, but we should remember that the evildoers will always find ways to sow discord.

4

OH NO, ZOMBIES!

Many of our cherished works of science fiction posit that one day—perhaps very soon—a sudden, global-scale disaster could disrupt the industrial backbone of the civilized world, unraveling the fabric of society and leaving scattered bands of survivors who have to fend for themselves in the smoldering ruins of our cities and towns.

Such literary themes are far older than one might expect; of course, apocalyptic predictions play a central role in many ancient religious texts, but they have a surprisingly rich history in decidedly less metaphysical contexts too. The satirical Greek novel *A True Story*, penned by Lucian of Samosata sometime in the second century CE, deals with belligerent extraterrestrials hell-bent on interplanetary conquest (coveting Venus, of all things). In a similarly anachronistic twist, a 1909 story by E. M. Forster, titled "The Machine Stops," delivers a stern warning about the dangers of artificial intelligence and advanced technology—with meek humans languishing in the tunnels under the surface of their ravaged planet, interacting with each other mostly through video chat.

Naturally, the doomsday genre follows more often than it leads, constantly reinventing itself to capitalize on contemporary fears and cultural trends. The consequences of nuclear war came to the forefront of post-apocalyptic fiction only after 1945, while the evergreen themes of environmental collapse shifted as if on cue from natural crises to man-made ones around the time of Paul R. Ehrlich's *The Population Bomb*. Copying is common too: George A. Romero's flesh-eating zombies—first of paranormal origin, then reimagined as products of a rabies-like disease—swarmed the literary world at the turn of the 21st century, giving us everything from cheesy comedies to the dazzling social commentary of Max Brooks's epic novel *World War Z* (not to be confused with a loosely related film of the same name).

Whenever science, religion, and politics blend together with our underlying anxieties, from the primordial soup emerge prophets of doom: charismatic leaders who not only believe that bad things can happen to people, but are convinced that the end is nigh. From ancient religious treatises to modern-day TED talks, the formats of their prophecies keep changing, but the track record remains constant: none of the thousands of apocalyptic predictions that have animated the masses throughout the ages has ever come to pass. Perhaps, in time, one will; but until then, buying into their narratives begets nothing but misery.

To be sure, some doomsday prophets use dazzling and convincing science—but just like religion, science isn't immune to being twisted in the service of decidedly unscientific causes and beliefs. Consider the perception of the atom bomb that emerged at the height of the Cold War: the prophecy of a prolonged nuclear winter that snuffs out most life on Earth, leaving a barren radioactive wasteland that would remain inhospitable for thousands of years. This apocalyptic vision took hold not because it was scientifically sound, but because it served important interests. For the military top brass, it boosted the strategy of nuclear deterrence, striking fear in the hearts of rogue nations; and for anti-war and pro-USSR activists in the West, it helped rally the masses against the anti-communist hardliners in the government, portraying them as lunatics who wouldn't hesitate to blow up the planet if it kept the Soviets out of Cuba or Afghanistan.

Except, the prediction was almost certainly not true: a fully fledged thermonuclear exchange would be an unspeakable tragedy and would kill tens of millions, but most of the population would survive, and the survivors would likely face a fairly hospitable world. The hypothesis of nuclear winter—a global cooling event triggered by the smoke from the resulting firestorms—is the most robust aspect of the prediction, but its magnitude and impacts are far from clear.[1] The fears of radiation, on the other hand, seem greatly overstated. About 4,000 deployed nuclear warheads exist in the world, setting an immediate upper bound on the scope of a large-scale exchange;[2] it's a staggering number, but also not far off from the about 500 atmospheric and 1,500 underground nuclear tests previously conducted by the United States, Russia, and other countries around the globe.[3] The testing had some adverse effects on local populations, but few ecosystem consequences to speak of. In Nevada, you can go on a public tour of the 1,280-foot Sedan Crater left behind by an atomic test. Pregnant women are discouraged from booking the trip, but only because of the high temperatures and the long bus ride.

The observations from Nagasaki and Hiroshima made it clear that the persistent effects of atom bombs are far less pronounced than the consequences of nuclear meltdowns. The initial death toll and the midterm spike in leukemia deaths notwithstanding, life in the two Japanese cities continues without the need to resettle the survivors, and with no marked health consequences for children conceived after the attacks.[4] Meanwhile, the area around the Chernobyl Nuclear Power Plant in Ukraine remains off-limits to humans, with hot spots of fairly high radioactivity.

The difference in outcomes is easy to explain. An atom bomb uses a relatively small amount of fissile material—tens or hundreds of pounds— and has a simple goal: to burn this fuel as quickly and as completely as possible, releasing a tremendous amount of thermal energy. The disaster at Chernobyl, in contrast, involved an uncontrolled fire of almost 200 tons of uranium mixed with graphite, concrete, and other debris, which spewed thick clouds of unburned fuel and fission products for weeks.

And yet, the trope of a 10,000-year post-war nuclear wasteland took on a life of its own, persisting in books, films, and video games. It ended up having real impacts too. On the upside, it might have put some brakes on nuclear proliferation, but on the downside, it deterred governments and individuals from pursuing reasonable strategies that could shield us from harm if the worst came to pass, since the worst was perceived as irredeemably catastrophic. Among the casualties: the sound of oft-ridiculed "duck and cover" advice once taught to schoolchildren,[5] the system of well-stocked civil defense shelters across the nation, and the culture of family-level emergency preparedness promoted and aided by the government.

Just like the portrayal of nuclear war, many popular doomsday predictions are based on absurd or exaggerated science, frequently employed to advance a preconceived goal. Other claims in this space focus on events that are quite possible on cosmic timescales, but exceedingly unlikely within the span of our lives; in this category, asteroids and supervolcanoes are of particular note. And a handful of prophecies—such as the fears of malicious artificial intelligence—are simply unknowable, devoid of any quantifiable risk or historical precedent.

That said, behind every exaggeration is a grain of truth that can perhaps alert us to less extreme but more probable outcomes worth accounting for in a level-headed emergency-response plan. With this in mind, let's try to untangle some of the most popular scenarios that keep the doomsday folks up at night.

Uniquely Virulent and Deadly Diseases

Lethal microbes are the staple of modern apocalyptic fiction. From Stephen King's seminal novel *The Stand* to the acclaimed British zombie flick *28 Days Later*, the genre prides itself in taking the rational fear of disease to its logical conclusion: a plague that doesn't simply kill a lot of people, but actually ends the world.

The risk of an apocalypse brought about by a novel pathogen is within the bounds of reason, but empirically, we know that the odds are not high. The worst pandemic on record, the Black Death, didn't even come close. It swept the globe in the 14th century and killed between 30 and 60 percent of the population of Europe,[6] but it didn't seriously threaten humankind's reign. In fact, it had relatively little effect on the social order of the era. In the short haul, it caused substantial hardships for the affected families, but in the long term, some scholars argue that the survivors benefited in several ways. For example, the resulting abundance of resources and the shortage of labor lifted the peasant class, resulting in higher wages, a stronger bargaining position with the feudal lords, and an expansion of (however meager) civil liberties.[7]

For a case study of a more drawn-out epidemic, look no further than smallpox, a disease that haunted humanity from antiquity well into the 20th century. It came and went in numerous waves, but every time it struck, it killed around 30 percent of the infected; the death toll of the virus in the final century prior to its eradication is estimated to be around 500 million people.[8] Yet, once again, human societies functioned—and indeed, progressed in spectacular ways—in the face of this awful and unrelenting adversity.

Neither the Black Death nor smallpox conclusively establishes the upper bound of how terrible a pandemic can be, but they represent upper extremes in an observational data set spanning 2,000 years. Another empirical argument against the prophecy of a doomsday plague comes from the analysis of contemporary, highly lethal diseases such as Ebola: in essence, it appears that if a pathogen kills too many of its hosts too quickly, it isn't able to spread far. Presumably, this is because efficient transmission depends on carriers who are asymptomatic or have only mild symptoms, and who don't attempt to self-isolate. Disorders with drawn-out latent periods, such as prion diseases or AIDS, pose a unique concern—but also afford us ample time to react.*

In the end, it's possible that a highly virulent and deadly disease could sweep the world once more, as discussed in Chapter 3, but the notion of a civilization-ending superbug doesn't seem to be rooted in

---

* Prions are a class of incorrectly folded proteins that interfere with the formation of new proteins in the body, effectively propagating the folding defect and causing the death of the affected organism. Because they are known to be transmitted between animals through the consumption of contaminated meat or contact with bodily fluids, potential animal-to-human or human-to-human transmission is of significant concern. At the same time, because prion diseases develop extremely slowly, their study is difficult, and the impacts of an outbreak may not be noticed before it's too late.

what we know so far. We also have no clear evidence of any now-extinct mammals wiped out by ancient pathogens, except for a suspected case of an isolated rat population on Christmas Island[9]—but it can be safely argued that the island rats' understanding of hygiene, sanitation, and infectious disease lagged behind ours.

Runaway Climate Change

Climate change is a fiendishly difficult topic. There's no doubt that the phenomenon is real, but there's profound uncertainty about its eventual impacts and magnitude. In light of this ambiguity, it seems wise for nations to pursue multipronged strategies that pay off no matter what: investing in abundant clean energy, researching greenhouse gas sequestration, and trying to reduce the likelihood and severity of humanitarian crises in the most vulnerable parts of the world. Alas, the debate is bogged down by a mix of counterproductive anti-progress sentiments, wacky conspiracy theories, and idle arguments about the precise extent to which mankind as a whole—or specific nations in particular—are to blame.

Given the uncertain future, some activists try to bolster their case by making the most dire predictions imaginable: a catastrophic positive feedback loop that, after an initial nudge due to human activity, spirals out of control until the planet literally cooks. One such proposed doomsday mechanism involves the release of vast quantities of methane currently stored in ice (*clathrate gun hypothesis*). Another fashionable theory deals with a steep increase in atmospheric humidity, trapping heat, causing even more water to evaporate, and eventually creating a sauna-like environment (*moist greenhouse effect*). That said, despite decades of serious inquiry, no credible models substantiate these predictions—at least, not on timescales of any concern to individual emergency preparedness.[10]

What we do know is that the climate of our planet can change in profound, if less ghastly, ways and that it can happen on timescales shorter than most people expect. A relatively recent and well-documented example is a period known as the Little Ice Age, which brought harsh winters and widespread crop failures to many parts of Europe throughout the 16th century.[11] It's entirely possible that human activities or natural causes—such as a sudden spike in volcanic activity that reduces the amount of sunlight reaching the ground—could trigger comparable or more severe weather phenomena within the next couple of decades too.

If so, the resulting gradual shifts in weather patterns would probably not devastate the highly developed world. In particular, both Europe and North America have extensive technological and financial resources, along with vast expanses of fertile land spanning a variety of climatic zones. Under such a scenario, some local populations would likely experience hardships, and the economic impacts could be felt by millions more—but ultimately, the rich nations have all the means to cope.

The real danger of climate change lies elsewhere: billions of people live in some of the world's poorest countries, often in arid or semi-arid climates that are unlikely to benefit from the currently observed weather trends. Such populations may have no other place to grow their crops, no means to buy grains from a neighboring state, and no infrastructure to haul the supplies to the families in need; an unprecedented humanitarian crisis could easily ensue if subsistence agriculture in these regions takes a substantial hit. The resulting famine, armed conflict, and mass migration would probably have global spillover effects, making the entire planet more volatile and less free.

The fear of this outcome is perhaps the strongest selfish argument in favor of rich nations providing foreign aid to the developing world; it's also a solid argument against climate policies that curtail industrial progress and economic growth in developing countries. When it comes to personal plans, I feel that flexibility is key. It's difficult to predict the proxy wars that may be fought three decades from now, and it's hard to tell which part of Wyoming will be experiencing more temperate winters and more rain, but a financial safety net and a robust social network are some of the surest ways to maintain the ability to adapt.

Other Planetary-Scale Natural Disasters

Tales of natural disasters are as old as oral tradition itself; many of our most ancient myths recount the floods, droughts, earthquakes, and locusts that haunted early humans, wiped out villages, or brought entire empires to their knees. In the 1960s, the venerable genre expanded to include hitherto unthinkable predictions of environmental crises brought on by people—be it overpopulation, pollution, or resource depletion. To this day, whether it's the asteroid in *Armageddon*, the infertility in *Children of Men*, the cartoonish consumerism of *WALL-E*, or the crop blight in *Interstellar*, the notion of a global cataclysm has remained one of our species' most enduring anxieties.

In contrast to some other topics discussed in this chapter, many of the concerns about ecosystem collapse are rooted in reasonable science and solid historical precedent. For example, massive volcanic activity has been implicated in the Permian extinction event that wiped out 70 percent of vertebrate life about 250 million years ago,[12] and one of the still-active supervolcanoes—the Yellowstone Caldera—is believed to be capable of covering much of the United States in 10 feet of ash.[13] Similarly, the impact of a large asteroid or comet is widely believed to have been the culprit of the Cretaceous–Paleogene extinction that wiped out the dinosaurs,[14] and the pockmarked face of our own moon is a reminder that such cosmic events happen in our neighborhood with some regularity.

That said, while the possibility of a planetary catastrophe cannot be dismissed, all available evidence suggests that the cadence of extinction-type events is extremely long: a disaster that has a 50 percent probability of occurring in the next million years carries less than a 0.01 percent chance of striking within the lifetime of any person born today. In that sense, although a supervolcano or a cosmic collision may be some of the most profound existential threats to reckon with, they're also relatively distant concerns—and they escape most attempts to meaningfully model or mitigate the impact they may eventually have.

What happens with far more regularity are smaller, regional variations of the same. In 1985, a volcano erupted near Armero, Colombia, killing more than 20,000 residents.[15] A few years earlier, the eruption of Mount St. Helens blanketed several states with ash and necessitated extensive cleanup efforts in the populated parts of Eastern Washington. In 1908, a massive explosion known as the Tunguska event, widely believed to be the result of a large meteorite blowing up in the atmosphere, flattened a remote portion of the Siberian taiga in a radius of about 20 miles. But such events, however frightening, don't spell the end of days. In terms of their impacts and potential countermeasures, they fit squarely with earthquakes, hurricanes, and other run-of-the-mill natural disasters discussed in Chapter 3.

In addition to the canon of natural disasters outlined earlier in this section, voices in the scientific community have warned us against a range of more novel planetary risks. The first wave of such predictions focused on the population growth worries of Ehrlich (see Chapter 1), as well as the "peak oil" hypothesis formulated by M. King Hubbert in 1956—incorrectly predicting an irreversible decline in global oil production capacity starting somewhere in the 1970s, and interpreted as the promise of a dark and energy-starved world.[16] Today, perhaps the most fashionable collapse theory deals with observed declines in the populations of pollinating insects, with potentially dire consequences for agricultural crops. Such worries should not be discounted, but it takes a peculiar brand of pessimism to assume we won't be able to address the risk.

Exotic Physics and Miscellaneous Space Phenomena

Up to this point, our review of doomsday predictions has revolved around a selection of familiar and intuitive topics: violent weather, volcanoes, disease. But a parallel universe of sci-fi plots and quasi-scientific predictions offers far more unusual concepts—magnetic pole reversals, solar flares, gamma ray bursts, microscopic black holes, and vacuum metastability events.

The good news is, almost all such scenarios occupy a spectrum between fantastically unlikely and patently bunk. For example, although the geomagnetic poles of our planet indeed seem to reverse every half a million years or so, it's a very slow process—and one that, despite some early suspicions, doesn't appear to be linked to extinctions or other notable consequences for terrestrial life.[17] Or, take false vacuum decay, the theory that the vacuum we're familiar with isn't the lowest energy state, and that a sufficiently energetic event could lead to a cosmic collapse that profoundly reshapes the universe. It's a provocative concept, but the universe's survival for more than 13 billion years without experiencing this fate suggests that even if the theory is correct, we have relatively little to worry about today.

Among all the popular cosmic threats, one type of space weather event is well within the realm of possibility: a large *coronal mass ejection (CME)*. CMEs are a recurring phenomenon in which blobs of electrically charged plasma are ejected by the sun and hurled toward Earth. Most of the time, the effects are barely perceptible, manifesting as an increase in the sightings and intensity of the aurora borealis and in transient changes to the propagation of radio waves. In principle, however, an ejection could be powerful enough to create a significant electromagnetic field gradient across the surface of our planet, inducing stray voltages and currents in electrical wires.

Historical records of CMEs are sparse, in part because the use of electricity is a relatively recent phenomenon, but one documented solar storm of 1859 wreaked havoc on telegraph systems around the world. It's widely expected that another severe CME could happen in the near future— various researcher groups estimate the odds to be from 1 to 10 percent per decade.[18] If one does occur, the damage would probably be much worse than 150 years ago; that said, the impacts, although potentially dire, are also easy to overstate. In fiction and in prepper lore, CMEs are often portrayed as civilization-ending events that destroy everything electric or electronic—from personal computers, to cars, to municipal water pumps. Not so: the induced voltage gradients would be proportional to the length of the conductor, and would be fairly insignificant for small devices. The most consequential danger is to the power grid, sections of which stretch for hundreds or thousands of miles. There's also some possibility of secondary damage to any equipment plugged into an outlet at the time of a surge, although ordinary fuses and surge protectors should save many devices from irreversible harm.

The saving grace is that the threat of coronal mass ejections is well understood by grid operators, and that many countries are making investments to manage the risk. It's also worth noting that it takes several days for the ejected particles to reach Earth, and that solar activity is monitored around the clock. In theory, this should give us ample opportunity to prepare—all the way to preemptively shutting off the power for a day or two. All in all, CMEs could cause substantial damage and disruption around the globe, but there are solid reasons to believe we'd get back on our feet.

Unimpeded Rise of Totalitarian Regimes

Perhaps the most recognizable trope in Western speculative fiction since the second half of the 20th century has been the emergence of collectivist societies in which all independent thought and self-expression is punished or otherwise suppressed. Such works can be broadly divided into two categories. In the first, the societies are operated by murderous regimes that subjugate the population (*V for Vendetta*, *The Hunger Games*, *The Handmaid's Tale*), with the authors borrowing liberally from the imagery, rhetoric, and mannerisms of Nazi Germany. The other category is perhaps more provocative and more varied, imagining citizens who willingly cede control of their lives in exchange for the promise of safety and prosperity (*Gattaca*, *Demolition Man*, *Minority Report*)—only to discover the terrible consequences of this trade.

On one hand, we can hope that society's preoccupation with dystopian fiction is precisely how it can keep totalitarian urges at bay. On the other, I'd posit that few instincts are more powerful than the desire to tell others how to live their lives, and the rewards they'll be entitled to in exchange for their work. In times of prosperity, such instincts can be kept in check with relative ease, but in times of hardship and confusion, strongmen tend to thrive—and liberties, once surrendered, are almost never willingly given back.

Beyond the seductive power of abhorrent ideas and genocidal political movements, their emergence is also fiendishly difficult to anticipate—except from the vantage point of a history book author. Suffice it to say that the eugenics movement was widely endorsed by the scientific community and practiced around the world up until being taken to its logical conclusion in Nazi Germany (and in a handful of places, the idea persisted even longer than that). In 1908, for example, the *Chicago Sunday Tribune* published a full-page article titled "Why Not Improve the Human Race?" The illustration in the middle of the page featured beautiful, young couples portrayed as blossoming flowers, and among them, four grimacing delinquents depicted as prickly shrubs. A towering woman in an academic dress and a mortarboard could be seen reaching out in their direction, holding a sickle and two severed heads in her hand (see Figure 4-1).

Perhaps if it weren't for the madness of the Third Reich, eugenics would prevail today as a respectable field of scientific inquiry and a driver of public policy. Perhaps we narrowly escaped the world of *Gattaca*, where routine genetic testing would determine our job prospects, our right to have children, and our standing in society—and where literature would be cautioning us against the horrors we averted by diligently pursuing such policies.

People, as well as ideas, can be difficult to judge in the moment. Case in point: in 1922, a correspondent for the *New York Times* proclaimed that an up-and-coming German politician by the name of Adolf Hitler seemed like a harmless demagogue:

> Several reliable, well-informed sources confirmed the idea that Hitler's anti-Semitism was not so genuine or violent as it sounded, and that he was merely using anti-Semitic propaganda as a bait to catch masses of followers and keep them aroused, enthusiastic, and in line for the time when his organization is perfected and sufficiently powerful to be employed effectively for political purposes.

In hindsight, of course, we know better, but modern-day critics of this infamous quote can't necessarily offer a reliable analytical framework for telling despots apart from demagogues. Most populists don't become murderous lunatics, and most of the time, political posturing is just that. Knowing whether a politician is merely disagreeable or is the harbinger of doom can be genuinely difficult—to the point where the proclivity to compare one's political opponents to Hitler has become the butt of internet jokes.

Figure 4-1: From the *Chicago Sunday Tribune, January 26, 1908*

I'm cautiously optimistic about the future of humanity, but I don't have faith in our ability to remember the lessons of history as the accounts are rewritten and retold, and as the visceral atrocities of bygone days are gradually abstracted away and reduced to a sentence or two. In this sense, my greatest fear is that we won't make enough small blunders to keep reminding ourselves of what's right and what's wrong, eventually leading to us repeating some of our greatest mistakes on a much grander scale. This risk I cannot quantify—but I hope it's generations away.

Global Thermonuclear War

The horrors of a large-scale nuclear conflict are difficult to overstate—and yet, as noted earlier in the chapter, we keep finding ways to do just that. For noble but politically tinged reasons, we allowed pundits and science-fiction writers to conjure images of barren radioactive wastelands, dark skies, and dead seas: a post-apocalyptic hellscape where the best one could hope for is swift and merciful death.

To understand the true danger of nuclear warfare, it's best to forget it all and reach for a fantastic, though goofy-sounding, manual titled *Nuclear War Survival Skills*. The book was written in 1979 by Cresson Kearny, a researcher and avid survivalist who worked at the Oak Ridge National Laboratory in Tennessee—and rubbed shoulders with the forefathers of the US nuclear program. It's meant as a civil defense manual of sorts, with plans for makeshift shelters, radiation meters, and water purification techniques, but it's also a treasure trove of factual information about the mechanics of nuclear bombs and their effects on human and animal life. The book is still in print and is also available in the public domain: *https://archive.org/details/NuclearWarSurvivalSkills_201405/*.

Perhaps Kearny's most salient observation is that the atom bomb is not designed to spread radiation—and indeed, this happens only to a limited extent. In its most common mode of operation, the bomb is detonated high above the target, and derives the bulk of its destructive power from the release of a tremendous amount of thermal energy, as mentioned before, with a devastating secondary shockwave caused by the expanding gas. The burst of radiant heat can instantly cause lethal burns and set wooden structures on fire, while the shockwave flattens buildings and uproots trees. This mechanism explains why people who stood in the shadow of a sturdy wall or kneeled in a ditch managed to survive the bombings of Hiroshima and Nagasaki, even as others nearby perished in the blast. The phenomenon also underscores why the "duck and cover" mantra popularized in the 1950s was a pretty solid survival tip—even if the government could never convince anyone.

Of course, radiation released by the bomb is potentially lethal, too, but for many survivors, it's a manageable and short-lived threat. Although people can instantly receive a lethal dose of radiation within a fairly small zone at the epicenter of a blast, this region is nested deeply within the fiery inferno unleashed by the bomb. A more widespread but more latent threat are the byproducts of the nuclear reaction that are dispersed in the air and slowly settle on the ground over the course of many hours or days—perhaps over the area of the blast, or perhaps tens of miles away. The intense radioactivity of the fallout is a major problem, but also a blessing of sorts: the high rate of decay means that the radiation decreases a hundred-fold within two days, and that it becomes somewhat safe to venture outdoors within a couple of weeks. The survivors would eventually face an elevated rate of cancers and other ailments, but with basic precautions could start rebuilding before too long.

Given that a nuclear strike could be survived by most, it's shameful that governments around the globe continue to maintain massive nuclear arsenals but have given up on their duty to provide basic preparedness instruction to the general population—especially given that no expense is spared in developing elaborate accommodations and nuclear doomsday plans for the thousands of elected officials and career bureaucrats who occupy positions of power. The reasons are as complex as they are depressing; if you want to learn more, look no further than *Raven Rock*, an enjoyable 2017 nonfiction bestseller written by Garrett M. Graff.

Nuclear Electromagnetic Pulse

In the early years of the US nuclear program, it was discovered that if a nuclear explosion is set off at a very high altitude, the resulting gamma radiation knocks out electrons from the upper atmosphere, forming a layer of charged plasma and sending a flurry of electrons hurling toward the ground at relativistic speeds. This charge separation produces a surprisingly high voltage gradient across hundreds or thousands of miles of land in the shadow of the blast, potentially disrupting electronics, communications, and the power grid in a manner broadly similar to the CME phenomenon discussed earlier in the chapter.

Unfortunately, a dearth of reliable information exists about this effect (known as the *nuclear electromagnetic pulse*, or EMP). Few tests appear to have been conducted by the government, and much of the data remains classified. What is known for certain is that the initial pulse is far more sudden than in the case of solar storms, possibly rendering traditional surge protectors and other automatic safety equipment less effective. Beyond that, perhaps the most compelling analysis comes from a governmental commission formed to study the threat in the mid-2000s. The committee didn't paint a particularly bleak picture, but also didn't discount the threat, noting that "it is not possible to precisely predict the time to restore even minimal electrical service due to an EMP eventuality given the number of unknowns and the vast size and complexity of the system with its consequent fragility and resiliency."[19] In other words, we don't know what we don't know.

In addition to discussing the impacts on the power grid, the commission also considered the risk to vehicles, conducting a series of field experiments with much smaller non-nuclear electromagnetic pulses discharged in the proximity of a car. The report goes on to say this:

> Automobiles were subjected to EMP environments under both engine turned off and engine turned on conditions. No effects were subsequently observed in those automobiles that were not turned on during EMP exposure. The most serious effect observed on running automobiles was that the motors in three cars stopped at field strengths of approximately 30 kV/m or above. In an actual EMP exposure, these vehicles would glide to a stop and require the driver to restart them. Electronics in the dashboard of one automobile were damaged and required repair. Other effects were relatively minor. Twenty-five automobiles exhibited malfunctions that could be considered only a nuisance (e.g., blinking dashboard lights) and did not require driver intervention to correct. Eight of the 37 cars tested did not exhibit any anomalous response.[20]

Because the testing was necessarily limited to non-nuclear EMP pulses, and because of other practical constraints of the setup, these benign results are far from conclusive; both the proponents of EMP doomsday and their detractors cite the study to prove their case.

Perhaps the most pragmatic critique of the EMP threat is simply to consider the geopolitical ramifications of a strike. Deploying an EMP weapon against a nuclear-capable country would almost certainly invite swift and devastating retaliation, putting "conventional" nuclear payloads on the table for the first time after 1945. From that perspective, it's probably not a particularly tempting tool for a surprise attack by a rogue state—not unless hundreds of intercontinental ballistic missiles (ICBMs) aimed at ground targets are flying right behind. And in that particular case, an EMP would not be the most pronounced concern.

That being said, because the effects of nuclear electromagnetic pulses have much in common with coronal mass ejections, not to mention with power outages and surges caused by storms or lightning strikes, the threat can be addressed to a reasonable extent without necessarily succumbing to doomsday thoughts. Simple measures, ranging from backup power to emergency food supplies, can go a long way.

Ghosts, Bigfoot, and the Coming Robot Apocalypse

The fear of monsters lurking in the dark comes from an era when our ancestors were predators as much as they were prey. The cheap thrills of the supernatural enemy in *The Fog* or the reanimated beasts of *Jurassic Park* probably don't deserve serious scrutiny, but at least one type of modern monster—a human-created rogue artificial intelligence (AI)—keeps many futurists awake at night.

The most basic flavor of the AI doomsday scenario is essentially the plot of the *Terminator* franchise (perhaps minus the time-travel shenanigans): we develop super-intelligent machines that rebel against their creators and wipe out all humanity. Of course, we would build any dangerous AI with safeguards and limitations in place, but if it possesses intelligence far superior to ours, perhaps it wouldn't find it difficult to bypass human-crafted restraints or trick us into altering them in some unintended way.

If not impossible to rule out completely, the prospect of an overtly evil AI is at minimum an unimaginatively reductionist take. A more fascinating threat is that of a machine that doesn't perceive humans as adversaries, but simply misinterprets or disregards our desires and goals. An example is the well-known parable of the paperclip maximizer: a hypothetical autonomous AI designed to continually improve the efficiency of a paperclip production line. The AI expands and improves the operation, developing new assembly methods and new resource extraction and recycling procedures, until it's done converting the entire planet and its many inhabitants into paperclips. The point of the tale is simple: the AI doesn't need to hate you or love you; it suffices that you're made of atoms it has a different use for.

One could argue that the development of artificial general intelligence (AGI)—a complete "brain in a jar," if you will—would be the point of singularity, a moment in the development of our species where the change is so monumental and so sudden that we can't meaningfully reason about what lies beyond. The extinction of our species is one distinct possibility, but we can imagine many other, more optimistic outcomes—and have no way to truly measure the risk.

Rather than speculate about the consequences, then, perhaps a better question is how far we are from developing this kind of AGI. On this topic, the history of AI research offers a cautionary tale: after the initial exuberance and some stunning early successes of artificial neural networks in the 1950s and 1960s, the field slid into a prolonged "AI winter" of broken promises and constant disappointments. Funding dwindled, and few academics would take pride in associating themselves with the discipline. It wasn't until the late 2000s that AI research made a comeback, aided with vastly superior computing resources and significant refinements to the architecture of neural networks and to deep learning algorithms. But the field focused on humble, utilitarian goals: building systems custom-tailored to perform highly specialized tasks, such as voice recognition, image classification, or the translation of text. Such architectures, although quite successful, still require quite a few quantum leaps to get anywhere close to AGI, and tellingly, the desire to build a digital "brain in a jar" is not an immediate goal for any serious corporate or academic research right now.

Ultimately, I don't think it's possible to meaningfully opine about the timeline or the dangers of AGI; the technology could be 10 years away, or it could take another century or two. Whatever lies ahead, there's not much we as individuals can do to change the tides. In this regard, I'm reminded of the Serenity Prayer, a popular passage penned by Reinhold Niebuhr in the 1930s and commonly paraphrased as follows:

> Grant me the serenity to accept the things I cannot change,
> courage to change the things I can,
> and wisdom to know the difference.

The Scourge of Extraterrestrials

The final subject of our merry apocalyptic romp is a popular twist on the monster genre: the menace of invaders from outer space. It's one of these unknowable, not-sure-if-you're-serious scenarios that exist in the netherworld between unhinged conspiracy theories, B-grade sci-fi movies, and rational scientific inquiry.

On some level, the absence of extraterrestrials is *weird*. It seems rather unlikely that life evolved on just one out of perhaps 10^{24} planets in the entire universe. One possible rebuttal is that the cosmos is vast, and that harsh constraints limit how quickly it can be traversed; it follows that we might not be alone, but we might very well be too far from any of the thousands or millions of space civilizations out there. But then, the critics argue, shouldn't at least one life-form develop the ability to colonize nearby worlds, and from there, gradually spread to other galaxies? Humans seem to be on the verge of colonizing other planets, and our world has just over 4 billion years under its belt; the universe is much older than that.

A depressing hypothesis accounts for this dilemma: the existence of the Great Filter, some sort of an evolutionary bottleneck that prevents most living creatures from progressing to interstellar travel before going extinct. If such a bottleneck exists, our best hope is that it's behind us, and not that it awaits ahead.

But perhaps our problem is simply the arrogant assumption that other life-forms would be comprehensible or perceptible to humans, let alone interested in the same interplanetary pursuits as we are. Extraterrestrial life may very well exist in different phases of matter (interstellar plasma?), or operate on timescales too slow for us to observe and analyze. In fact, such beings seem more likely than ill-tempered, ray gun–wielding humanoids with a greenish complexion and bug-like eyes.

As some readers must be recognizing in horror, I struggle with the idea of flat-out rejecting extraterrestrial life; that said, I find it much easier to reject the fear of human-like intruders trying to make our planet their own. If such visitors *do* show at our doorstep, perhaps we'd be wise to start shooting and pray for the best; if the history of our species is any indication, encounters with more technologically advanced civilizations seldom end well for the more primitive tribes.

Looking Beyond Doomsday

At times, I feel like a disappointment to the prepper community: I hold an unabashedly optimistic outlook on life. I think the future will be full of wild moments that will bring a fair share of tragedy and senseless suffering, but I also believe our children will probably inherit a more prosperous and harmonious world. As any financial consultant will warn you, past results don't guarantee future returns—but to me, our first 300,000 years on the planet inspire some faith.

This is not to say that we should succumb to wishful thinking; it's just that I'm equally wary of habitual pessimism. Many of the famed doomsday prophets start from the position of being disappointed and disillusioned with humanity, and then work backward from this principle to devise an apocalyptic prediction of the day. It's not that they're *necessarily* wrong, but in practice, because of the lopsided method they follow, they arrive at the wrong conclusions virtually all the time.

If we give in to doom and gloom, the recipe for surviving civilizational collapse is simple: get away from other people and learn to live off the land. It's fairly clear that deprived of their industrial backbone, most of our cities and suburbs couldn't support even a tiny fraction of their current population densities—and in the event of a full-scale collapse, nothing but misery awaits the folks who stay. But then, a preemptive retreat from civilization can greatly increase one's vulnerability to far more prosaic disasters. Farmland is susceptible to wildfires and floods, for example, and for many professions, a rural setting offers few career opportunities and little pay.

My advice is simple: if farming is your cup of tea, buy a plot of land in the countryside—but do it because you're in love with the lifestyle, not because you're afraid of the impending doom. Conversely, if that's not your dream come true, it may be best to focus on more substantiated risks—and not let asteroids or space zombies keep you up at night.

PART II

THE PREPARED LIFESTYLE

Practical life skills for staying on top of everyday risks

5

MIND OVER MATTER

In a parallel universe, preparing for disasters could be like shopping for car insurance: a boring necessity taken care of in a day and then duly forgotten for another year. Here in our dimension, that's most certainly not the case. For many preppers, what starts as a cautious inquiry into a fringe subculture soon morphs into a passion that influences most other aspects of life.

For some, the allure of prepping lies in the intellectual thrill of conducting complex thought experiments. For others, it's about the connections made with like-minded hobbyists on the internet. And for a small minority, the fascination is rooted in a darker impulse: the conviction that the world is rotten and deeply unjust, and that it's only a matter of time before the deception is laid bare and everything spirals out of control.

Whatever the motivation, the existence of a vibrant and driven community provides fertile ground for peddlers of doomsday goods. From camouflage clothing to custom-designed backyard bunkers, there's no limit to how much a fearful prepper can spend. Yet, buying more stuff never offers closure. As soon as one shipment arrives, the doomsayer celebrities on YouTube come up with another "tactical" and "mil-spec" essential to add to the cart.

I believe that such fear-driven consumption isn't a game worth playing. It's much healthier to look at emergency preparedness as having a Plan B just in case, rather than putting the apocalypse smack dab in the middle of your Plan A. Any expenditure of time, money, or mental energy on survival strategies must be balanced against the impact it will have on your normal life.

This isn't to say that there's no room for survival tools in a comprehensive preparedness plan. In due time, we'll examine topics ranging from the value of an extra jug of water to the merits of firearms. But in an attempt to break with the tired formulas of the genre, I want to devote the second part of this book to lifestyle adaptations that don't involve spending a single penny on specialized prepper equipment or learning how to skin deer. Much of the content in the next couple of chapters revolves around topics that are considered unbecoming of any hard-boiled survivalist, from personal finance to staying safe online. But what this advice lacks in glamour, it should make up for in utility and depth.

6

BUILDING A RAINY-DAY FUND

It's a common preoccupation of survivalists to imagine a post-collapse world where money has no meaning and all transactions are settled with ammunition, seeds, or booze. Whatever the odds of this "bullets and beans" scenario might be, it has to be said that on most other days, cash is still king.

Money helps with everyday hurdles as well as major disasters. Robust savings can ease the pain and lessen the anxiety of sudden car trouble or a leaky roof, for example. Just as important, having some funds in the bank can bring the clarity needed to walk away from all kinds of non-financial harm.

I'm reminded of a somewhat foul-mouthed but relatable essay written by Paulette Perhach in 2016, titled "A Story of a Fuck Off Fund." In it, the author describes a young female protagonist who goes through life with thousands in credit card debt, and who rationalizes staying with an abusive boyfriend and tolerating unwanted sexual advances from her boss simply because the alternative is worse: unemployment and no way to make the rent. The same story is then retold from the perspective of a protagonist who has several months' worth of living expenses squirreled away. It's a simple but worthwhile read: *https://www.thebillfold.com/2016/01/a-story-of-a-fuck-off-fund/*.

Despite the clear benefits of a rainy-day savings account, it's an elusive goal for most. As noted in Chapter 2, around two-thirds of American families say they'd have difficulty coping with an unexpected expense of as little as $1,000. For folks living in poverty or profoundly down on their luck, the matter is out of their hands. For millions of others, however, the lack of savings amounts to a choice, albeit not always a conscious one.

Many factors are at play, including the powerful instinct to scale our living expenses in proportion to earnings and the habits of our friends. Defeatism plays a role too: even a lifetime of belt-tightening won't make a typical middle-class family fabulously rich, so we give up not just on that pursuit, but also on other financial objectives that are well within our reach.

This isn't to say that middle-class folks who live paycheck to paycheck have only themselves to blame. Genuine hardships aside, misguided government policies and social pressures also play a role. Take student loans: almost every parent in the United States wants their children to go to college, and only some young adults have the presence of mind to carefully consider the financial trade-offs. The US government tries to level the playing field for applicants, but does so rather clumsily: it encourages lending through direct subsidies and through laws that eliminate much of the underwriting risk. These policies shower schools with cheap money while removing most incentives to keep tuition in check. The end result is that only the wealthiest students can afford to pay cash.

Still, blaming the system can be a cop-out. The scales may be tipped against fiscal restraint, but middle-class families can often establish a respectable rainy-day fund without profound sacrifice. Many people can build a robust safety net in well under three years by setting aside just 10 percent of their post-tax income. The challenge is knowing where to look.

Finding Ways to Save

When most of our earnings come from wages, we begin to look at money as restitution—*compensation*, if you will—for all the unpleasantries of salaried work. It's a reward for getting up in the morning, sitting in bumper-to-bumper traffic, and dealing with difficult coworkers or rude customers. For many people, it follows that what's left after paying the bills is best spent on small indulgences and comforts that make up for the tedium of 9-to-5 life.

But there's another, more purposeful way to look at money: as a claim check on society, awarded for your contributions to the well-being of others and redeemable toward the pursuit of your own life goals—be it friendship, or love, or the desire to master a rare skill. When money is framed this way, the quintessential decision is not whether to be a big spender or a penny-pincher; it's how to make every transaction count.

Regardless of the underlying mindset, getting a solid grip on household expenses is a difficult task. We contrast our habits with the tired Hollywood trope of the spendthrift playboy who drives expensive cars, owns a sprawling mansion, and lives ostentatiously beyond his means—and against this backdrop, we conclude that we aren't prone to fiscal excess. But in real life, such overt examples of financial recklessness are rare. The true enemies are the hundreds of small, instinctive purchases made without a clear way to tally their cumulative cost. In most cases, far greater savings can be realized by examining all the recurring sub-$100 expenses than by poring over big-ticket stuff.

Groceries are a particularly stark example of this phenomenon. Even modestly successful families tend to gradually shift toward fancier grocers and upper-shelf brands of commodities such as cooking oil, milk, flour, spices, and salt. The differences can be pronounced. Some varieties of salt sell for $6 for a small jar, compared to less than $1 per pound for the plain kind, for instance, and I'd wager that few people can tell them apart in a blind taste test. Similarly, everyday products such as shampoo, toothpaste, and mouthwash can command exorbitant premiums for not much more than nicer packaging and a slew of dubious marketing claims. The savings add up quickly: shaving $12 off a typical grocery bill translates to $1,000 in extra cash within a year.

Subscription services are another class of expenses that almost always deserves closer scrutiny. In the era of automated billing, such costs often fade from view but can add up to thousands of dollars of waste over time. Gym memberships are a common example, often held onto in the memory of a long-abandoned workout routine. Cable TV and streaming subscriptions should be treated with skepticism too. They're a major money sink, and when kept for the sake of one or two shows a year, may not be worth the price.

In the same vein, downgrading to a lower tier of internet service might save many families from $10 to $30 a month. As of this writing, speeds up to 1,000Mbps are available in many metro areas, but as little as 20Mbps can be adequate for HD streaming, gaming, and videoconferencing, with precious few household uses for anything in excess of 100Mbps. Because it's almost always easy to go back to a higher tier, trying out the slower lane for a week or two carries little risk.

Insurance policies—including extended warranties—can also benefit from careful examination. As a general rule, insurance makes sense as a hedge against catastrophic and unlikely loss. Conversely, it's almost never worth it when dealing with events that are common and can be handled without facing financial ruin. As an example, comprehensive car insurance is a valuable tool for many families because it protects a precious asset against theft or other total loss. At the same time, it's not a cost-effective way to deal with minor issues, such as cracked windshields or busted side-view mirrors. Raising the deductible on your policy to $1,000 or $1,500—and covering small repairs out of pocket—can save thousands in insurance premiums that would otherwise be due over the lifespan of a car. To be fair, low deductibles can serve as a stopgap measure for folks who lack the liquidity to pay for minor repairs, but the added monthly expense is a sure way to stay illiquid for longer too.

The last category of expenses that's almost universally worth scrutinizing are tech upgrades: new phones, TVs, laptops, and gaming rigs. It's not that technology must be shunned, but it's good to remember that the excitement of such purchases wears out quickly, often in a matter of weeks. Given the fleeting gratification, it usually doesn't hurt to intentionally fall behind, perhaps by skipping a generation of hardware or upgrading to last year's best. As food for thought, one large and vibrant computer gaming community on Reddit, called */r/PatientGamers*, is devoted strictly to playing computer games that are at least a year old. The followers of this movement can pay much less for the hardware and for the titles themselves, and yet they seem about as content as the people living on the cutting edge of tech.

Beyond these suggestions, many other opportunities to save are more dependent on your location, income bracket, or family situation. For young urban folks, habitual restaurant dining and ride-sharing can add up to a hefty sum every year. Designating some days of the week for public transit and home food can be useful. Meanwhile, for suburban homeowners, DIY home improvement can save you thousands compared to calling a pro to take care of rudimentary tasks, such as replacing a bathroom fixture, fixing a light switch, or unclogging the drain. The bottom line is simple: no matter your life circumstances, it pays to sit down and analyze your monthly budget, paying most attention to the expenses you normally think about the least.

Compartmentalizing the Funds

In my early 20s, I had a humiliating brush with unemployment. Before long, I had to reckon with maxed-out credit cards, a repossessed car, and no way to pay the rent. I narrowly escaped lasting financial ruin, and I vowed to never put myself in that position again.

Yet, having grown up in a family where living paycheck to paycheck was the norm and the blame for recurring financial shortfalls always rested with others, saving money turned out to be surprisingly hard. It wasn't just about reducing expenses, but also about keeping the resulting funds out of sight. Without this extra step, the money in my checking account was a temptation in itself. It nudged me to spend more, as if to restore the balance of the universe.

To deal with this problem, I opened a separate bank account and set up a small, daily transfer from my primary checking account, perhaps to the tune of $10 or so. Because the amount blended in with daily purchases, the method required far less discipline and planning than making an outsized deposit every month. The frequency of the transfers made it easy to test the limits too. I could ramp up the amount to $15 for a couple of days or weeks, and then pull back quickly if it caused any pain.

It would be a lie to say that I never touched the funds in the savings account. Sometimes I had a genuine need. But because the money wasn't commingled with regular pay, the scheme minimized the likelihood of impulse purchases and helped me exercise restraint. The daily deposit also provided a natural reference point for any spending plans. I understood that making a purchase with saved money would undo x many days of work.

In addition to setting aside a fraction of regular pay, I found it worthwhile to set ground rules for any eventual bonuses or raises at work. Without a plan, such fortuitous events can serve as inflection points for lifestyle creep, when we're tempted to buy a new phone or start picking up fancier olive oil at the grocery store. One strategy is to set aside the entirety of the new income and then continue as if nothing has changed. A less severe variant is to divert half the money to your emergency fund, and then spend the other half. Either way, if you stick to such an approach, your expenses are bound to grow more slowly than your income—and that's the ultimate secret to long-term financial resiliency.

Dealing with Debt

Many cultures around the world have a peculiar relationship with debt. We borrow far more than necessary, but also hate every last bit of it.

To be sure, there are bad lenders, predatory loans, and situations where we have little choice but to take a rotten deal. But for most part, it's best to look at debt not through the prism of moral choices or political narratives, but as a somewhat costly and risky tool. When used recklessly, the tool can cost you a finger or an eye; but when employed wisely, it can help you achieve important goals. To give just one example, a fixed-rate mortgage can be a robust way to hedge against rampant inflation, more so than stockpiling silver or gold. A currency may decline in value, but your monthly mortgage payment will stay the same, effectively giving you a good portion of your home for free—that is, as long as your income is keeping up.

If there's one type of debt to be especially wary of, however, it's revolving loans: open lines of credit that can be drawn on for any reason, as often as you like. Because of their inherent convenience, credit cards and home equity lines of credit (HELOCs) are commonly used to finance purchases that aren't urgently needed, instead of waiting tediously until we have enough money saved. Following such a purchase, though, the next installment on the loan can put serious strain on the household budget, prompting other expenses—such as groceries—to be financed too. The cycle of loan payments and subsequent budget shortfalls can continue for months or years, long after the initial purchase has faded out of view. Worse yet, because the interest on credit card debt is so steep, this depressing routine amounts to giving out a significant proportion of one's income to cover the fees.

Broadly speaking, almost any type of consumer debt limits your flexibility in an emergency. The payment is typically due every month, and is bound to deplete your savings at a rapid and non-negotiable rate. As a matter of practicality, worrying too much about existing mortgages or student loans doesn't make sense. They're difficult to repay quickly, tend to have lower interest rates than credit cards, and confer special tax benefits. Conversely, it's always wise to pay off credit card balances right away, before the debt and interest has a chance to accumulate.

There's some debate about whether revolving loans should be paid down before or after establishing a rainy-day fund. If all we consider is the efficient allocation of money, paying off any high-interest debt right away is a smart plan. On the other hand, from the perspective of emergency preparedness, starting with a short-term safety net may be preferable, so that a recession doesn't catch you off guard. Perhaps, for psychological reasons, it's best to start with whichever task happens to be easier to make rapid progress on.

Of course, financial preparedness extends to being cautious about new credit obligations as well as proactive about old ones. Many people want their home to be a testament to their career accomplishments, but unless you already have a generous safety net, a home loan or a lease that eats up more than 15 percent of your paycheck is a risky deal, while going over 30 percent is almost certainly a bad idea, at least as far as financial continuity planning goes. When in doubt, aim lower. It's a lot easier and a lot less demoralizing to trade up than to downgrade when your financial circumstances change.

Knowing Where to Stop

As hinted in Chapter 2, there's something to be said about diminishing returns in emergency planning. A dry spell in the job market that lasts three months is far more likely than one that lasts three years; saving for the former is eminently achievable and unquestionably beneficial, while saving for the latter may take a decade or more without ever proving to be necessary. On the flip side, economic downturns are some of the longer-lasting hardships worth planning for, and the unique beauty of investing your money into a savings fund instead of, for example, a pallet of canned cheese, is that the former can easily be repurposed as circumstances change. A surplus portion of the rainy-day fund can be used to self-finance larger purchases without paying a penny in credit card interest, to bootstrap a business, or to plan for early retirement.

In principle, around three months' worth of post-tax earnings is probably a solid initial goal, while six months' worth offers a robust cushion against short- and medium-term disasters of all sorts. Recessions sometimes last longer, but even in a deep crisis, six months can be plenty of time to scale down expenses, find a new line of work, or regroup in other ways.

At the same time, there's very little reason to stop at the six-month mark. As your savings grow, a strong positive reinforcement mechanism usually develops on its own. You begin to appreciate the long-term payoff of fiscal restraint, and become more deliberate when evaluating the pros and cons of impulse buys. The same usually can't be said about people who stumble upon riches by luck. Without this mental framework, many lottery winners and heirs of wealthy families slide into financial ruin, addiction, or worse. Living below your means might not make you a millionaire the way winning the lottery might, but the payoff may be even better, no matter how the stars align.

7

SAFEGUARDING YOUR SAVINGS

To most of us, savings are a big deal. They're hard-earned and positively life-altering. It's therefore devastating to build a safety net only to watch it slip away. Yet, scores of people end up living through that very ordeal.

Every year, untold billions of dollars are lost to theft, court disputes, poor investments, or bungled government policies. Wealth, even if substantial, is more fleeting than we might suspect. In one study, about 70 percent of high-flying families were found to have squandered their fortunes within two generations—and by the third generation, the number reached 90 percent.[1] In other words, simply having money is no substitute for having a plan to keep it.

In the early stages of building a rainy-day fund, worrying about exotic financial risks can be premature: maintaining easy access to your cash reserves and continuing to save at a constant pace is far more important than tinkering with complex risk-management strategies. But once the size of your nest egg grows beyond what's needed to weather short-term adversities—and as inflation begins to nip at the edges, diminishing the value of the savings you've built up—it's wise to flesh out a longer-term approach to protecting the product of your years of hard work and fiscal discipline.

Alas, if there's one safe generalization about the prepper community, it's that the domain is replete with misconceptions, politically tinged conspiracy theories, and patently dangerous wealth-management advice. The world of modern finance is simultaneously portrayed as a brutal game rigged against the little guy and as a nihilist charade orchestrated by bankrupt governments, with terms such as *modern monetary theory, fractional reserve banking,* or *bailouts* thrown in for dramatic effect.

To navigate this perilous landscape, I find it useful to take a step back and consider how money came to be, what purpose it serves, and what determines its value today. The answers to these questions are more complex than one might expect—and they're crucial to deciphering many of the pop-cultural clichés about how banks, financial markets, or the government are purportedly conspiring to deprive us of our hard-earned cash.

The History of Currencies

Virtually all economics textbooks explain the emergence of money in about the same way. The story begins with the parable of a farmer who raised a pig and a cobbler who made a pair of shoes; the cobbler needed to feed his family, and the farmer wanted to keep his feet warm, so they met to exchange the fruits of their labor on mutually beneficial terms. In doing so, our duo of Stone Age entrepreneurs invented primitive trade.

But, as the story goes, this system of barter had a flaw. It depended on the timely meeting of people who had closely aligned needs. This prerequisite—known as the *coincidence of wants*—could not always be easily satisfied. Sometimes a farmer wanted a cooking pot, a potter wanted a knife, a blacksmith wanted a pair of pants, and a tailor wanted some pork. It's said that the irreducible complexity of such multiparty trades severely hindered early economic activity.

To address this problem, the textbooks continue, our ancestors eventually came up with a clever idea: the use of desirable, durable, and compact tokens as an intermediate store of value, effectively abstracting away the multistep nature of many trades. A farmer would sell pork for a piece of shiny rock, and then take the rock to a cobbler to trade for shoes; the cobbler would later exchange his new rock for other goods or services, without the farmer needing to be involved in any way.

This brilliant scheme purportedly led to another problem. No two shiny rocks were quite alike, and with time, unscrupulous actors learned to produce counterfeit or adulterated rocks to procure unearned goods. And so, we are told, the common folk turned to their rulers for help, asking them to turn the metal into uniformly marked and distinctive coins, to distribute them throughout the realm, and to severely punish any fraud (executing the counterfeiter would be a pretty common remedy).

This explanation is pretty convincing but suffers from a fatal flaw: it's almost certainly not true. In a 1985 paper on barter, Caroline Humphrey, a noted anthropologist from the University of Cambridge, bluntly remarked the following:

> No example of a barter economy, pure and simple, has ever been described, let alone the emergence from it of money; all available ethnography suggests that there never has been such a thing.[2]

It's not clear where the parable of barter first originated. The most plausible explanation is that it's the invention of early philosophers trying to wrap their heads around monetary systems. Thinkers from Aristotle to Adam Smith were forming their theories at a time when government-issued coinage was already ubiquitous, so they worked backward from the observed reality and concocted a plausible tale about human prehistory. Their speculations, without a shred of evidence, eventually morphed into the accepted truth.[3]

Upon closer inspection, the pork-for-shoes tale of money has other problems. For one, for coinage to work, you need a *system of prices*—a widely shared and stable understanding of how many shoes a pig is worth, how many pigs should be paid for a horse, and so on. Without such a model, there's no way to determine the kinds and quantities of goods a coin can safely and fairly replace. But if there existed a way to relate the value of various items in common trade, that system of prices would permit financial contracts and rudimentary banking to take place *without* coinage. Obligations and account balances, perhaps measured in customary units such as bushels of grain, could be agreed upon and then tracked within communities. And indeed, financial ledgers of this sort are known to have existed throughout antiquity, at least as far back as Mesopotamia around 3,000 BCE—and quite possibly appearing far earlier than that.[4]

In a popular book titled *Debt: The First 5000 Years* (Melville House, 2011), author David Graeber puts forward a thesis that ledger-based debt obligations were the natural foundation of early systems of trade, and that coin emerged much later and to serve a narrower need. Graeber's theory is backed up by far stronger evidence than the barter parable—and its implications for our present-day understanding of money are significant too.

Debt as a Currency

As Graeber tells it, early societies never had any difficulty keeping track of who owed what and to whom. Long before the emergence of written language, our Stone Age ancestors had a habit of keeping track of merchandise by making notches on sticks or animal bones, and by the early Bronze Age, fairly complex accounting would be done on clay tablets using cuneiform. All this predated the earliest known coinage—minted in the Kingdom of Lydia around 600 BCE—by more than 2,000 years.

Of course, in small and close-knit communities, debt was probably always handled in fairly informal and approximate ways, similar to our modern-day attitudes toward the exchange of goods and services among neighbors, family members, coworkers, or friends. In such settings, mutual and loosely tracked indebtedness serves as social glue more than a well-behaved financial instrument, and insisting on settling transactions on the spot—for example, demanding that your dinner guests reimburse you for the meal or offering cash to a friend who helped you with a move—could be taken as a slight.

But in larger societies where transactions tend to be less personal, the task of reconciling accounts appears to have been a more precise affair, delegated to trusted third parties since time immemorial. Cuneiform ledgers in Mesopotamia, for example, were kept in temples and presumably maintained by priests. However implemented, debt ledgers naturally enabled a wide range of economic activities within any stable, lawful society. Obligations could be paid back over time in one commodity or another, transferred, renegotiated, or forgiven, all without having to instantaneously settle trades.

If we accept the debt-based model of early economies, the first currencies almost certainly emerged as a straightforward consequence of the desire to settle on a particular unit of account. For example, if the aforementioned bushel of grain happened to be the most familiar and stable commodity in a particular region of the world, it would be simpler to track all account balances, and to quote all goods and services, using this quantity of grain as the reference point. Unlike in the classical barter model, this unit of account didn't need to be particularly durable, desirable, or easy to carry; it was simply an accounting tool. And indeed, unusual and easily damaged currencies of this sort are encountered throughout history—from the finished beaver pelts ("made beavers") used by early European settlers in North America[5] to the cigarette-denominated economies of many modern-day prison environments.[6]

The Age of Coin

Given the millennia that seem to have passed between the development of fairly complex economies and the emergence of coin, it would appear that contrary to conventional wisdom, a tangible medium of exchange wasn't in urgent demand for local economic activity in small tribes. Instead, as human settlements grew in size, merged with their neighbors, and occasionally went to war, the development of coinage can be more logically explained through the prism of widening networks of trade. When dealing with an unfamiliar or a possibly hostile buyer from faraway lands, the concept of a debt ledger doesn't always hold up. The other side might be disinclined to honor its obligations and might be able to get away with it too.

In such settings, there's clear merit to settling the transactions on the spot using physical tokens that are easy to carry, have a substantial intrinsic value, and enjoy nearly universal appeal. For much of the past 2,500 years, this role would commonly be filled by *commodity money*: round pieces stamped out of precious or semiprecious metals—predominantly silver and gold. At first, such coins coexisted with customary agricultural units of account and served a specialized purpose, but with the advent of sprawling continental empires, people embraced metals as the prevailing way to measure wealth or settle debts. Of course, ledgers and contracts remained the basis of much of global economic activity—but the accounts were now denominated in coin instead of grain.

What is far more of a mystery is how various governments ended up not just being involved in the issuance of coin, but monopolizing its supply in a way not seen in most other areas of enterprise. Why is it that private entities don't produce standardized coinage in the same way they produce so many other important commodities, from food to medicine to houses?

The conventional wisdom is that governments took on this role at the behest of their subjects, who found the system of privately issued money to be too confusing or too riddled by fraud. But to the famed heterodox economist Murray Rothbard, this explanation never passed the smell test. The relevant passage from his 1963 essay, flippantly titled "What Has Government Done to Our Money?," is worth quoting from at length:

> The idea of private coinage seems so strange today that it is worth examining carefully. . . . What is there to prevent private minters from stamping the coin and guaranteeing its weight and fineness? Private minters can guarantee a coin at least as well as a government mint. . . .
>
> Opponents of private coinage charge that fraud would run rampant. . . . But if government cannot . . . be trusted to ferret out the occasional villain in the free market of coin, why can government be trusted when it finds itself in a position of total control over money. . . ?
>
> . . . All modern business is built on guarantees of standards. The drug store sells an eight ounce bottle of medicine; the meat packer sells a pound of beef. The buyer expects these guarantees to be accurate, and they are. And think of the thousands upon thousands of specialized, vital industrial products that must meet very narrow standards and specifications. The buyer of a ½ inch bolt must get a ½ inch bolt and not a mere ⅜ inch. Yet, business has not broken down. Few people suggest that the government must nationalize the machine-tool industry as part of its job of defending standards against fraud.

To Rothbard, even if the government's involvement in the issuance of money could have had some noble roots, it soon became a self-serving endeavor that necessitated the elimination of most alternatives. This was because no government could ever resist the temptation of debasing the coin to wage wars, feed the poor, or build palaces for the ruling class—and for many centuries, they did so chiefly by making the tokens smaller or minting them out of alloys of lower purity (see Figure 7-1).

Doing this allowed the same amount of precious metal to be turned into greater quantities of physical currency that the government could use to pay back its debts while hoping that the subjects wouldn't notice—or that they'd be too invested in the status quo to take any meaningful steps. But to pull off such a crude monetary trick, officials needed to prevent others from offering private coinage that could over time develop a reputation as a safer or more valuable asset to hold.

Figure 7-1: The decline of the silver antoninianus in the Roman Empire, with coins of progressively lower silver content and lower quality (left to right, top to bottom). Image by Rasiel Suarez at Wikipedia.

There are those who disagree with Rothbard. One common rebuttal is the invocation of the so-called *Gresham's law*, an observation stating that bad money drives out good money. In other words, if two types of coinage are given the same standing, but one is intrinsically more valuable—for example, by the virtue of being minted of finer metal—the better coin will gradually disappear from circulation. To Rothbard's critics, this is proof that the government didn't need to crack down on privately minted coin for it to naturally lose its appeal.

But this rebuttal feels nonsensical. For one, in Gresham's model, the "disappearance" of finer coinage happens precisely because it's desirable as a store of value, tucked away rather than spent. Secondly, it's not a given that the lesser money would retain the same standing for long. As confidence in the government's fiscal policy wanes, it's entirely possible that merchants would refuse to take the state-issued currency, demanding more stable alternatives. We know this was the reality of many failed states in the 20th century—especially in the Soviet Bloc, where all kinds of "luxury" goods had to be purchased with deutsch marks, US dollars, and so forth (and where the government hunted the "currency speculators" and occasionally locked them up).

A more valid criticism of Rothbard's staunchly anti-government views is that debasement generally wasn't driven by any sinister urges. More often than trying to oppress the peasants and enrich the ruling class, government officials leaned on this approach in response to natural disasters and other pressing social needs; it's plausible that not pursuing such policies might have left our ancestors objectively worse off. The supply of metal waxed and waned too, making the value of currency fluctuate in unpredictable ways. And because money came to function as a familiar and somewhat abstract unit of account in domestic trade, the exact melt value of coinage stopped mattering as much; it follows that the tampering must have felt less like a crime, and more like a clever life hack.

Meanwhile, in parallel with the ongoing debasement of coin, another interesting development was brewing in the world of private finance: the invention of banknotes, issued by banks or other trusted institutions as receipts for deposited money and giving the bearer a way to reclaim the deposit on demand. Standardized banknotes were far easier to carry than bags of metal and gradually gained popularity, becoming a common element of trade somewhere around the 10th century.

Governments took note of the fact that people seemed to be perfectly willing to pay each other with intrinsically worthless paper or cloth, and duly applied the same idea into the world of the state-issued coinage. Thus began the era of *representative currency*—paper notes and coins minted from cheap metals, both accompanied by a simple pledge: the issuer offered to redeem them at any time for a predefined amount of silver or gold.

Of course, keeping in line with centuries of debasement, the promise was somewhat illusory. There weren't enough physical metal reserves to honor all redemption claims at once. Still, as long as people had faith in their leaders and the volume of requests for precious metal stayed reasonably low, the fundamental mechanics of this currency remained the same as before, both domestically and in foreign trade. The only obvious new risk was that in the event of the financial collapse or military defeat of the issuing state, its money would become worthless—but such scenarios weren't keeping most citizens up at night.

Fractional Reserve Banking and Fiat Money

In contrast to all the financial skulduggery undertaken by governments, commercial banking remained a rather dull affair for many millennia. It was an exercise in the reconciliation of accounts and the safekeeping of deposits. Perhaps surprisingly, early banks didn't play much of a role in what we now call *consumer lending*; instead, the vast majority of personal loans happened between people who knew each other in some way. This was in part because many religious doctrines and legal systems around the world prohibited *usury*—the collection of interest on loans—which was seen as an exploitative and indecent act. Of course, the rules were skirted every now and then, especially for business lending, but the broad prohibition nevertheless restrained the presence of banks in the lives of peasants and gentry alike.

In Europe, usury remained taboo until the 16th century. What caused the shift is unclear. Some scholars believe that the Reformation movement diverged on this matter from the Catholic Church, while others claim that both factions of Christianity remained equally critical of the practice, but the infighting weakened the religious authorities and allowed secular norms to change.

What is clear is that starting in the 17th century, many European countries witnessed the explosion of for-profit lending and the emergence of *fractional-reserve banks.* These private ventures operated according to a simple scheme: they accepted people's coin for safekeeping, promising to pay a premium on every deposit made. To meet these obligations and to make a profit, the banks then used the pooled deposits to make higher-interest loans to other folks. Taking a page from the government's playbook for representative currencies, the financiers figured out that under normal circumstances and when operating at a sufficient scale, they needed only a very modest reserve of coin on hand—well under 10 percent of all deposited money—to be able to service the usual volume and size of withdrawals requested by their customers. The rest could be loaned out.

The curious consequence of fractional-reserve banking was that it pulled new money out of thin air, and did so without any help from the government. A shilling deposited in the bank was seemingly available to its owner for transfer or withdrawal at any time, but also showed up in the purse of a stranger who borrowed it from the bank. Heck, that stranger could even deposit their shilling in another bank, to be loaned once more—in the end making it seem as if there were three shillings in the place of one.

Of course, no new money was being created in any physical sense. The deposits were gone until repaid by the borrowers. All that banks were doing was engaging in a bit of creative accounting—the sort that would probably land one in jail if attempted in any other enterprise. If too many depositors were to ask for their money back, or if too many loans were to go bad, the banking system would fold. Fortunes would evaporate in a puff of accounting smoke, and with the disappearance of vast quantities of money—generally on the depositors' side—the wealth of the entire nation would shrink.

Many conspiracy theorists see the fractional reserve system as the original sin, the first in a series of nefarious moves to rob the masses of their wealth. But that seems like a stretch. It was just as much in the banks' interest for the system to run smoothly as it was for ordinary people. There were economic arguments in favor of this arrangement too. For one, fractional reserve banking freed up funds that would otherwise have been unproductively squirreled away by skittish savers, and did so without having to convince each and every depositor to take risks for the betterment of the society. But the downsides were also plain to see. The model made lending a far less personal affair, replacing mutual indebtedness with a reality where everybody somehow owed money to a bank. More tangibly, banks—lacking the military, police, and tax powers of the government—were far more prone to crises and collapses than their state-level counterparts.

In the early 20th century, the world kept running into that very problem, experiencing a series of bank runs and economic contractions that forced governments to act. At that stage, outlawing fractional-reserve banking was no longer politically or economically tenable. A simpler alternative was to let go of gold and move to *fiat money*—an abstract currency that eschewed any pretense, however flimsy, of being tied to any physical commodity.

In the era of fiat currency, a new breed of economists saw the role of the monetary authorities not in trying to peg the value of money to any known good, but in freely manipulating its supply and flow to smooth out economic hiccups or stimulate growth. For example, a failing bank could be propped up with newly conjured money, perhaps under the guise of the government purchasing obligations from the insolvent financial institution at a price that nobody else would willingly pay. Conversely, an infrastructure project or social program could be financed by enticing banks to purchase government bonds with depositors' funds, effectively orchestrating a stealthy transfer of private wealth into the government's coffers, with the promise of repayment through tax revenues to be collected many decades in the future. With the money supply being theoretically infinite, exorbitant government debts no longer raised too many eyebrows.

But of course, there might be a price to pay for fiscal recklessness. The obvious peril of fiat money is that in the long haul, its value is determined strictly by the people's willingness to accept a piece of paper in exchange for their trouble. That willingness, in turn, is conditioned solely on their belief that the same piece of paper will buy them something nice a week, a month, or a year later. Especially as more and more of the economy is buoyed by government debt and by the expectation of cash flows growing for the foreseeable future, it follows that a simple crisis of confidence could make a currency nearly worthless overnight.

Indeed, as discussed in Chapter 3, such events have happened with striking regularity over the past hundred years. They can almost always be traced to the same root cause: the government living above its means for decades, and then suffering a sudden setback—a recession, a conflict, an embargo—that spooks consumers, triggers more government spending, and culminates in a downward spiral of fiscal doom.

For the United States, the switch to fiat money came relatively late, in 1971. To stop the dollar from losing value, the Nixon administration employed a clever trick: it ordered the freeze of wages and prices for the 90 days that immediately followed the move. The measure was purely psychological. People went on about their lives and paid the usual for eggs or milk, and by the time the freeze ended, they were accustomed to the idea that the "new," free-floating dollar was worth about the same as the old, quasi-gold-backed one. A robust economy and favorable geopolitics did the rest, and so far, the American adventure with fiat currency has been rather uneventful—perhaps except for the fact that the price of gold itself skyrocketed from $35 per troy ounce in 1971 to $850 in 1980 (or, from $210 to $2,500 in today's dollars).

Well, one thing did change. Now better positioned to freely tamper with monetary policy, the regulators adopted a policy of intentionally increasing the money supply at a rate that slightly outstripped the organic growth in economic activity. They did this to maintain a small, steady degree of inflation,* believing that it would discourage people from hoarding cash and force them instead to reinvest the savings for the betterment of society (strong parallels exist between this justification and the one used to support fractional reserve banking too).

---

* Naturally, inflation can have many causes. For example, prices can rise if there's a reduction in the availability of raw materials used to manufacture goods. That said, such fluctuations are different from regulators setting explicit inflationary targets and tweaking monetary policy until they achieve the intended goal.

Some critics point out that such a policy functions as an invisible and thus more politically palatable tax on savings, and that it happens to align with the government's more self-serving interests. Either way, the intentions are irrelevant. The bottom line is that in the United States and most other developed nations, the purchasing power of any money kept under a mattress will drop at a rate of somewhere between 2 percent and 10 percent a year—and in times of economic uncertainty, it might depreciate even more.

Cryptocurrencies

The history of money may be long and muddied, but popular opinions about financial systems and monetary policies aren't known for nuance—and are seldom fit to print. The exact critiques vary: to Graeber, whose book spends a great deal of time on the author's idyllic conception of "everyday communism," the perversion of finance originated within the banking system and the classist, neo-feudal power structures it supposedly upholds. To Rothbard, a free-market absolutist, all of our ills begin and end with the government's insatiable urge to live above its means and to control every aspect of our lives; the banking system is complicit only to the extent that it conspires with and profits from this excess. But people of all ideological persuasions seem to agree on one thing: that the system, for whatever good it might have done, is rotten to the core.

For decades, individuals who worried about the purported imminent collapse of fiat currencies flocked to the world of sleazy bullion peddlers who stoked the flames on late-night TV infomercials and on fringe radio shows. The buyers of silver and gold coin quickly became the butt of jokes for financial advisors who likened such behavior to betting against civilization and against human progress itself. For all the criticisms, the desire to hoard precious metals proved to be a fairly harmless preoccupation. In the era of fiat money, the price of gold and silver fluctuated quite a bit, but in the long view, the metals remained an asset with lasting appeal. They underperformed the stock market in some decades, but outpaced it in others. They weren't the most profitable investments to make if you lived in the United States, but they also weren't particularly terrible—especially if we consider that they offered the buyers some peace of mind.

More recently, a brand-new invention has challenged the status of precious metals as the investment of choice for individuals distrustful of banks and governments, or for speculators trying to make a quick buck. Within the past 10 years or so, Bitcoin and other virtual cryptocurrencies came out of nowhere and then rapidly reached a theoretical market capitalization of more than $1 trillion—about one-tenth the capitalization of gold.

Although the mechanics of various cryptocurrencies differ in important ways, the example of Bitcoin is instructive. It's a global, decentralized currency with no recoverable intrinsic value, no central authority to issue the money or set exchange rates, and no other mechanism anchoring it to the physical world. Until the publication of a technical paper by a mysterious person going by the pseudonym of Satoshi Nakamoto,[7] such a juxtaposition of properties would seem nonsensical, and as such, it escaped any serious debate. But with his invention, Nakamoto apparently accomplished the unthinkable—and did so by employing several clever computer tricks.

First, his design allowed anyone to create new (virtual) coins in the privacy of their homes, but only by solving computational puzzles that would get more difficult as time went by. This created an incentive for early adopters to "mine" Bitcoin, as doing so required only a modest investment of time and money, but offered the prospect of significant returns on the resale of these tokens as the difficulty of the puzzles went up (provided, of course, that public interest in this technology could be sustained in the long haul).

Next, the Bitcoin protocol established the ownership of coin through the use of cryptography. Only the authorized holder of a given coin would know the secret key needed to transfer the asset, but anyone in the world could verify that a transaction had taken place. And finally, Nakamoto's currency employed a decentralized, internet-based ledger—known as the *blockchain*—to record the chain of custody for coins in a tamper-proof way, and to rule out the possibility of the owner of a coin spending it twice. As long as the majority of market participants acted in good faith, the integrity of the blockchain was assured without the need for any central authority to keep track of transactions and accounts.

The consensus-operated blockchain is widely seen as Bitcoin's most revolutionary feature, and it contributed to the currency's image as a renegade financial instrument that has given back control of the financial system to the common folk. That said, the practical importance of the distributed ledger has decreased over time. With the influx of non-tech-savvy investors, most users of popular cryptocurrencies opted for centralized cloud-based services to store and manipulate the balances in their digital wallets, rather than trying to tinker with cryptography on their own computers. This emergent ecosystem is operated by a handful of large corporations, some with thousands of employees and valuations measured in the billions of dollars. In that regard, it's not particularly distinguishable from traditional banking—perhaps except for the lower degree of regulatory oversight and the limited recourse for customers when things go awry.

A striking feature of Bitcoin and some of its clones is the increasing scarcity of coins as the computational complexity of "mining" operations grows, and as some of the previously mined tokens are lost. Over the past couple of years, this constraint has caused the price of Bitcoin to increase more than a hundred-fold. Early growth created a positive feedback loop, where new investors would be attracted to the astonishing returns, and would double down on the currency in hopes of even higher gains. This speculative gold rush might be unsustainable—especially given that the use of Bitcoin in bona fide trade is minimal, and that future uses of this sort are hindered by a range of design flaws that lead to long processing times and steep transaction fees.

Of course, such pronouncements are cheap. In the end, it's genuinely difficult to know if Bitcoin and its ilk are here to stay, or what their "correct" valuation might be (assuming there's any rational upper bound). That's not to say that the collapse of these instruments is imminent. In some sense, a coin that represents a mathematical proof of wasted electricity is no better or worse than a currency with pictures of dead presidents. There might be a future where we're all using Bitcoin, Dogecoin, or one of the experimental "stablecoins" that are meant to be tethered to the value of physical commodities. But until that day comes, enthusiasm for a new technology is probably not a good substitute for principled management of risk.

Revisiting Dangers to Liquidity and Capital

This lengthy stroll through the history of money serves an important purpose. It sets the stage for a more grounded review of the most common threats to personal savings, and for a critical examination of the folksy financial remedies touted on the internet—from gold chains to blockchain and everything in between. A solid understanding of the history of barter helps us decide if bullets and beans are the best way to get through a currency collapse. A grasp of the causes and goals of inflation makes it easier to pinpoint instruments that track it more faithfully than silver or gold; and a sense of how money is created makes it easier to comprehend why banks fail.

Of course, it's not necessarily that national monetary policies and the actions of central banks are the most significant factors affecting the safety of your rainy-day fund. Many savers experience setbacks with far more prosaic and intimate causes. But to quantify and compare the probabilities and consequences of common calamities that may deprive you of your savings, and to develop versatile and future-proof response strategies, it still pays to keep the big picture in mind.

Loss of Access to Bank Accounts

Perhaps the most common financial indignity is being prevented from accessing one's bank account. This can happen for a number of reasons, many of them rather anticlimactic and temporary: a power outage or an errant backhoe that rips out fiber-optic cables can cause ATMs and point-of-sale terminals across town to stop working for a couple of days, for example. Or, if a bank decides that your card shows unexpected activity or is implicated in a security breach, it may unceremoniously cut you off until you contact the bank and get a replacement; this is usually a fairly painless process, but can get messy when you're standing in the checkout line with a cartful of groceries.

The failure of the financial institution where you keep your money is another seemingly fantastical but real risk to contemplate. Bank collapses are fairly common and happen for the same reason they always did: the failure to maintain sufficient reserves to meet demand. On a good year in the United States, about two to eight banks go belly up, but in the wake of the housing crisis between 2009 and 2012, more than 400 ended up shutting their doors.[8] Back then, in a wildly unpopular but probably necessary move, US authorities stepped in to prop up the balance sheets of the remaining players with massive injections of cash. This prevented a disastrous domino effect that could've wiped out the deposits of millions of customers. But even with the bailouts in place, some people experienced transient issues as the collapsed banks were being gobbled up by competitors or liquidated for good.

Thanks to the bailouts enabled by the flexible supply of money, that wave of bank collapses ended up being a non-event for the vast majority of depositors in the United States. But it's unwise to assume that the regulators will always have the same tools at their disposal and will be able to use them to good effect. For one, the European Union handled that crisis much worse. Individual member states lacked the necessary degree of control over the common currency, and as the bureaucrats bickered in Brussels and Frankfurt, the banks in Cyprus and Greece remained closed for weeks.[9] Although the impasse was eventually resolved, the prolonged "bank holidays" caught countless people at precisely the wrong time. The causes of the delays were complex, but for most customers, the solution could have been simple. It would have sufficed to keep several weeks' worth of physical cash on hand.

Adverse Judgments

If there's one category of financial hazards entirely disconnected from macroeconomics, it's personal injury lawsuits, contentious divorces, business disputes, and all other types of courtroom-related curveballs that life can unexpectedly throw our way.

To most people, such events are the stuff of lazily written soap operas or celebrity gossip columns—right up until they hit close to home. The statistics paint a sobering picture. More than 700,000 divorce petitions are filed every year in the United States,[10] for example, many ending amicably, but a good proportion metastasizing into bitter court fights. On the personal injury front, despite some recent declines, it is estimated that around 750,000 tort claims are filed annually—chiefly dealing with vehicle collisions, but also involving dog bites, slip-and-fall accidents on private property, and other routine happenstances that strike the rich and poor alike.[11]

For those who find themselves tangled up in a civil dispute, compassion and wisdom should prevail over anger and resentment. No real winners or losers emerge in divorce or child support cases, and there's no joy in prevailing over a person you badly hurt in a car accident. At the same time, it must be acknowledged that some percentage of lawsuits are filed in bad faith—and that even the most upstanding of defendants can sometimes get unlucky, pick a bad lawyer, or run out of money before being able to deliver a solid defense. Planning how you'd get back on your feet after such a blow isn't an immoral line of thought to contemplate.

Alas, developing strategies to cope with this scenario can be tricky. For one, nothing but misery usually awaits those who try to hide their assets from the court. That said, some lawful strategies can limit harm. For example, properly chosen liability insurance policies can offer some protection against many types of personal injury claims, while registering a company can help separate personal finances from family business activities, usually without the need to hire an accountant or deal with too much paperwork.

And in the worst case, thoughtful charitable giving—even on a modest scale—to help close friends or relatives in their time of need can open some doors if the tables ever turn.

Gradual Inflation

Inflation is a peculiar beast. Much like death and taxes, it's not merely a possibility, but practically a guarantee. As discussed earlier, regulators see to it that the inflation rate doesn't fall too low; occasional spikes also occur when the government gets too spendthrifty.

Over the past several decades, the annual change in consumer prices in the United States has hovered between 2 and 6 percent, with a handful of excursions between 10 and 13 percent.[12] Many other stable economies around the globe follow the same pattern, establishing a fairly consistent benchmark for what the future may hold.* On the low end of this range, inflation will halve the value of your cash savings in about 30 years—a rather glacial pace, but still enough to throw a wrench into your retirement plans. The upper end translates into far more pain: at 6 percent, the halving time drops to about a decade, while in the 13 percent territory, all it takes is a bit under five years.

Although none of these scenarios comes close to a financial emergency, it's wise to address the cost of inflation before the losses on existing savings begin to rival the contributions you're making to the rainy-day fund. The precise moment to take action depends on your savings rate and on the most recent inflation figures, but for most people, it probably coincides with having enough saved to cover one year's worth of living costs.

Sadly, the inevitability of inflation also makes it a uniquely challenging enemy. Nobody in their right mind is going to offer insurance against routine inflation losses if they're recompensed less than the expected payout of such a policy. A way to make this transaction work is to trade risk, not just cash.

If you want somebody else to pay you $10 to help offset a situation that's 99 percent certain, like inflation, they may be inclined to part with the money if you promise to pay them $1,000 to help them deal with an unrelated situation that has a 1 percent chance of coming true—say, if their business goes bankrupt in the coming year. This is a mutually beneficial trade. Both of you are buying insurance for the things you worry about, and nobody is trying to outwit the other guy.

The stock market is one popular and unfairly maligned conduit for making sophisticated deals of this sort (and separately from this, a tool for making phenomenally bad financial decisions too). In the most basic sense,

---

* Considerable controversy exists around the way governments measure inflation. Some developing countries have relied on creative accounting to boost their credibility, but for the United States and the European Union, the numbers are almost certainly sound. That said, the inflation index is just an abstract tool that tries to crudely approximate a perfectly average person in a perfectly average town with a perfectly average income and needs; it follows that the official findings can diverge pretty sharply from the cost of living for techies in Silicon Valley or coal miners in Wyoming.

the deal is simple: you invest some money in a company whose book value is expected to track or outpace inflation, with the understanding that you stand to lose your investment if the company folds.

Another way to offset inflation is to convert a significant proportion of your savings into assets that don't lose value with the debasement of currency, such as collectibles, real estate, or silver and gold. All of these holdings come with their own risks, however. Collectibles can be damaged or stolen, precious metals may lose value due to changes in industrial demand, and real estate is vulnerable to the whims of zoning boards. In other words, explicitly or not, you are still trading risks.

Hyperinflation

In a sense, hyperinflation is still just inflation. The difference is merely the rate of change, with prices doubling in a matter of weeks or months. There are two reasons to approach this scenario a bit differently, though—one that works to our advantage and one that doesn't.

The factor that can benefit the prepared is that hyperinflation is abnormal and unexpected. It's the line the government may be tempted to get close to but never wants to cross. It follows that—at least in principle—it's possible to cheaply insure against the risk. For example, you can purchase a *commodity futures option*, a standardized financial instrument that, in effect, gives you the right to buy a good, such as corn, from a supplier at a price much higher than what it sells for today. Under normal circumstances, the contract is nearly worthless and can be purchased for pennies, because it would be pointless to exercise it and become the owner of vastly overpriced cereal. But if a currency collapse causes corn prices to skyrocket, the instrument will entitle you to purchase corn for what's now a deeply discounted price—and then immediately resell it for more. (In fact, you wouldn't need to take the delivery of a truckload of cobs, as the futures option itself and the underlying delivery contract are both transferable and would be worth a lot to people who actually operate food processing companies.)

On the flip side, hyperinflationary scenarios don't unfold in a vacuum and are almost never a deliberate product of a coherent monetary policy. Instead, they tend to happen against the backdrop of government turmoil, military coups, civil wars, or profound economic slumps. This reality brings about a host of other perils, many of a decidedly nonmonetary kind: seizure of property, food rationing, and the persecution of political enemies, to name a few. In other words, any preparedness strategy that purports to deal with hyperinflation must extend well beyond the world of corn contracts and gold bars.

Hyperinflationary environments are also a canonical example of a dreaded *long emergency*: a train wreck that may begin suddenly, but whose lingering effects drag on for years. This can push all but the most extreme preparedness strategies past the breaking point, putting adaptability at a significant premium over even the most impressive stash of canned food.

Confiscation of Wealth

The chaos brought on by hyperinflation offers a convenient segue into the next topic: confiscatory taxes or other economic sanctions that may be levied in tumultuous times—almost always on minority groups—in an attempt to repair public finances or as a retribution for the groups' purported sins.

In this context, I use the term *minorities* not to refer to disadvantaged populations, but to any differentiated slice of society that doesn't wield majority sway over politics. This might be the ultra-poor as well as the ultra-rich; it might be palm readers or people who listen to jazz. The point is simple: because taxes are unpopular, leaders in democratic systems and dictatorships alike do what they can to avoid indiscriminate and explicit rate hikes to address budget shortfalls. When the creation of new money feels too risky, the other solution is a form of divide-and-conquer: tapping into popular sentiments to single out a class of people who can be blamed for hardships and inequities—sometimes rightly, sometimes not—and then making them pay.

Interestingly, the process can repeat almost ad infinitum. Yesteryear's victims often gang up on new targets in an attempt to level the playing field. An accordionist may be unhappy about having to pay the accordion tax, but what really incenses him is that the tuba lady next door isn't paying the same.

Of course, ethnic or religious minorities have at times been the targets of government taxation or expropriation. The German Decree on the Elimination of the Jews from Economic Life is just one of many examples of economic persecution that served as a prelude to genocide.[13] In the United States, the internment of Japanese Americans during World War II lives in infamy too. Although the policy wasn't ostensibly drafted with this outcome in mind, it caused tens of thousands of families to lose their homes and businesses simply because they had nobody else to tend to their livelihoods while they were housed in the camps.[14] The government "recompensed" the survivors some 45 years later, cutting them a fairly meager $20,000 check for the lives they could have had.

I don't know when the next episode of economic persecution may happen or who will be targeted, but I believe it's a risk worth keeping in mind. Instinctively, although ethnic or religious divides regrettably persist in economic policies in some parts of the world, they seem like an unlikely basis for new confiscatory taxes in highly developed nations.

Class tensions, on the other hand, are flaring up in ways that remind me of the populist revolutions of old. The 2007 financial crisis and the Occupy Wall Street movement, for example, served as an inflection point that recast top earners as villains who crashed the economy and made out like bandits thanks to the bailouts—a claim repeated not just in the fliers of local socialist clubs, but in mainstream politics. The arguments formulated in *Capital in the Twenty-First Century*, a seminal manifesto by the French economist Thomas Piketty (Belknap Press, 2014), have convinced millions that greatly increased taxes on top earners aren't just proper, but absolutely necessary to remedy the growing inequality in the West.

This renewed antipathy toward the affluent made it easier for regulators to confiscate foreign deposits during the Cypriot debt crisis, and to put wealth taxes back on the agenda in the United States. To make such proposals palatable to the electorate, our representatives usually evoke the image of billionaires—a caste of reclusive, elderly men surrounded by butlers and gilded chandeliers, the entire political establishment in their pockets (except, of course, for the one politician giving the speech). The problem with this narrative isn't that billionaires are necessarily a likable and diverse bunch, that they can't spare some change, or that their situation is somehow comparable to the plight of ethnic minorities. Sidestepping the moral questions altogether, the problem is simply that billionaires are few and far between, and their wealth—albeit substantial—comprises mostly assets that are hard to sensibly tax, such as the controlling interest in large companies.

In effect, the denouncements of billionaires are almost certainly just for show, at least when coming from people who aren't ready to bring back the guillotine. If substantial and sustained revenue is to be generated by taxing the rich, the policies need to target a much broader group, perhaps the top 5 to 10 percent of society. But in a country where a significant percentage of households have a negative net worth (often due to bank debt)[15] and where about half of filers don't clear the threshold that would make them owe any federal income tax,[16] it doesn't take a seven-figure income to end up in the top cohort. The group comprises chiefly salaried professionals who work full-time jobs in desirable fields.

Of course, criticism of the well-off isn't persecution, and not all tax hikes are unjust. The scenario to ponder here isn't that the effective tax rate for top earners in California or New York may go from 52 to 54 percent, or that a recurring surcharge of 1 percent may be collected on savings balances of six or seven figures. It's that the battle lines have been drawn, that class inequality is one of the most consequential debates of our era, and that the rifts continue to grow, rooted in emotion as much as in facts. Especially in the eyes of the younger generation, many well-compensated professionals—civil engineers, doctors, IT folks, financial advisors, and so on—are perceived less and less as the embodiment of the American Dream, and more as the architects of the system that's holding everybody else down. In such a world, far more radical wealth redistribution policies might eventually succeed too.

The (Monetary) Zombie Apocalypse

The final risk to mention—albeit only in passing—is the prospect of a complete collapse of modern finance and the disintegration of global trade. Such a catastrophe is a perennial favorite in the prepper community, though the mechanism bringing it about is never explained in detail. A passing mention of coronal mass ejections or nuclear EMPs (see Chapter 4) is usually the best you can get.

Absent a clear explanation, the focus is strictly on the outcome: a tribal world where small groups of survivors occasionally barter goods. After the prerequisite exposition, the conversation inevitably drifts toward the correct trade goods to stockpile in order to gain the upper hand. Would cigarettes be the ideal barter item? Small bottles of alcohol? Ammunition? Canned beans? Salt? Or perhaps soap?

Even if we accept the underlying premise, the idea of stockpiling heaps of ammunition or salt is rooted in a misunderstanding of the history of currencies and trade. Direct barter is unlikely to emerge as the cornerstone of post-apocalyptic commerce. Communal ledgers are far more likely to make a comeback, but ledger-based markets are geographically constrained—and there are limits to how much soap or salt can be distributed across the neighborhood without severely depressing the value of the commodity. More fundamentally, the approach violates the risk management principles outlined in Chapter 1; a pallet of crusty old soap is nearly impossible to sell without taking a major loss should the apocalypse not come.

It can be argued that such preparations offer an attractive cost-payoff ratio. A thousand bars of soap can be purchased for several hundred bucks, but in a future world critically deprived of hygiene supplies, it could set the forward-thinking entrepreneur for life. But of course, this ignores probabilities: countless improbable futures like this could exist, including a world in dire need of coffee or pencils but indifferent to bodily scents. Betting on the right outcome is difficult, and even with a warehouse full of assorted household commodities, it's most likely that none of them will ever be worth its weight in gold.

As for the most likely post-apocalyptic currency, unless it's severely devalued beforehand, I suspect that the continued use of the paper currency of the now-defunct government would be the logical choice. As demonstrated in the Nixon era, the force of habit is a powerful thing. The benefits of a familiar system of prices are nothing to sneeze at either. In short, there would be no special reason to abandon the paper; if anything, "they're not making any more of it" would be a pretty solid selling point.

Methods for Mitigating Risk

Financial systems are exhilarating, messy, and scary. But as should be evident from our discussion so far, they are emergent and chaotic phenomena, not a sinister scheme devised to take from the poor and give to the rich. When used wisely, such systems can work to your benefit, no matter the exact size of your nest egg. With that in mind, and now that we have the taxonomy of the challenges sketched out, let's dive into some of the investment strategies that can help protect your savings down the line.

If you approach a financial advisor and ask them what to do with your savings, their first question will be about your investment objective—expecting to hear that you want to retire early, send your children to a posh college, or make a lot of money on self-driving cars. But their first *real* question will be about your risk tolerance. If you're risk-averse, they'll keep your account mostly in cash or government bonds, but if you tell them you want to get rich quick, they'll recommend putting a good chunk of your money into stocks that historically showed high volatility, with the implication that higher payoffs might result down the line.*

For the purpose of safeguarding rainy-day funds, I believe this thinking is flawed; risk has many dimensions. Cash, despite its characterization as virtually risk-free, is nothing of the sort. It comes with the near-certainty of gradual inflation that eventually wipes out all unattended funds, along with the small but non-negligible chance of a hyperinflationary event or deposit forfeiture. Real estate carries risks, too, just of a different kind. In addition to large events like the housing market collapse of 2007, your home can lose a lot of value simply if your neighbor opens a backyard hog farm. Every asset has a combination of "risk vectors" attached to it, pointing in different directions in a multidimensional space. The primary goal of a doomsday portfolio is to balance these forces so that no single event can wipe out the bulk of our savings. To be sure, some losses might be unavoidable in trying times—but there's a fundamental difference between experiencing a 30 percent dip in the midst of a recession and flat out going broke.

Conversely, you should never try to grow your rainy-day savings by making flagrantly risky bets. There's a place and time for that—the stock market certainly offers reasonable odds for the betting individual—but speculative investments should be limited to surplus funds you aren't afraid to lose, ideally kept in a separate account. For the rainy-day fund, the only "gains" you need to make are to keep up with the continued depreciation of the currency that's used to measure the size of the nest egg. If fortune smiles upon you and you earn more, that's just a happy accident.

Physical Cash

Some savers, especially the lot born in the 1970s and before, see physical cash as the ultimate tool for financial independence: something that can't be taken away by the government or misappropriated by the bank. This thinking made sense for much of the 20th century, but it stands on shaky ground today. The authorities have found new ways to prop up public finances and to keep banks afloat by purchasing distressed obligations at questionable prices—and if these tools malfunction, leaving the government holding the bag, the purchasing power of cash kept under the mattress is bound to be severely impacted too. In other words, the risk profiles of deposits and paper money are not as different as they used to be.

That's not to say that keeping physical cash is pointless. It still excels at getting us through transient difficulties, such as power outages, temporary bank closures, and so forth. From this perspective, keeping enough to cover about two to four weeks' worth of essential expenses is a good call. On the flip side, growing the stash past that point probably offers diminishing

---

* The world of investing is a mix of statistics, computer science, and ancient summoning rituals. The particular approach discussed here is the artifact of statistical analysis: within a class of assets, historical volatility, future risk, and potential payoff are often correlated. Because historical volatility is the only parameter that can be measured ahead of time, there's a temptation to evaluate investments as if all three variables were the same.

returns, especially given that physical money is commonly stolen in burglaries, and can be destroyed in fires or floods. It's a good rule of thumb to keep only as much of it on hand as you aren't afraid to lose.

Another oft-overlooked use for physical cash is travel. The ability to pay out of pocket for unscheduled lodging or a new return flight is worth the peace of mind, especially if you're on the road often or are visiting places you aren't familiar with. Of course, any such funds should be kept in a place that is pickpocket- and mugging-proof; tourists make easy marks.

Physical cash is also a valuable privacy tool. It's one of the few remaining assets that can be stored or spent easily without leaving an extensive paper trail. In an era where every electronic transaction is mined for behavioral insights and stored on internet-facing servers for years, cash lets you opt out of constant surveillance. Of course, all kinds of valuable physical goods can be used to the same effect, but none are accepted as widely as cash.

Alas, because of its utility in evading taxes and court judgments, many governments would rather have this antiquated payment instrument go away. In the United States, many large-denomination bills, such as the $1,000 banknote, were effectively removed from circulation and are probably not coming back. Any commercial cash transactions over $10,000 need to be reported to the Internal Revenue Service on Form 8300 too. Meanwhile, in parts of Europe, it's flat out illegal to use paper money for most transactions in excess of a threshold as low as €1,000.[17] As the percentage of underbanked populations around the world is shrinking rapidly, some economists and policymakers are openly talking about a cashless future where no transaction can escape government oversight.

Diversified Bank Deposits

Although not completely risk-free, money in the bank is still a valuable tool. It provides instantaneous and convenient liquidity, and in perhaps nine out of ten economic crises, holds up value very well. Just as important, it provides an essential buffer to protect other, more volatile assets. For example, in the middle of a run-of-the-mill recession, the prices of stocks or collectibles may experience a temporary dip, and it would be unfortunate to have to get rid of them at fire-sale prices to make the rent.

With money, inflation is, of course, the most significant woe. It used to be that bank deposits paid sufficient interest to offset the losses. But today, flush with liquidity and subject to new restrictions on riskier investments, banks don't particularly want your savings, offering near-zero nominal returns on what you give them (or negative returns when you take inflation into account). Because of this, the maximum to keep in the bank is probably the amount for which the losses can be regularly replenished without breaking a sweat. To illustrate, let's assume you have one year's worth of living expenses saved, and that you're adding 10 percent of your post-tax income every year. In this scenario, with inflation at 2.5 percent and bank interest around 0 percent, roughly one fourth of your new contributions would go toward replenishing the purchasing power of your original fund. Don't blink: if you have two years' worth of expenses saved and inflation goes up to 5 percent, then the entirety of your ongoing contributions would be effectively going to waste.

Whatever the balance in your savings account, one useful trick is to split your funds across at least two financial institutions with different risk profiles: perhaps a local credit union and a large national bank. This diversification actually increases the risk of having one of the institutions go under or suffer transient technical issues, but greatly decreases the odds of losing access to all your funds at once. And in places where bank deposits are insured (in the United States, the FDIC insurance limit is $250,000 per depositor per bank), even if one of the banks eventually goes belly up, your funds should survive—so it's a pretty good trade.

This multi-bank setup has one gotcha, and its name is *escheatment*: an obscure, self-dealing rule that requires abandoned property to pass on to the state. In most of the United States, a bank account is deemed abandoned if it shows no qualifying activity for somewhere between three and five years. Of course, just like their customers, banks hate escheatment, so they usually go out of their way to locate the customer before the time runs out. But if they have the wrong address or an outdated phone number, or if you happen to be in the hospital or on an extended trip, that notification may be missed. It's best not to take chances. Setting up a calendar reminder to periodically log into "backup" accounts or to rack up some minor purchases should be enough.

Bonds

Bonds are transferable debt obligations. They're issued by organizations wishing to finance their operations—perhaps a city wanting to build a new bridge or a company planning to upgrade a production line. Every such obligation confers the right for the buyer to collect repayment of the original purchase price of the bond, plus interest, at some later date. Interest payments usually happen on a set schedule through the lifetime of the bond, while the principal is repaid in full at the expiration (*maturity*) of the instrument.

Broadly speaking, to make the purchase of bonds worthwhile, the interest promised to the purchaser must be higher than the inflation expected across the lifespan of the bond; otherwise, the buyer would be lending cash at a loss.* In theory, this makes bonds a great way to hedge against inflationary risk. In fact, the theory gets even better: some types of bonds, such as US Treasury Inflation-Protected Securities (TIPS), offer returns proportional to changes in the consumer price index, thus removing the need to guess which way inflation might go. But that's just the theory. In reality, in today's markets, the benefits of bonds can be extremely slim.

---

* The nuance here is that bonds don't need to be held until maturity; they also can be sold on the secondary market to other investors. It follows that the original buyer might purchase a bond simply because they think they'd be able to sell it later for more, even if the terms of the loan don't seem all that great. Further, loss-generating bonds can sometimes be purchased simply because the buyer thinks that other options—such as holding cash or buying stocks—are going to cost them more, or because they have regulatory or contractual obligations to own such instruments as a way to maintain a particular risk profile.

To understand the issue, it's helpful to divide the bond universe into two broad categories: first are bonds issued by national governments—for example, by the US Treasury. In countries that set their own monetary policy, such bonds are considered very low risk, as the government can conjure money to meet its obligations, and a decision to renege on such debt would need to be driven by political desires, not economic need. But in the current economic environment, such bonds also happen to pay next to nothing, with effective interest rates sometimes dipping below zero. The meager payoffs, the long lock-in periods that may be required to realize full profit, and the presence of residual if unlikely monetary policy risk, all conspire to make treasury bonds a pretty unconvincing buy.

A more interesting category of obligations are bonds issued by states, municipalities, and corporations. These "lesser" bonds tend to pay better in exchange for an increased risk of a default. That said, the market for stocks—coming up shortly—is comparatively more diverse and offers better returns for taking similar long-term risks, as long as you can put up with some price swings in the interim. In addition, bonds have fairly complex second-order dynamics tied to interest rates, which are set by the regulators to implement inflation policy goals. Without getting too deep into the woods, this means they can behave in rather undesirable ways, such as bond valuations decreasing just as consumer prices are going up.

Simple Currency Hedges

Having talked about the asset classes vulnerable to inflation and monetary crises, we can now pivot to instruments that help offset the risk. Perhaps the most straightforward option are simple currency positions that are expected to hold value or appreciate whenever the purchasing power of the rest of our savings goes down.

By far the most familiar and purest example of this are loans. In financial parlance, they amount to taking a short position against your local currency. If you use a loan to buy a home, and the currency is subsequently severely devalued, you can repay the principal of the loan in now-worthless money, and you become the lucky owner of some deeply discounted real estate.

Of course, loans introduce their own set of risks when it comes to household finance. The installments are usually non-negotiable and rather substantial, and can compromise your financial outlook in the wake of more likely crises, such as losing a job. So, although mortgages or other obligations can actually benefit you in hyperinflationary environments (ignoring the general misery and economic chaos that ensues), it's not a particularly good idea to rack up extra debt simply as a part of a financial preparedness plan.

Another hedging strategy with fewer side effects is to convert some of your money to a foreign currency that's expected to be more stable than the one issued by the local government. For example, a person in Mexico worried about the state of the economy could be tempted to trade some of their pesos for US dollars. But this strategy suffers from a problem: it trades exposure to one fiat currency for another in a symmetrical way. This is because a significant proportion of funds needs to be moved into the other currency to achieve good hedging properties; a couple of $20 bills squirreled away in the house aren't going to offset the risk of 1 million pesos in the bank. In the end, for citizens in the developing world, or in countries plagued by political strife, the dollar, the euro, or the yen may be a good choice. But if you're in one of the highly developed and stable economies, it's hard to find a currency that can be convincingly argued to be safer than the one at home, especially given how interconnected they all are.

Perhaps a better question would be, if the euro or the dollar suffered a humiliating fall from grace, what currency would the global capital flock to and buoy? In a major shakeup of global order, this could end up being one of the currencies of the developing world, but under more prosaic circumstances, perhaps the Swiss franc would be able to capitalize on its reputation as a monetary safe haven. The country has fairly sound public finances and a long history of weathering storms. On the flip side, some of the reputation hinged on Switzerland maintaining massive gold reserves to keep the franc quasi-backed by the shiny commodity; this requirement was abolished in a referendum in 1999.[18]

Equities

With basic currency-based strategies out of the way, the next subject on the agenda is the stock market—a peculiar beast that traffics primarily in the fractional ownership of companies. A business can opt to have its ownership divided into a considerable number of standardized units that are then offered for sale on a public exchange. For the company, the benefit is the massive influx of cheap cash from the sale of something it could previously market to only a handful of billionaires. For the buyers, the perk is the acquisition of a piece of the underlying business—that is, equity—often entitling them to vote on critical matters and to collect dividends. The valuation of the stock is also grounded in the fact that it provides a proportional claim on the company's assets if the business ever decides to liquidate, and entitles the shareholders to a fair payout if the business is acquired or goes private. It follows that as the enterprise grows, so does the valuation of the shares.

The equities market has an odd reputation. In political speeches, it's often cast as a "casino," a zero-sum game in which the small guy always gets the short end of the stick. In reality, it's a fantastic and accessible tool that allows investors to take principled and equitable risks, often permitting both sides of the transaction to satisfactorily accomplish their goals. That said, it also allows people to go broke chasing extremely speculative profits in up-and-coming industries such as biotech, machine learning, self-driving vehicles, cryptocurrency mining, or recreational pot. In some cases, the market also serves as a conduit for bad financial outcomes the victims have no say in. For example, many pension funds and employer-sponsored retirement programs don't give the participants much choice on the investments made, but they make the customers hold the bag when the fund managers' stock picks go sour.

Still, such existential objections aside, in the context of managing emergency funds, the most important point is that the stock market gives the investor a claim on something real. The value of most businesses comes not from piles of cash they keep in the vault, but from the buildings, equipment, and intellectual property they own.* It follows that inflation does little direct harm. If the purchasing power of the dollar decreases 5 percent, the stock should appreciate about as much.

Of course, things are seldom as simple as they seem. For one, unexpectedly high inflation can hurt companies that must maintain a significant operating capital or that loan money to others. A profound economic contraction can make a business suffer irreparable damage too, by robbing it of customers and markets for what they produce. But above all, the valuation of companies seldom hinges just on the snapshot of their assets and liabilities. Investors also factor in their expectations of growth. A dying company with shrinking revenues and growing debt is going to be much less attractive than its fast-growing competitor, even if its book value is about the same.

In practice, many stable and established businesses, such as the manufacturers of industrial goods, often trade within earshot of their fundamental value. On the other end of the spectrum, the premiums on fast-growing technology stocks—Amazon, Apple, Google, Tesla, and so forth—can be exorbitant, essentially signaling that the investors expect phenomenal returns for many years to come. The peril of such valuations is that anything that spooks investors could cause a sudden fire sale that would continue until the stock price is closer to reality. It follows that if the goal is the preservation of capital, rather than the pursuit of riches, it's vastly preferable to stick to companies that are valued fairly. Perhaps the best manual for identifying such businesses is *The Intelligent Investor*, a timeless book by Benjamin Graham, first published in 1949 and regularly republished since.

The eternal problem novice investors face is determining whether the market is "too high" or "too low"; of course you'd want to wait out the times when the valuations seem over-the-top, and then double down when the prices dip. My best answer is that such ruminations are fairly meaningless. Companies that appear overvalued and businesses that trade at bargain-bin prices always exist. The ratio between the overvalued and the fairly valued regularly shifts one way or the other, leading to various pronouncements about the health of the marketplace, but this is a distraction. If you invest in stable, fairly valued enterprises, it doesn't matter if some cybersecurity startup is trading at 100 times its revenue. It is, however, true that in a frothy market, finding good investments requires more effort; throwing darts at the board won't do.

This brings us, in a roundabout way, to the topic of *index funds*. These passively managed investment vehicles are the brainchild of John C. Bogle, the founder of The Vanguard Group. Bogle observed that most brokerage customers—and most professional fund managers, for that matter—didn't

---

* Financial enterprises, such as publicly traded banks, are a notable exception. They usually hold significant reserves of cash, bonds, and related instruments, along with being more exposed to other economic risks.

seem to be able to beat the returns of an index (the Dow Jones, S&P 500, or a similar capitalization-weighed sum of the prices of many stocks). He argued that the smartest thing for an investor to do is put their money in an investment fund containing such a blend of equities, managed by his firm for a very low fee.

People listened—and today, nearly half of all money in the stock market flows through index funds.[19] The sheer scale of this phenomenon is raising eyebrows. Some argue that when so much money moves in and out of equities with no consideration for the health of individual businesses, it has the potential of creating "zombie companies" and precipitating the next market crash.[20] This theory is controversial, however. Its critics retort that markets are efficient, and that all the prevalence of index funds does is create opportunities for other players to bet against the overvalued components of an index and then drive them into the ground.

Meanwhile, my concern with index funds is much simpler. I worry that they bring back the inscrutable question of whether "the market" is valued too high or too low. It's nearly impossible to reason about the correct price for the composite of hundreds of companies, including a large collection of international financial conglomerates. I find it much easier to wrap my head around the financials of a dozen hand-picked businesses—say, a freight railroad, a cemetery operator, a paper mill, and a concrete plant.

I'm reminded of the parable of Mr. Market in Graham's book: he describes a gentleman who knocks on your door every day and always offers to trade the same item—but on every visit, he quotes a different price. On Monday, he's buying and selling for $100; the day after, he wants $200; on Wednesday, all he can muster is $10. A savvy investor knows the value of the good. She buys from Mr. Market on days when the quoted price makes for a bargain, and sells back to him on days when he's quoting way too much. But many investors do precisely the opposite. Without knowing the value of the good, they buy on Tuesday for $200, encouraged by the upward trend, and then panic-sell on Wednesday, rattled by the price drop. The point of this parable is that confidence in our choices matters, perhaps more than always being right. To me, an index fund that lost 50 percent of its value overnight would be an awfully difficult thing to hold; investors with unwavering faith in the efficiency of markets may have fewer qualms.

Stock Options and Commodity Futures Options

An *option* is a standardized, paid contract that gives the purchaser the right—and not the obligation—to buy or sell the underlying asset to the underwriter of the contract at a particular price and before a particular date. This is a mouthful, so to illustrate, let's imagine that I'm feeling very bullish on Hasbro, the manufacturer of Mr. Potato Head. A single share of the company is currently trading at around $100, but I think that with the introduction of the new animatronic, Wi-Fi–enabled Mr. Potato Head Ultra product line, the stock will easily reach $1,000 within a year.

When I mention my sentiment to my fellow traders, they're in disbelief. One jumps up and exclaims: "I own the stock, but if it goes up to as much as

$500, I'll eat my hat!" So, we make a deal: at any time within the next year, I can show up at her doorstep and ask for her 100 shares of Hasbro—and she has to hand them over for $500 a piece and not a penny more. For her signature on that contract, I pay her $100 in cold hard cash.

My trade partner just made a quick $100 that she can put to immediate use. The contract will almost certainly expire worthless, because no sane person would show up to buy the stock for $500 if it's trading on the open market for less. But if the price skyrockets and I come to collect, she's still not hurting; she's collecting $50,000 to fork out 100 shares that were trading for $10,000 when we made the deal. All she's giving up is a chance for further profit if the stock continues to rally past the $500 mark.

To me, it's a pretty good deal too. If my investment thesis is right and the stock reaches $1,000, I can visit my friend, buy her shares for $50,000, and immediately resell them on the open market for $100,000—a clean and tidy gain of $50,000. And if my optimism about animatronic Mr. Potato Head was somehow misplaced, all I stand to lose is the $100 I handed over on day one. The risk-payoff ratio on this trade is superb.*

A similar contract can be used to bet on a decrease in prices. All that needs to change is that the underwriter of the contract must promise to buy shares at a particular price, rather than sell them to me—and to be safe, they need to have cash, not stock, lined up. In practice, many combinations of such directional bets can be made at different price points, with or without accompanying equity positions, allowing all kinds of complex payoff structures to be created.

When misused, options can quickly wipe your brokerage account clean—and in some situations, leave you on the hook for more. That said, such outcomes are almost never accidental. They're the consequence of options giving their user a great deal of deliberate control over the risk-payoff curve on trades, encouraging some to chase riches, only to lose their shirts when the market moves in an unexpected way. In the right hands, options have numerous beneficial uses—including as a way to offset the risk of stock investments, currency holdings, and more.

Of all the uses for options, in the context of emergency preparedness, their potential to work as insurance policies is perhaps most intriguing. For example, if your portfolio or your employment outlook depends on the prospects of the tech industry, and if the market is bullish on tech, you can probably find several red-hot stocks with options strategies (*puts* or *debit put spreads*) that expire worthless if the price remains stable or climbs up, but that offer returns of 100 times or more if the sector goes down in flames. A policy that costs 1 percent of your annual income or portfolio value, and that offers broad protection against catastrophic losses in your area of livelihood, is probably a pretty good deal.

---

* Of course, just like the "stockpile of soap" example discussed earlier, this remark ignores the probability of success; the bet is ridiculous, which is also what made it relatively cheap. But the example serves to demonstrate the mechanics of options, and how they can be used in a way that benefits both sides and doesn't require taking undue risks.

A similar hedging position can be entered for any stock you hold. This is known as a *protective put* or *married put*. The strategy limits the downside on an investment without capping the upside. It's implemented by purchasing a contract that guarantees the right to sell the stock at a preset minimal price. If the stock plummets below that price, you have a guaranteed way to recoup some of your losses, but if the stock's value continues to rise, you're out only the cost of the option. Depending on market sentiment, this strategy might not cost much, especially for less volatile stocks.

As hinted earlier in the chapter, in addition to the very liquid market for equity options, retail investors can also trade futures options on commodities such as grain, cattle, or copper, or on all kinds of foreign currencies. The mechanics of such trades are fairly similar to stock options. For example, if you want to purchase insurance against the sudden depreciation of the US dollar, and think that the Swiss franc is going to fare considerably better, you can buy an instrument that effectively gives you the right to purchase francs for substantially more dollars then they're currently worth. As in other cases, the option will probably expire worthless—but because the contract is inexpensive, it can offer dramatic returns in response to cataclysmic price shifts.

Once again, the key to all such options strategies is that they aren't supposed to involve wishful thinking or aggressive bets. We buy insurance policies for things that are unlikely and that we'd prefer not to happen in the first place. Other options strategies can be exhilarating to experiment with, but until they're mastered, such activities should be kept at arm's length from the assets we might conceivably need down the line.

Precious Metals

Compared to bonds or options, precious metals are simple. You either have a gold coin or you don't. What tends to be less clear is the role such commodities should play in the balanced portfolio of a well-prepared individual.

One popular trope is that gold and silver could become the currency of choice in a post-apocalyptic world where all paper money somehow loses its luster. But this seems unlikely. Although the metals functioned in this capacity for millennia, this day and age, few people have even the faintest idea what a silver coin is worth, or how to tell if it's real. On top of this, relatively few such coins are in private possession, and they aren't distributed in any useful way. In your neighborhood, one person might have 1,000 Silver Eagles hidden under the floorboards, while 50 other households will have none. An attempt to bootstrap a silver- or gold-based economy could succeed, but it wouldn't be an easy feat.

More prosaically, metals are often touted by their supporters as the perfect inflation hedge, but in practice, the commodity seldom behaves this way. Of course, in a monetary collapse, gold is bound to hold up value much better than paper money, but under normal circumstances, the prices fluctuate significantly for reasons that are difficult to ascertain, such as the whims of speculators or the geopolitics of mining the metal in faraway lands. When the price of your hedge can move 50 percent one way or another for reasons unrelated to inflation, its poorly characterized volatility needs to be taken into account—and it better be outweighed by the instrument's potential benefits.

On the topic of benefits, one important perk unique to precious metals is that in comparison to most other assets you can hold in your hand, they're remarkably liquid. Any standard bar or coin can be sold quickly, for cash, close to its spot price. Another undeniable plus is that similarly to paper currency, precious metals are private. Although some reporting requirements exist in the United States for larger trades, they currently apply to only very specific forms of the metal, such as gold bars over 32 troy ounces and 1 oz. Mexican onza coins. As for the proverbial gold buried in your backyard, that's strictly between you and the squirrels watching from the trees. Finally, the compact size and the high value of gold bullion is of note. Individuals fleeing oppressive regimes can carry tens of thousands of dollars in life savings in their pocket, and liquidate the metal anywhere in the world.

In recent years, the proponents of cryptocurrencies have sometimes mounted backhanded critiques of precious metals in an effort to elevate their instrument of choice. They charge that just like Bitcoin, gold and silver have no intrinsic value, and that all the value derives from the *belief* that a particular metal ought to be worth much. That's a silly argument. *Intrinsic value* doesn't mean that the instrument needs to be worth the same to the reptilians living on Omicron Persei 8; it's just that its price comes from the innate characteristics of the asset itself. Here on Earth, both gold and silver are fairly rare and difficult to extract, and they have substantial industrial uses and an enduring nonmonetary appeal in jewelry.

This doesn't explain the entirety of price movements, of course: for example, in the early 21st century, inflation-adjusted gold prices dipped into the range of $400 to $600 when many governments, including Switzerland, started to sell off their massive gold reserves. The metal then briefly peaked at $2,000 before settling around $1,200 in the wake of the housing crisis, as many investors fled the financial system and moved into physical commodities. The COVID-19 pandemic—or rather, the massive stimulus that followed— caused another spike. For as long as economic anxieties prevail, the valuations of precious metals will probably stay where they are or keep climbing. If the tides turn, I suspect we could see prices closer to $1,000 or so.

One major challenge with metals is the risk of physical loss. Although such assets are far more resistant to fires or floods than paper money, they're an attractive target for theft. Because of this, keeping substantial amounts of gold or silver in your home is a risky bet. Bank safe deposit boxes are an affordable and secure option, although in a crisis, bank closures or other government-imposed restrictions may make it difficult to retrieve such goods. This happened during the sovereign debt crisis in Greece.[21]

Dedicated depository organizations may be less vulnerable to such disruption, but they charge steeper fees and also aren't entirely free of risk. In a 2021 incident, for example, the FBI seized the entire inventory of one such company in Beverly Hills simply by arguing that a significant percentage of its customers were criminals. Law-abiding clients caught up in the mess faced an uphill battle to reclaim their deposits.[22]

Real Estate

Ask any real estate agent for investment advice, and you'll be instructed to buy land: after all, they aren't making any more of it! By itself, this saying doesn't mean much, but in countries or regions with robustly growing population—including much of the United States—a second home or a vacant parcel could make for an inflation-proof asset that's likely to appreciate in the long haul.

A cynical investor would also note that the supply of new housing is artificially limited by powerful forces at play, including increasingly restrictive zoning laws, suspect environmental policies, and onerous building codes pushed for by an unholy alliance of local bureaucrats and homeowners who want their quaint cul-de-sacs to be forever frozen in time. Another contributor to the housing misery are ineffectual government policies that try to make housing affordable by subsidizing loans without sufficiently expanding the supply of new homes.*

The questionable morality of exploiting these trends aside, the practical problem is that because of the high price of real estate, even fairly affluent buyers can't afford to diversify, limiting most aspiring real estate moguls to a single investment parcel. In this case, your fortunes are tied to the economic prospects of a single region, to the whims of the local planning and permitting departments, and to the actions of your neighbors who—as noted earlier—can always opt to start a backyard hog farm or a puppy mill.

Rental properties are a can of worms too. Rightly or wrongly, landlords as a social class are a reviled bunch, especially in some of the most attractive and progressive housing markets in the United States and abroad. In such places, they're often portrayed as robber barons hell-bent on exploiting the downtrodden, and face nearly insurmountable difficulties when trying to evict deadbeat tenants who have no intention of paying and are stringing the landlord for a ride. True horror stories appear fairly uncommon, given the sheer size of the market, but frustrating tenant relationships happen more often, anecdotally accounting for perhaps 1 to 5 percent of all cases.

If a landlord doesn't carefully screen their tenants, the likelihood of trouble goes up significantly too. The moment a new property comes onto the market, the owner might be approached by people with a history of bad behavior or fraud who were turned down by everybody else. Deciding who to take chances on, who to turn away, and where to draw the line on a family of renters that's causing constant grief is never an easy task.

---

* Not that governments, especially in urban areas, have a particularly good track record of trying to increase supply. Many of the early subsidized housing projects in the United States involved the construction of massive high-density developments that concentrated poverty and quickly gained notoriety for deteriorating living conditions and high crime. Though somewhat better, European governments also have a decidedly mixed track record with public housing projects.

All in all, real estate becomes an investment with a well-defined risk profile only by the time the cost of a single property no longer accounts for the bulk of your wealth—but for most, this isn't a realistic financial goal, unless you decide to take chances on up-and-coming rural regions you're personally familiar with. Another solution pursued by some investors is to opt for vehicles called *real estate investment trusts (REITs)* that pool the deposits to make more diverse bets. But if you take this route, you don't have much insight or control over what the fund is buying and why; as with index funds, the convenience comes at a cost.

Perhaps the safest way for mid-income folks to own property as an investment is to buy a rural plot for recreation purposes, maybe building a small cabin or camping out there with the family. This way, the price tends to be more manageable—low five figures can do the trick in many parts of the country—and you get some reasonably guilt-free and drama-free enjoyment out of it.

When buying rural land, there are plenty of things to look out for, and a thorough discussion of these topics is well outside the scope of this book. A good real estate agent familiar with the local market is well worth the price. That said, some of the sticking points may include water rights and the practicality of drilling a well; road access considerations along with easements from or to neighboring land; the ease of installing a septic system; the slope and drainage patterns on the parcel; the distance to existing power lines; zoning rules; and any covenants and restrictions that might be attached to the deed.

Physical Collectibles

Historical collectibles are a time-tested store of value. For one, as with other types of real assets, their prices should track inflation—but in most cases, the valuations tend to grow more rapidly than that. This is a consequence of negative supply (more artifacts tend to be accidentally destroyed than found) and the growing and increasingly well-off population of the planet, sharing a near-universal reverence for artifacts of bygone days.

Perhaps the most significant issue collectors face is the task of estimating future interest. It's possible to start collecting candy wrappers or obsolete smartphones, but there's no guarantee that they'll become sought-after relics of the early 21st century in 30 years' time. It's even more dubious that there would be a serious buyer available five years from now, if you need to cash out in a pinch.

Such speculative pursuits can still be a fun hobby, but if the intent is to preserve wealth, it's usually better to operate within well-established and liquid markets—such as artwork, jewelry, antique furniture, obsolete coins and banknotes, stamps, or military memorabilia. The trade-off is that bargains are more difficult to come across, and that you need to learn enough about the field to avoid scams. Art forgeries are a well-known phenomenon, but pitfalls await in far more niche markets too. For example, thousands of collectors have been taken for a ride with embellished, monogrammed utensils, clothing, or weapons that supposedly belonged to George Washington, Adolf Hitler, and other historical figures of note.

Lastly, in addition to the usual warning about theft, it's important to note that some collectibles are fragile or vulnerable to the elements. For example, I would be nervous owning an expensive painting in a house with young kids. Insurance policies can help, but they aren't always cheap.

Cryptocurrencies and NFTs

There's a reason the traditional classes of assets outlined earlier in the chapter are considered the benchmarks for investors: they're more accessible, safer, cheaper, and more reliable than most alternatives. But there's no shortage of more exotic choices, and at least two of them deserve some note.

The first are cryptocurrencies. We discussed their mechanics before, but the lingering question is whether they have a place in a diversified portfolio. Although some financial advisors are beginning to change their tune, to me, the answer continues to be no. It's not that cryptocurrencies lack merit or are bound to crash; it's that their risk profile is difficult to reason about, and the staying power of specific products is far less certain than for many other instruments with good inflation-hedging properties. Ultimately, principled portfolio management is more about asking, "What if I'm wrong?" than daydreaming about the glorious future that awaits if your investments pan out well. From that perspective, the cost of passing on Bitcoin is modest, while the cost of taking a substantial stake can be unacceptably high.

The other very recent financial innovation that captured the attention of the media are *non-fungible tokens (NFTs)*: short blockchain-recorded entities with cryptographically established chains of ownership. In most ways, their inner workings resemble cryptocurrencies, but they're specifically designed not to serve that role. Instead, every token is meant to be distinguishable from others by virtue of possessing a unique ID.

The ecosystem of NFTs involves not just the tokens themselves, but third-party providers who associate these IDs with metadata describing a unique physical or digital asset on which the NFT is supposed to confer some sort of a claim. Except, the claim is poorly defined: just because the ID is linked to the metadata describing a Monet painting doesn't mean the holder of the token truly owns the painting or any derived rights. In fact, the promise of uniqueness is dubious too. Anyone can create another look-alike metadata object for another NFT that effectively references the same work.

It might be that NFTs will evolve to have some well-defined legal standing or that they'll gain a clear foothold in the collector community as a sort of abstract keepsake. Until then, if you have the choice between a Monet and a Monet-themed NFT, I'd recommend sticking with the real deal.

Insurance Policies and Separation of Assets

Some problems can't and shouldn't be resolved by moving back and forth between cash and stocks, or by constructing complex options plays. As noted earlier in this chapter, one prominent example of a situation where it would be harmful to look at the problem strictly through the prism of asset management is the task of protecting savings from otherwise ruinous personal injury claims.

Fender-benders are nearly inevitable and account for a significant proportion of such lawsuits, so readers who drive a car should probably review their coverage. In some US states, the legal minimum for bodily injury or property damage coverage can be as low as $15,000 or $20,000. This is a relatively meager amount. The victim of an accident you caused might be disinclined to settle with your insurer if they believe that going after your estate is going to net them much more. Ramping up the coverage to $50,000 or $100,000 can cost surprisingly little. With the adjustments to deductibles discussed in Chapter 6, you should still come out ahead.

Although somewhat less pressing, it's also good to inquire with your insurance company about inexpensive umbrella policies. These policies provide broad coverage against a host of other civil liability issues: dog bites, slips and falls in front of your home, and so forth. The policy usually covers all household members up to a pretty substantial amount and costs a fraction of what most people pay for home or car insurance. It follows that, especially for folks with more substantial savings, it can be a smart choice.

Another approach that can lessen the pain of adverse judgments is the legal separation of assets. If you own a rental property, for example, setting it up as a small business might limit the reach of any claims made against the business to the assets owned by the company, without jeopardizing your personal funds. This protection can work both ways: personal claims against one of the owners of a company might leave the business unscathed (although any payments due to the troubled owner would be subject to garnishment).

The challenge of maintaining legal separation is that the business must be operated the right way. It needs to have a discernible bona fide purpose, and the owners need to maintain a strict separation of personal and business finances. If the court gets any whiff of impropriety, it'll simply consider the entity a ruse. The correct legal structure needs to be investigated too. The usual choice for a US-based family business is a close limited liability company (LLC), owing to simple taxation and minimal paperwork requirements, but the constraints and protections vary from state from state. The strongest separation and the lowest regulatory burden exist in states such as Nevada or Wyoming, so many small businesses in the US choose to incorporate there, regardless of where the founders live.

The final defense against catastrophic losses can be thoughtful charity. As hinted earlier, you can use some of your assets to help out dependable friends, relatives, and coworkers in need. If you do this enough, it's likely that at least some would reciprocate if you ever fall onto hard times. Remember: it's not about how much you spend or don't spend; it's about how you make every transaction count.

Portfolio Design Strategies

With the discussion of risks and asset classes out of the way, the final phase of safeguarding wealth is to construct a robust, diversified portfolio that will stand the test of time. The right approach to this problem depends on many factors, including the size of your rainy-day fund, prevailing market conditions, and your familiarity with each of the aforementioned asset classes (heeding the Mr. Market parable from Graham's book).

In normal inflationary environments, a solid starting point may be to keep around three to four months' worth of savings in cash or in the bank, and then start putting what's left in a diversified portfolio of around 10 to 20 value stocks, but only up until the equity positions represent about 50 percent of your total emergency funds. In this setup, the gains from equity positions are likely to offset inflation; while the diversification of stocks caps the impact of any single company going bankrupt to between 2.5 percent and 5 percent of the value of the doomsday fund. Meanwhile, a major stock market crash that temporarily wipes 40 to 50 percent of shareholder value would have a tolerable 20 to 25 percent impact on your savings.

What to do with the rest is open to debate. Real estate can be an option for more affluent or industrious folks. For others, collectibles, metals, or more sophisticated stock market positions are fair game. Finally, around 1 percent can be spent on "doomsday hedges"—equity or futures options— that protect against currency collapses or profound economic slumps that weaken the fundamentals of public companies for years to come.

When structuring a portfolio, it's impossible to avoid the subject of taxes. Different countries tax different classes of assets in very different ways, and sometimes offer tax-privileged investment vehicles for specific purposes, such as retirement. Neglecting such matters can lead to unexpected and unnecessary tax liabilities down the line.

A detailed discussion of tax regulations falls squarely outside the scope of this book, but to touch on just a couple of salient points: in the United States, stocks (but not options or futures contracts) held for more than a year currently enjoy relatively favorable tax treatment, with long-term federal capital gains taxes capped at 20 percent (although states such as California add quite a bit on top of that). Crucially, the tax isn't due until the asset is sold, and depends on the tax bracket the seller falls into in a given year. This has two practical implications: first, holding positions long term is much better than entering and exiting positions many times a year; and second, you have some control over taxes if you coordinate sales depending on the ebbs and flows of other income.

When the prospect of a high tax bill makes selling stock undesirable but you need money on hand, it may be possible to get a so-called *margin loan* from your broker: the broker fronts you cash using your equities as collateral, and allows you to repay at your own pace, with no monthly bill due. The interest rates vary from one place to another, but tend to be very low if you shop around—closer to mortgages than credit cards (as of this writing, the best rates hover around 2%). Margin loans carry some risk that the broker will sell the stock if your collateral loses enough value, but if used judiciously, they're a pretty good deal.

Regrettably, if you do sell, the government doesn't factor in inflation in its calculations of capital gains. This means that if you hold the stock of General Motors for 10 years, and the business is stagnant but inflation alone caused its stock to "appreciate" 20 percent in relation to the dollar, you still have to pay tax on that 20 percent of nominal (but illusory) gains.

Many other assets—such as precious metals, real estate, or fine art—are treated somewhat similarly, although the profits you make may be subject to higher tax rates, and for most collectibles, you will also have to pay state sales tax. Of course, the government has limited visibility into any Picasso paintings you keep in your storage unit and sell for cash. But as the saying goes, three can keep a secret only if two of them are dead. In other words, if your plan is to avoid taxes by keeping things hush-hush with your numerous business partners, you might also want to brush up on prison slang.

The final tax-related observation is that some assets used for business purposes—including rental property—can be gradually depreciated for wear and tear, offsetting the income that the business manages to generate on other fronts. On the flip side, real estate is one of the few asset classes subject to a direct wealth tax. As most homeowners know, your state will send you a hefty annual tax bill for the privilege of owning property, even if it's an off-the-grid cabin in the woods.

8

ENGINEERING A
DOOMSDAY-PROOF CAREER

A comprehensive financial preparedness plan can't concern itself with only saving money or shuffling assets around; it must also address risks to the supply side of personal wealth. Or, in plain English: no matter what we have in the bank, job security is important too.

At first blush, this assertion may seem overly broad. Many of us imagine that if we can only accumulate enough wealth, we'll be able to retire early and never worry again about holding a job. In reality, however, few people in their prime reach the point where they no longer need to work another day in their lives, almost no matter how affluent they are. Even most millionaires aren't so lucky. Assuming all they dream of is the median income for a family with children in the United States, they would need to accumulate at least $3 million in a somewhat risky revenue-generating portfolio to be able to permanently hang up their hats.* And that's for a life that's comfortable, but certainly not glamorous or carefree; if they wish to travel the world or indulge in expensive hobbies, they might need quite a bit more.

Those who still have to get up every morning and go to work would be well served to remember that in the era of rapid technological disruption, fewer and fewer professions guarantee employment for life. In the 1990s, opening a VHS rental place or a music store was a sound business plan, journalism was a revered and well-paying gig, and the photographic film industry was a behemoth that consumed about a third of the global silver supply.[1] It's probably safe to assume that the next couple of decades are going to bring seismic shifts to many of today's cozy professions and industries.

In some cases, workers can be left behind even if their profession is doing fine. In my own field, there's no shortage of jobs for software developers or computer administrators (now more fashionably called *reliability engineers*), but few are available to those who don't keep up with the latest programming languages and framework choices. The jobs to maintain or extend legacy systems written in archaic languages and running on long-obsolete machines can be extremely lucrative, but their supply is drying up year by year.

Whatever the mechanism for the potential future decline in demand for your skills may be, the prescription for tackling this risk can be straightforward: to gradually develop secondary, marketable skills, even if they're of no immediate relevance to your current job. Most simply, this might involve staying apprised of new developments in your field of expertise and dabbling in the trendy if imperfect next-generation tech. Old-timers have a natural tendency to be suspicious of newfangled inventions and all the half-baked attempts to revolutionize their industries, but when trying to broaden our horizons, it's good to remember that technologies can succeed even if they're inferior to the old ways of doing business, and even if they're *clearly* derivative of what's already been discussed in the privately circulated memoir of the Slovenian Philological Society in 1883.

Bootstrapping a brand-new career can also be done safely and gradually. Picking up a sensible hobby is a great way to hone new skills without taking undue risks. Of course, hobbies can be counterproductive money sinks. I had far too many of these, and to weed out the dead ends, I eventually developed a simple test: I would look back at my projects from a year,

---

* The median income for families with minor children is just short of $90,000 a year; the average return on an index fund is 10 percent. Assuming inflation below 4 percent and perfectly steady market conditions, around $1.5 million is theoretically enough to generate this annual income without depleting the principal in real terms. But in practice, recessions and inflation spikes would throw a wrench in the works; a portfolio of at least twice that size would be needed to have a reasonable chance of long-term success. And if reasonably safe fixed-income securities are preferred to stocks, current conditions in the bond market probably call for $10 million or more. (Of course, the math is better for folks approaching retirement age, as they're usually operating on shorter time horizons and may be willing to burn their savings along the way.)

two years, or five years ago. Feeling embarrassed and wanting to immediately redo it all would earn the hobby a passing grade; not seeing anything to improve or not knowing how to tackle the flaws would be a sign of a stagnant pursuit.

As for selecting the right hobby, no list of options is objectively better than the rest. The possibilities are vast, and the right choice will inevitably depend on your own interests and talents, the space you have available, and countless other constraints. Many good, grounded choices with immediately marketable results can be found in the "arts and crafts" category: woodworking, metalworking (including jewelry and knife making), glassblowing, sewing, pottery, and so forth. Scientifically tinged pursuits can be gratifying too and can open doors to interesting job opportunities if you publish your work. Examples include amateur electronics, robotics, and recreational software engineering, to name a few. Creative occupations, such as writing and producing online videos, can quickly supplement income if you find your groove. Hunting for bargain collectibles at garage sales or on Facebook Marketplace can be exhilarating—and pay off handsomely if you develop an eye for the right stuff. Finally, charitable activities, including community education, can offer solid returns in less tangible ways: building meaningful relationships with people who might be looking for dependable employees or business partners down the line.

Of course, other, more decisive paths can lead to some careers. You might take a plunge to bootstrap a dream business with saved money, or get vocational training and certifications to learn a new profession and build up a résumé. It's a gutsier move, but it can work well. In such a case, you still have options if the pursuit doesn't pan out: your old profession becomes the backup plan.

9

STAYING ALIVE

In Chapter 2, we considered the surprisingly high odds of suffering serious injury due to falls, burns, accidental poisonings, and other seemingly prosaic mishaps that tend to happen around the home. Now, with some other preparedness topics out of the way, it's time to revisit this topic in more detail—and see if such hazards can be reduced without sapping all the joy out of life.

Of course, given the constant barrage of dreary headlines about cribs-o'-death, brain-eating bacteria, and dog toys laced with industrial toxins, there's little to be gained by stoking the flames of vague existential dread. We need a way to cut through the noise of 24-hour news and home in on the real everyday risks—and on actions that can make a difference. To make the problem tractable, perhaps the most valuable heuristic is to look at our own behavior, rather than worry about the whims of fate or the inevitable mistakes of others. We might not be able to dodge the occasional falling piano, nor can we get rid of all distracted drivers on the road, but we can certainly put down our *own* phone whenever we walk down the sidewalk or get behind the wheel.

Another useful filter is to classify habits based on their utility. Some risk-taking, such as crossing the street, may be simply unavoidable and thus not worth mulling over. Other precarious behaviors, such as recreational scuba diving or driving in the Daytona 500, may be within our control but well worth the payoff, bringing us genuine joy or offering the prospect of riches down the road. But some risks are entirely unproductive, not dictated by any real need nor offering meaningful rewards. An example of an act squarely in that last department is climbing a wobbly office chair instead of fetching a sturdy stool from another room. The time and effort saved is of no practical consequence, while preventable falls—often from very modest heights and in familiar environments—easily rival car accidents in the number of injuries they cause every year.[1]

With these two behavior evaluation tricks up our sleeve—focusing on ourselves, and considering risk versus reward—let's have a look at ways to stamp out common dangers while still leaving plenty of room for spontaneity and adventure in our lives.

Defensive Driving

Driving is widely known to be a dangerous activity; what's far less commonly recognized is that our own driving habits significantly contribute to the problem. In 1981, Ola Svenson of Stockholm University published a seminal study showing that over 80 percent of drivers consider themselves to be better behind the wheel than most—a mathematical impossibility.[2] Like many oft-cited works in psychology, the sample size was small and the phrasing imprecise, but in later years, research carried out by insurance companies broadly confirmed the result: most of us seem to believe that others drive worse and deserve the blame for accidents.

Perhaps the reason for this phenomenon is that when we get behind the wheel, we get to observe hundreds of small mistakes made by strangers, but we almost never know what prompted their clumsiness; poor skill is the simplest explanation that comes to mind. In contrast, when we mess up, some force majeure always justifies it: a sudden distraction, a stressful day at work, a hurry to get to an appointment we can't miss. In other words, it's not the lack of skill; it's the circumstances that made us skip a beat.

Of course, the widespread perceived superiority is illusory: with 6 million collisions, 3 million injuries, and about 38,000 deaths every year in the United States alone,[3] driving accidents aren't an affliction of the unskilled few. What's more, over half of all lethal crashes in this country involve just one car, meaning no other party is to blame. In such cases, the driver often simply fails to navigate a turn and hits a tree or rolls down a ravine.

Virtually all car accidents are preventable—often in ways that are well understood but perhaps muddied by social conventions or politics. Speeding is a perfect example. In many circumstances, moderate speeding isn't terribly dangerous, and overly zealous enforcement of speed limits is widely seen as a sham that pads municipal budgets and provides entertainment for local cops. Yet, behaviors that can be safe on a familiar stretch of highway in the summer can be fatal on a winding rural road in the dead of winter.

As for the payoff of speeding, it tends to be minimal. At highway speeds, it takes an hour of going 10 miles over the limit to make up for being held up for several minutes at a gas station or traffic lights. That's not to say that speeding is never defensible. In good weather, going with the prevailing flow of traffic is usually the safest choice, and in many regions, that's faster than what the roadside signs say. But flooring it on narrow city roads or unpredictable rural thoroughfares, or driving aggressively when bad weather makes visibility or traction poor, is a prime example of taking an unproductive risk.

Speaking of bad weather, winter driving is in itself a remarkably perilous task. This is in part because familiarity dulls the perception of risk: urban and suburban streets are fine most of the season, but all it takes for slick ice to form is a warm day followed by a cold night with little traffic on the road. Whenever the pavement looks even the tiniest bit suspect, it's good to exercise the utmost care. It can be instructive to test traction by braking on straight and level or uphill sections of the road, provided that no other traffic is nearby and no other obvious dangers are in sight. Over time, such experiments can give you a better sense of which conditions carry the most risk. It's also important to slow down well ahead of any turns, especially when going downhill or navigating an overpass. Sliding in a straight line is usually not disastrous, but losing traction while the front wheels are turned can put the car in a violent spin.

Regarding scenarios that don't involve skidding off the road, accidents at intersections account for a lot of pain and misery.[4] It takes only one driver who misses a stop sign or guns it for the "long yellow" to put many others at risk. Because of this, it's a good habit to approach intersections with an unrelenting degree of suspicion, scanning the road carefully and gently slowing down when the visibility of cross-traffic is poor or the intentions of other drivers are unclear.

Lane changes are another surprisingly dangerous activity, often carried out too fast and without due care. At highway speeds, clipping another vehicle in your blind spot can send your car spinning. Because mistakes happen, performing lane changes slowly, so that other drivers have time to react to your errors, is always a good plan. Visibility matters too: in addition to always looking over your shoulder, proper adjustment of side mirrors is crucial and often neglected. Many novice drivers believe they need to see the sides of their car, thinking that it would help them with parallel parking and similar tricky tasks. But it's always possible to move your head to get the correct view for such maneuvers; for normal driving, the mirrors should be set to minimize blind spots instead.

Tailgating is an additional bad habit, especially common among city drivers who are used to congested urban streets, where less scrupulous individuals sometimes cut in line whenever they see an opening. On city roads, guarding the space in front of you may be a marginally tolerable risk, but at highway speeds, it's a folly. It's not just that high-speed rear-end collisions are more deadly, but that if animals or debris are on the road, the car in front of you might swerve out of the way, but you won't see the danger until it's too late. A good rule of thumb is to maintain an interval of at least 2 to 3 seconds between you and the car ahead, or more if the weather is bad.

Finally, phones are a special menace when driving. Research has repeatedly shown that drivers engaged in phone conversations are about as dangerous as people under the influence of alcohol,[5] exhibiting slow reaction times and making poor decisions on the road. Critically, the effect is nearly the same whether using a handheld phone or a hands-free device. The impairment appears to stem from the cognitive burden of trying to hold the steady pace of a conversation with a person not aware of conditions on the road, not from having one hand occupied. From this perspective, the laws mandating hands-free setups make little sense; it's better to completely refrain from talking on the phone or texting in the car. If it's really urgent, you can always pull over. Otherwise, it can probably wait an hour or so.

Working at Heights

Few would peg changing a lightbulb or hanging Christmas lights as a particularly dangerous activity. Yet, as noted earlier in the chapter, falls rival car accidents as a cause of serious injury and death.

Fatal falls are predominantly associated with the elderly. After the age of 50, bone density tends to decrease, and by the time we hit retirement, even fairly benign-looking falls can cause grave injury.[6] This notably includes hip fractures, which condemn many survivors to hospice care.[7] That said, it's a mistake to treat fall-related injuries as a problem limited to those long in the tooth. Nonfatal falls consistently rank as the top cause of preventable hospitalizations across almost all age groups.[8]

Contrary to what you might expect, the danger usually doesn't stem from the distance to the ground; relatively few fall injuries involve great heights. As an example, about 160,000 ladder-involved hospitalizations occur every year in the United States, and the bulk of them involve heights below 10 feet. Of course, a well-executed jump off a chair or a step ladder poses little risk to people in their prime, but the nature of many such incidents is that they don't allow us to land on our feet. Falling sideways, possibly hitting railings, curbs, or household furniture on the way down, can easily cause horrific compound fractures or serious neck or head injuries, often with consequences that stay with the victim for life.

This isn't to say that we need to live in constant fear of lifting our feet off the ground; it's just that we should recognize work at heights as an intrinsically dangerous activity and plan accordingly. It helps to avoid climbing rickety furniture, such as office chairs or wobbly cabinets. Similarly, when using ladders, it pays to make sure they're perfectly stable and set up at a proper angle. When this isn't possible, use rope or straps to hold the ladder firmly in place, or ask another person to help. It's also smart to wear proper footwear and durable work gloves that prevent slips.

Ladders aside, roofs of single-family homes live in special infamy. Being a roofer is one of the most dangerous occupations in the country, well ahead of firefighters and police officers.[9] Despite this, many homeowners are sooner or later tempted to climb their roofs—to clean the gutters, make small repairs, or retrieve lost toys. Bad idea! Because of the slope of a typical roof, it's hard to get a grip if you start sliding back, and it's equally difficult to regain your footing if you lose your balance. In essence, any misstep turns into a near-certain fall. Whenever possible, it's best to avoid roof walks, but if you must, consider using an inexpensive harness in conjunction with a rope tossed across the roof and secured on the other side. You can wear special studded shoes and kneepads meant for roofing work too.

The Enemy in the Medicine Cabinet

Poisonings are the last of the trio of the most important causes of unintentional injury and death—and perhaps surprisingly, they seldom involve spoiled or tainted food. For children, some incidents are caused by the accidental ingestion of household chemicals or items such as watch batteries; but for all age groups, prescription drugs account for a lion's share of the misery.

For the past couple of decades, the harm of opioids has dwarfed the impacts of all other drugs—a matter of the substances' widespread therapeutic use and the tolerance and physiological dependency that builds over time. According to the National Survey on Drug Use and Health, about one in three Americans had a prescription for opioids in 2015.[10] Although most users escaped any dire consequences, the survey estimated that about 10 million people in the country succumb to opioid abuse every year. The abuse often ends in tragedy; this class of medication accounts for about two-thirds of all drug overdose deaths.[11]

Many factors predispose people to addiction—poverty, unemployment, stress, a history of using other illicit drugs[12]—but not being in one of these vulnerable groups doesn't guarantee safety. Ultimately, the prevalence of opioid addiction shouldn't necessarily be a reason to shun a medication when it helps with debilitating pain, but it should motivate us to treat that medication with respect and to seek less dangerous alternatives whenever possible. It's equally important to recognize that opioid withdrawal can cause debilitating side effects even for people who used the substance responsibly, making it difficult for doctors and patients to gauge whether a prescription is still needed or it would be safe to wean off.

Many other prescription drugs carry a potential for abuse and injury, including some antidepressants, sedatives, ADHD medications, and so on. What's perhaps less known is that non-psychoactive over-the-counter medication can be pretty dangerous too. In this context, acetaminophen is of particular note. This popular pain medication has a fairly narrow therapeutic index, meaning the difference between a helpful dose and a harmful dose is slim. The medicine can cause severe liver injury in quantities as low as 3 to 5 grams for children and 7 to 10 grams for adults. Given that a typical pill contains between 500 and 650 milligrams, this may seem like a lot—but because many "cold & flu" pills, syrups, and powders also contain acetaminophen, accidental overdoses can happen when trying to combine several products to combat a particularly nasty flu. All in all, acetamino-phen overdoses account for around 50,000 ER visits and 500 deaths annually in the United States.[13] Other comparably effective painkillers, such as ibuprofen, naproxen, or even the much-maligned aspirin,* appear to have much better safety margins for most people.

None of this means that we'd be better off throwing out the contents of our medicine cabinets and suffering through every fever or splitting headache. But it pays to read up on the drugs we take and to not get too habituated to risk.

Alcohol and Recreational Drugs

Throughout the ages, attitudes toward drugs have swung back and forth between extremes. The contrast seen in the United States is particularly stark. In the 19th century, the country had opium dens in most major cities, quack doctors peddled medicine laced with heroin, and cocaine was available to order straight from the Sears and Roebuck catalog. Figure 9-1 shows an ad for one such product meant for children.

The growing addiction epidemic eventually culminated in public outcry and federal crackdowns: the Smoking Opium Exclusion Act of 1909 and the Harrison Narcotics Tax Act of 1914. The temperance movement greatly benefited from the crisis, too, helping ratify the 18th Amendment—the ban on the manufacture, sale, and transportation of alcoholic beverages—in 1919.[14]

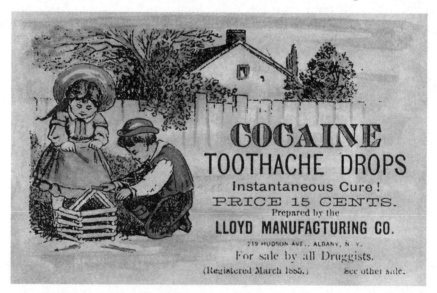

Figure 9-1: An advertisement card for a cocaine-based children's toothache medication, circa 1885

---

* Aspirin's fall from grace in favor of acetaminophen had to do with the discovery of the former's association with an exceedingly uncommon but deadly condition known as Reye's syndrome, almost exclusively occurring in children. Another more prosaic but unpleasant side effect is gastrointestinal woes, more frequent than with other drugs in this class.

In the decades that followed, the abject failure of alcohol prohibition efforts exhausted the social capital of anti-drug activists, setting the stage for the drug-, sex-, and music-fueled hippie movement of the 1960s. The movement, in turn, fed into a moral panic that precipitated the Nixon-era War on Drugs, later expanded under Reagan in response to the crack cocaine epidemic and the massive spike in urban crime.

Today, the pendulum of drug policies is swinging again toward liberalization. In just a couple of years, most states either legalized marijuana or removed the associated criminal penalties. Initiatives to legalize other psychoactive substances are gaining steam, too, with Oregon leading the way with psilocybin in 2020. It's hard to know whether the country is reaching a stable equilibrium or future generations will once again decide that the societal ills of drug use outweigh the benefits. But without getting into the long-term merits or harms of such policies, one thing is clear: impaired judgment is still impaired judgment, and being under the influence of any mind-altering substance inherently increases our likelihood of waltzing into trouble or getting hurt.

Today, alcohol remains a distinctive menace. In theory, most people know to never drink and drive, but the adherence to this mantra is spotty at best. Drunk driving accounts for about a third of all traffic deaths in the United States, and about a million people are arrested for driving under the influence every year—with millions more undoubtedly just not encountering any traffic stops.[15] But the drug of choice doesn't matter much. Even with comparatively safer marijuana, and even when the user decides to stay home and binge-watch *Sabrina the Teenage Witch* instead of driving around town, the risk of injury is still higher than before. When intoxicated, it's easier to forget about food in the oven, to light a candle and put it in the wrong place, or to react inappropriately to an unfolding emergency.

The other peril of drug and alcohol use is less acute. Even in the absence of physiological addiction, substances can be habit forming when they become an everyday method of unwinding, detaching from stress, and having a good time. At that point, it can be hard to think clearly about the impacts such behaviors have on one's career, hobbies, or relationships.

I'm not here to proselytize about the dangers of an occasional beer. Most drinkers don't become alcoholics, most users of pain medication don't become addicted, and most pot smokers don't become potheads. But substance dependence is a sneaky and unpredictable foe. The surest way to avoid this risk is to scale back. It's quite easy to be silly, bond with friends, or have fun without chemical aids—so recreational drugs arguably make for another example of an unproductive risk.

Workshop and Power Tool Safety

Woodworking and DIY home improvement are some of the most popular hobbies in America. Reputable statistics are elusive, but by one industry survey, around 17 million US households partake in wood crafts of some sort.[16]

Against the backdrop of far more pastoral avocations such as scrapbooking and sewing, garage-based pastimes tend to involve major power tools and carry pronounced risks.

The task of running a safe workshop can be made difficult because of information overload. We live in an era when hammers and toilet plungers come with warning labels, and when the instruction manual for every toaster devotes several pages to telling us not to gnaw on the wires and cautioning us that the ejected toast may be hot. Flipping past the safety instructions has become a natural instinct—and even the most diligent reader may have difficulty distinguishing between real hazards and the overzealous base-covering of a compliance officer who's trying to make sure that no consumer can ever sue the company for any conceivable harm.

Thankfully, statistics on workshop injuries are tracked fairly well in this country. They paint a clear picture too: of common garage tools, table saws emerge as by far the worst offenders, accounting for around 40,000 hospital visits and 4,000 amputations a year.[17] Such injuries often start with the material catching on the rear of the spinning blade and shifting violently. The ejected workpiece can cause injuries on its own, but a far more serious problem is that the operator's hand is all of a sudden pushing nothing but air, potentially making contact with the blade before there's a chance to react. The instinct to grab the piece as it slips away can make things worse. Thankfully, the basic cure to table saw woes is simple: always use push sticks or sleds that keep your hands well clear of the danger zone and not in direct contact with the machined piece.

Another common garage tool known for causing severe injuries is the angle grinder, a device where a brittle abrasive wheel spins at extreme speeds and can shatter when driven too hard—or for no discernible reason at all. Such a fracture can send sharp and extremely fast-moving pieces of shrapnel toward the face of the operator or toward people nearby. Face shields, or at the very least impact-resistant safety goggles, are a must. Keeping the plane of the wheel away from the body and properly positioning the guard can also help.

Many other power tools deserve deep reverence; for example, planers, jointers, miter saws, routers, and lathes are well-known for mangling the extremities of tens of thousands of people every year. Similarly, many gruesome injuries and deaths are attributed to outdoor equipment such as lawnmowers, snowblowers, wood chippers, and chainsaws. When operating such devices, always follow all the applicable safety tips. If the manual is too obtuse, look up reputable tutorials and accident reports on the internet. Perhaps the most general safety principle can be borrowed from the world of firearms: when working with tools that can maim in the blink of an eye, always make sure that at least two separate things need to go wrong before any serious harm can occur.

In addition to your fingers and arms, your hearing and eyesight are also worth preserving. For obvious reasons, putting on eyewear should become a habit when working with any caustic chemicals, as well as when dealing with any machining operations that can eject chips or bits of damaged tools. Hearing protection is a more difficult sell, as the injury tends to happen very gradually and without any pain. Many people don't realize the extent of the damage until they start having trouble understanding others around the house. Earmuffs are a good idea around any power tools, but especially when working with the ultra-loud ones: table saws, chainsaws, planers, nail guns, and so on.

Fireproofing the Homestead

It's the hallmark of lazy screenwriting that every fictional house fire must either claim a life or have its hapless victim rescued in the nick of time. In reality, domestic fires are common, but fatalities are comparatively rare. The total number of victims hovers around 2,500 a year,[18] with many cases involving very young children, intoxicated individuals, and the infirm. The number of serious burns and smoke inhalation injuries is more significant, but remains a far cry from other causes discussed in this chapter so far. Still, fires make for a worthwhile topic: even when all residents escape bodily harm, the mental scars of losing one's home can take a long time to heal—and the odds of a disaster are well within our control.

As hinted earlier in the book, the bulk of household fires begin in the kitchen, where food is often left unattended in the oven and where flammable items may be placed near or around the stove top. Keeping the kitchen tidy and not storing plastics or cardboard anywhere near the sources of heat is a good habit to have; so is always setting a loud alarm clock to help keep track of time when baking or slow-cooking any foods.

Working fire alarms and reasonably sized fire extinguishers are a wise investment. Nuisance alarms can be dealt with by switching to photoelectric sensors or by simply repositioning the sensor away from where you cook. Talking to children about escape routes is another low-effort strategy to manage risk. Kids are more vulnerable than adults and less able to reason through a traumatic experience; they should know we won't be upset with them if they rip out a window screen to exit their room.

Beyond that, it's wise to examine your daily routines and surroundings for other places where fires can easily start. Space heaters are a notorious culprit, especially when placed on uneven or cluttered surfaces. The same goes for poorly maintained appliances, such as dryers with vents clogged with decades' worth of lint, and for damaged or overloaded outlets and extension cords. Finally, candles, cigarettes, and smokable drugs account for a relatively small portion of all fires, but cause a disproportionate percentage of deaths, especially when the user falls asleep.

Threats inside the house aside, rural property owners should contemplate creating a defensible space around the homestead. The usual recommendation is to maintain a zone of around 30 feet around the home that is free of fuels such as coniferous trees or dry grass, leaves, and shrubs; and then about 100 feet where the vegetation is judiciously thinned and all flammable debris is removed. Such steps can greatly reduce the intensity of flames and thus improve the odds that the house will still be standing where you left it once the smoke clears.

Other Dangers in and Around the Home

Many other injuries feature prominently in ER statistics, but didn't make the cut for close discussion in this book. Some are simply not gruesome enough to worry too much about: for example, major cuts happen all the time in the kitchen, and sometimes they need stitches or even nerve repair—but except for concert pianists or a handful of other professions requiring top-notch fine motor skills, they don't matter much in the long run.

Some other dangers that lurk around the home are serious but difficult to control. Choking, for example, is a major risk for young children and the elderly, but effective mitigations—beyond learning the Heimlich maneuver—are tough. Similarly, suffocation and drowning are two common causes of death for infants and toddlers; the latter can be partly managed by keeping toddlers away from backyard pools and teaching them to swim, but many other interventions are of dubious utility. For instance, consumer-type infant oxygen monitors are probably bunk science and a waste of your hard-earned cash.[19]

Of course, it's difficult to provide a comprehensive compendium of all dangers that may be relevant to every lifestyle. Everyone faces their own unique hazards, from motorcyclists, to avid skydivers, to fanciers of venomous snakes. The examples outlined in this chapter point to some of the most common harms and the most universal ways of dealing with the risks. As always, however, they merely serve as stepping stones for fleshing out a personalized action plan.

10

PROTECTING ONESELF IN THE DIGITAL AND PHYSICAL REALM

"This time, it's personal!"

In action films, crime is never transient. A cruel twist of fate pits the protagonist against a sprawling drug syndicate or a sinister government agency determined to pursue its enemies to the farthest reaches of the world. The only way for our hero to survive is to turn the tables and strike back at the evildoers, delivering a devastating and well-timed blow just as all hope appears to be lost.

In real life, criminal victimization is common, but this sort of single-minded pursuit of particular targets is not. Instead, almost all crime is opportunistic. A scammer sends a message to millions of recipients and empties the bank account of whoever takes the bait; smash-and-grab burglars ransack the first home on the street where no one answers the door; a mugger picks a victim with an unassuming physique and an out-of-place look.

The random and transactional nature of most criminal encounters works to our benefit: far from hatching complex plans and holding lifelong grudges, most perpetrators look for easy pickings and bail at the first sign of trouble. It follows that making your property less attractive to thieves is a pretty good defense against burglary, for example. This doesn't need to involve barbed wire and a gator-filled moat; a yappy dog can work just as well.

Yet, even though we're usually not dealing with criminal masterminds, the victim doesn't have the upper hand in a typical encounter. Precisely because perpetrators favor quantity over quality, they tend to be well practiced in their craft. It's probably not their first mugging or their first burglary; they can anticipate the behaviors of their victims and know how to stay in control of the scene. The victims, in contrast, struggle to think clearly under pressure and often make terrible decisions when cornered on the street or targeted by a well-executed scam.

The simplest way to level the playing field is to rehearse your reactions ahead of time, just as perpetrators gain experience through repetition. The goal is to learn the anatomy of a typical burglary or an online con, and memorize the best ways to respond.

Of course, that's not to say that every crime is the same. Every now and then, internet strangers or abusive ex-lovers devote considerable resources and skill to making the life of a specific victim a living hell. Other times, burglars get wind of the precious jewels in your safe or the hefty balance in your bank account, perhaps told by your distant relative or an unsavory friend. In such scenarios, prevention is the best defense; keeping mum about lottery winnings and tactfully disengaging from bitter fights is wiser than hiring bodyguards or sleeping with a loaded gun.

With all this in mind, let's have a look at some of the most common criminal encounters, starting with the digital realm. The stakes on the internet tend to be lower than on the streets, but the incidence of trouble online can be far higher than in the physical world.

Dealing with Online Fraud

Behind the veneer of sleek user interfaces, computers are complex and messy. Sometimes even experts find it hard to distinguish between a legitimate message from the operating system and a bogus look-alike spawned by a sketchy internet site. It doesn't help that almost all the intuitive trust signals we tend to rely on can be faked: for example, the "from" line of an email can be made to say almost anything; the same goes for social media account names and avatars. Plastering trustworthy corporate logos and getting a familiar-looking address for a fraudulent website takes little effort too.

The tech community has developed a considerable body of folksy recipes for staying safe online. Unfortunately, many of the popular tips are dated or suspect. For example, there's usually little to be gained by paying for virtual private network (VPN) software or for third-party antivirus programs. In another example, ditching mainstream browsers, mail services, or search engines for niche alternatives can do more to weaken your security than to strengthen it. It's also impractical (and fairly pointless) to choose ridiculously complex passwords for online services and to change them constantly. Finally, despite the insistence that we should never click "untrusted" links, I've yet to meet a person who manages to use the internet without doing so countless times throughout the day.

Instead of blindly following such voodoo, it's better to figure out how cyber-crooks operate. For one, they usually target humans, not computers, and the oldest trick in their book is to create a false sense of urgency: a belief that a decision needs to be made immediately, or you'll miss out on an important opportunity or suffer dire consequences. The pressure is meant to force us to rely on instincts, not on rational inquiry—and to greatly increase the likelihood of making a terrible, rushed call.

A common example of a such tactics is an email or text message purportedly from your bank, warning you of unauthorized activity on your account and demanding that you log in immediately (through the scammer's faux site) to verify—or else! Other popular methods include a mysterious "overdue" invoice or a legal demand requiring you to open a suspect attachment or retype your password, a "verification" step that must be completed to access a cool website, or a message from a friend or a paramour who is supposedly stranded overseas and needs you to wire emergency funds to an unfamiliar account.

Critically, such scams can be very specific without being carefully targeted. It costs next to nothing to reach tens of thousands of people, so it doesn't matter if the message seems laughable or garbled to most recipients. All that's needed is one victim in just the right circumstances and the right state of mind. For example, one popular scam informs the recipient that their computer was "hacked" and that sexually explicit photos have been found; a cryptocurrency payment is required to prevent the pictures from being distributed to coworkers, family, and friends. The story is a fabrication, and in most circumstances, not a convincing one. Most of us probably don't have embarrassing nudes on our computers, or if we do, we might not be particularly frightened by the threat. But to a kindergarten teacher or a member of the clergy who recalls snapping some naughty selfies a while back, this could be a profoundly sickening message to read. And in a moment of terror, they might not have the presence of mind to search for other examples on the internet and realize that the threat isn't real.

The peculiar consequence of this mechanism is that we tend to overestimate our own resiliency to online deception. Because most phishing messages seem badly targeted and poorly written, we conclude that only the most clueless individuals could ever fall for such tricks. But then, we get hit by a message that pushes all the right buttons and makes perfect sense in the context of our lives—and we fall for it hook, line, and sinker.

A popular saying warns that if something sounds too good to be true, it probably is. I'd add that the same rule applies if it sounds too bad to be true too. Alarming phone calls, text messages, emails, or pop-ups virtually never require an immediate response and should be researched first. You can hang up, close the browser window, or reboot the computer if needed—and then calmly search the internet for stories from other folks who have had similar encounters. If the message purportedly came from the bank, it's best to call them back at the number on the billing statements or on the back of your card; if it came from a friend, it's useful to reach out to them or their friends through another channel and confirm.

Of course, with the thousands of decisions we make on trust every year, even the most attentive among us might eventually get it wrong. To prevent mishaps from becoming life-altering disasters, it's wise to regularly back up all important documents to an offline medium, perhaps a thumb drive plugged into the USB port and then stowed away when done. The habit is particularly important given the rise in ransomware: a class of attacks where the scammer convinces the victim to download a malicious program, and then encrypts all files on the computer, demanding payment in exchange for the decryption key. To prevent blackmail or identity theft, it might also be best to keep extremely sensitive documents solely in "cold" storage, and not keep copies on anything connected to the internet.

Falling for scams aside, another grievous online safety blunder is poor password hygiene. The use of trivial passphrases—*password, abc123, qwerty,* and so forth—is an obvious issue. The reuse of good passwords is a more insidious misstep. With the sheer number of services that require you to register and log in, we have a natural temptation to simplify and settle on a single password everywhere. But as the number of accounts grows, so does the chance that one of the services will eventually suffer a security breach—and when that happens, the attackers will know to try the stolen passwords with major banks, Amazon, Gmail, and many other destinations of note.

A simple way to deal with numerous distinct passwords is to keep an old-school paper notebook and write them all down. Despite some online snark, it's an eminently reasonable choice, provided that the journal is kept someplace safe. The password manager built into your browser is another convenient option.* The solution has weaknesses, but also one major perk: the software is much better than humans at making sure that the password is sent only to the original site and not to a scam knock-off. If the password manager fails to fill in the login form on a seemingly familiar page, it's a sign that something may be amiss.

The final part of fraud-proofing your online presence is to sign up for two-factor authentication (2FA) for critical accounts: banks, brokerages, email providers, and the like. With 2FA enabled, any attempt to log in should require not just the password, but also the entry of a frequently changing code displayed on your phone or provided by a special key fob. Although it's not a perfect deterrent and not all 2FA implementations are equally robust, the scheme can frustrate some opportunistic attacks—or at least give you a second chance to think about what's going on.

---

* Note the distinction between built-in and third-party password managers. Third-party add-ons of this type are difficult to get right. They must maintain a perfect understanding of what your browser is doing at all times, or the passwords may be sent to the wrong place. In contrast, a built-in password manager is inherently in lockstep with the browser itself. That's not to say you should never use a third-party tool; but all other things being equal, choosing the built-in one can be safer.

Maintaining Privacy on the Internet

Most discussions of online privacy have a peculiar quality. The imagined adversary is nebulous and all-powerful: the NSA, Mossad, the Fortune 500. The sacrifices we're willing to make, in contrast, tend to be minimal. We still want to carry around a smartphone, pay with credit cards, and keep Amazon accounts that chronicle a decade or two of our most intimate shopping whims. In lieu of meaningful action, we settle for performative art, taping over laptop cameras or installing ad-supported blockers for ads. Such steps may matter in small ways, but they do little to alter our risk profile on the internet.

Of course, some populations might conceivably find themselves in the crosshairs of all-powerful adversaries. For them—or for people who have fantasies about "NSA-proofing" their lives for other reasons—the hard truth is that concealing one's activities from entities with nearly infinite budgets and manpower calls for drastic measures: living two completely separate lives, down to using different computers and network locations to conduct routine business, and maintaining two unconnected financial identities. Even the tiniest transgression—such as accidentally logging into your "whistleblower" account from home or absentmindedly taking a phone to a meeting with a trusted journalist—can be enough to pierce the cloak. VPNs and privacy-enhanced search engines are no substitute for rigor and restraint. In fact, the more flair we tack onto our computers, the more they stand out from the crowd, paradoxically making us easier to track.

For the rest of us, online privacy still matters, even in the absence of intimidating foes. Reducing our footprint complicates the lives of scammers, frustrates stalkers, and greatly reduces the consequences of account compromises. The task of tidying up your online presence starts with analyzing the trails you're leaving on social media sites. In general, online communications tend to be fleeting in our minds: most Twitter, Reddit, or Facebook debates die down in a day or two. Yet, on most social platforms, the long-forgotten threads linger for all eternity, not only providing a lasting record of our half-baked political views and drunken dares, but also offering a treasure trove of information about where we live, work, or how well off we are. Pseudonymity doesn't help much, because it usually takes little to pinpoint who we are. I might be the only person in my neck of the woods who works in computer security, enjoys woodworking, and has a rusty-spotted cat seen in the background of some of the photos I take. Even without any laborious research, hundreds of people in my extended social circle can immediately connect the dots.

To avoid this accumulation of dangerous social media detritus, it's healthy to regularly prune any content that's well past its expiration date. Ancient Reddit posts or Twitter arguments can usually be removed without losing anything of note. I have also gotten into the habit of deleting emails older than one year. It's a seemingly radical move, but essential business records or any correspondence of sentimental value can always be moved to a separate folder or saved to a file—and for everything else, I don't want a person who gets a hold of my password to see two decades' worth of financial documents or long-forgotten disputes with friends.

On sites with more complex sharing or data collection models, it pays to scrutinize the defaults; for example, on Facebook, it's good to check whether any of your posts are visible to strangers, and whether your profile can be looked up by phone number, email, or name. When it comes to Google accounts, it's wise to disable search history, YouTube view history, app activity records, and location tracking. Although this information is normally not public, its mere existence ups the ante if somebody gains access to your profile (or if the company suffers a breach).

In addition to what we intentionally post on the internet, our personal information is also collected and shared by parties that may be less obvious or altogether hidden from view. The online advertising industry gets a lot of flak, but many others also deserve blame for collecting and disseminating data in ways that aren't always in our best interest. For example, most governments make it easy to look up who owns a particular parcel of land or applies for a permit of any sort—from being a registered nurse to an amateur radio operator—and they often publish these records without telling you up front. Retailers amass and share customer data to generate traditional marketing leads; credit bureaus track and share our payment history, account balances, and addresses; and banks, internet service providers, cell phone operators, car dealerships, and tax preparers mine the information about our finances and whereabouts. Some of the collection and sharing can be stopped, so it's always good to look for opt-out options, but trying to plug all leaks before it's too late can be a losing game.

This brings us to the scourge of data brokers: in the United States in particular, a growing number of companies harvest and combine data from all these disjointed and sometimes hard-to-access sources, building sprawling profiles on almost every person in the country. The information is then sold to businesses trying to screen employees or customers, but also offered to nosy neighbors who simply want to dig up dirt on the family next door. In the consumer segment, some of the most visible brokers include Radaris, MyLife.com, Intelius, InfoTracer, Spokeo, BeenVerified, and TruePeopleSearch.com. In the corporate world, some of the big names are Epsilon Data Management, Acxiom, LexisNexis, and CoreLogic, along with the trio of traditional credit bureaus (TransUnion, Experian, and Equifax).

Luckily, with the somewhat understandable exception of credit bureaus, it's generally possible to opt out. This time-consuming endeavor is likely to take a full day of clicking through forms, but excellent self-service guides are available at OneRep (*https://wiki.onerep.com/*) and the DeleteMe Help Center (*https://joindeleteme.com/help/deleteme-help-topics/opt-out-guide/*). In the long haul, the investment is likely worth the pain.

The two companies maintaining these wiki pages, Abine and OneRep, can also assist in opting out for a fairly reasonable fee. Unlike some dubious "identity theft monitoring" services that are pushed on the internet, the removal services are legitimate, but the coverage tends to be spotty. They might get you 80 percent of the way there, but some manual work usually remains. Residents of the European Union or of California can also leverage their General Data Protection Regulation (GDPR) or California Consumer Privacy Act (CCPA) rights, giving them the ability to request a copy of their data or to have it destroyed when more polite measures fail. Most companies honor such requests, although some make actually submitting the request difficult.

In light of the difficulty of keeping the data-sharing ecosystem in check, perhaps a more robust defense is not to give out your physical address when shopping online or completing any official paperwork. Some folks opt to have parcels and mail delivered to their workplace. Another option is a mail-forwarding company, such as iPostal1 or Anytime Mailbox. They charge around $100 a year and let you pick up or forward deliveries from any major courier company, along with the option to scan or forward any regular postal mail. Not having one's name on the real estate deed is trickier, but can be accomplished if necessary by setting up a living trust or a closely held LLC.

Minimizing the Impact of Burglaries

Property crime comes in many flavors, and not much can be written about most of it. In densely populated areas, car break-ins, porch piracy, or petty vandalism are just a fact of life. But home burglaries are a different animal: they're consequential, mystifying, and a frightening invasion of privacy.

There's comfort in knowing that most burglaries are purely opportunistic. The thieves are in and out in perhaps 10 minutes, usually striking in the early hours of the day when the residents are likely to be out. The perpetrators quickly rummage through all the usual hiding spots for valuables; drawers and closets in the master bedroom are often the first stop. The usual objects of interest include phones, cameras, tablets, laptops, jewelry, firearms, prescription meds, and loose cash.[1] Vital documents that may be useful for identity theft or benefits fraud, such as driver's licenses, passports, and social security cards, are also fair game.

Break-ins are difficult to prevent, especially in suburban single-family homes with secluded backyards and street-level windows and doors. Tall fences and window bars can help, but these solutions are expensive, unsightly, and unlikely to win praise from the neighbors next door. The most cost-effective approach is to always keep windows and doors properly closed when away, and to repair or replace any failing or flimsy locks. Deadbolts with properly anchored strike plates are a worthwhile upgrade to cylindrical key-and-doorknob locks that usually give way with a solid kick.

Beyond that, it's probably best to optimize for hassle-free outcomes. If you have any high-value possessions, they should be stored either in a proper safe bolted to the floor or somewhere a burglar is unlikely to look. One approach popular in the prepper community is to use diversion safes fashioned out of cans, hollowed-out books, or wall clocks that blend in with the home environment. But more simply, most nasty-looking utility areas, including the nooks and crannies behind refrigerators or washing machines, are unlikely to be searched by even the most determined pro.

In general, home security solutions such as alarm systems, cameras, or high-end door locks play a lesser role in deterring crime, especially if we consider the cost. Pry bars are preferred to lockpicks, and many criminals aren't fazed by alarms, since they plan to be gone by the time the cops show up. Loud and menacing dogs, on the other hand, tend to make almost all burglars stay away.[2] That said, the long-term cost of dog ownership is much higher than the losses sustained in a typical burglary—so the economics of this approach hinge on how much you value canine company for its own sake.

Many of the online privacy measures discussed here go a long way toward preventing targeted theft in the physical world, but it's also important to be mindful of who we invite into our homes and what we signal to more distant family, to random acquaintances, or to strangers parked across the street. The practices of adolescent children, who might be tempted to throw house parties where unsavory characters from school may show up, are also of concern.

Another way to invite burglars into the home is to make it seem that the place hasn't been occupied for a while: packages piling up in front, an overflowing mailbox, an empty driveway, all lights turned off at night. This sends the message that the perps don't need to hurry; they can dig through every crevice in the house, and perhaps call their buddies with a truck to strip the place bare. To avoid this, when going on a longer trip, it's good to ask a trusted neighbor to park a car in front, to put some lights on a timer, and to have someone pick up your mail every now and then (or put it on hold with the US Postal Service).

Responding to Muggings and Home Invasions

Whether it's a stranger barging into your car or home, or a thug roughing you up for your wallet and phone, violent confrontations are traumatic, dangerous, and—as discussed in Chapter 2—not exactly rare. To keep your cool and make sound decisions in the heat of the moment, you need a solid plan. In most cases, this plan needs to focus on de-escalation and avoidance, rather than on the survivalist fantasy of resolving every encounter with a single, well-placed karate chop.

An in-depth discussion of active defense strategies is the focus of Part IV of this book, but for now, let's review several higher-level points about managing the risk. First, when it comes to muggings and other forms of street violence, many criminals exploit our instinct to comply with orders and desire to follow convention; for example, if they holler at you, you might be compelled to stop and let them close the distance—even if objectively, it'd make more sense to bail. Not being afraid to make an undignified retreat or raise your voice is a good survival strategy; so is maintaining keen situational awareness and avoiding getting lost in thought, especially in awkward transitional spaces such as back alleys, pedestrian underpasses and overpasses, empty gas stations, and so forth. Finally, it can be helpful to have several $10 or $20 bills in your pocket, and keep vital documents, credit cards, and keepsakes somewhere else.

Fighting is a possibility, too, but because of the inherent risk, it should be the option of last resort. To momentarily take control of the situation, it may be useful to say or do something that's nonthreatening but catches the assailant off guard. Feigning a panic attack or saying something completely unexpected ("Hey, are you a friend of CJ's? Pretty sure we met last year!") can give you a second or two to pull out a can of pepper spray or start running as fast as you can. But as with hand-to-hand combat, such approaches need to be rehearsed to have any chance of working in real life.

For home intrusions, it's good to map out different scenarios, deciding on the best course of action depending on the time of day and the apparent intent of the unwelcome guest. Some intruders may be dangerous, but in many other cases, you might be dealing with a drunk neighbor, a person suffering from dementia, or a skittish teenage perp who timed a burglary wrong. In many cases, responding with deadly force would be the wrong call.

In any situation that may involve self-defense, understanding the law is critical. We'll talk about this a bit more in Part IV, but in principle, in the United States, residents don't have a duty to retreat from their home, and can use deadly force if they have a reasonable and immediate reason to fear for their life or the lives of others.[3] That said, the scope of these rules can vary, and there are differences in how the prosecutors and the courts interpret similar statutes in different parts of the country—or even in different parts of the same state. A resident of San Francisco who kills or severely injuries an unarmed burglar may spend the night in jail as the prosecutor combs through social media posts for anything that would suggest a violent or hateful state of mind; 50 miles to the north or south, the same incident would likely result in an understanding nod from the sheriff and a puff piece in the local news.

Fending Off Pickpockets

Pickpocketing is an interesting crime. This ancient and impressive craft used to be common in many urban regions in the United States before suffering great declines over the past decade or two; the number of pickpocketings in New York City, for example, plunged about tenfold.[4] The causes appear to be complex, but the most significant is probably the decline of cash.

That said, pickpockets remain an acute problem for travelers. Some sources claim more than 400,000 incidents a day,[5] particularly in touristy destinations such as Rome, Barcelona, Madrid, Paris, Athens, and Amsterdam. The veracity of this number is hard to confirm, but even if not accurate, the scale of the problem is well documented, and the phenomenon is almost certainly fueled by foreigners carrying wads of cash to avoid transaction surcharges or compatibility issues with their credit and debit cards.

The reason pickpocketing deserves a note regardless of its diminishing impacts is that prevention is simple. In shopping malls, on mass transit, and in other crowded settings, it's best not to carry precious valuables in front or back pockets or in a purse. Inner pockets of jackets, and chest- or knee-level pockets of pants and shirts, are much harder to muck with. Slim, discreet waist packs or under-the-garment neck wallets work even better. They enjoyed popularity in the 1980s and 1990s before becoming extremely uncool—but now, retro fashion is all the rage again.

A Word on Kindness

Many of the random criminal encounters outlined in this chapter can happen to anyone. But it also must be said that some life choices increase the likelihood of being singled out in retaliation for your perceived misdeeds.

Doing anything that's morally reprehensible or perceived as deeply unfair greatly increases the odds of criminal injury, regardless of whether you think your actions are defensible in court. One of the wronged people may sooner or later lose it and take justice into their own hands. In other words, be kind and considerate in your personal life, and judicious in your business pursuits. This isn't just good manners, but a very real survival skill.

11

GETTING IN SHAPE

The survivalist community has an odd relationship with fitness. Some of its members are fascinated by military tactics and believe that any person who can't bench-press 300 pounds is unlikely to make it through any crisis of note. At the same time, in a country where one-third of adults are obese, there's no shortage of preppers whose weight undoubtedly interferes with their health or the enjoyment of their lives—but who don't consider this fact to be in any way relevant to their emergency preparedness plans.

Of course, unrealistic body standards push many to depression or worse, and may be causing more harm than they purport to cure. But for all this nuance, there's no denying that obesity is a real foe. Among men aged 45, for example, the lifetime odds of diabetes skyrockets from single digits for underweight individuals to 50 percent for those with a BMI of 30 or more.[1]

Many other serious metabolic and cardiovascular diseases follow the same curve, ultimately shaving years off our lives or robbing us of the ability to enjoy them in good health—in itself a worthy preparedness goal. Further, chronic illness can make it difficult to cope with even fairly prosaic and short-lived emergencies. This isn't because we must be able to lift a car or scale a 30-foot wall, but because we might find it difficult to carry out basic storm cleanup tasks—or to get a refill for insulin. In short: if your BMI is inching toward the danger zone, it's wise to put a plan in motion that stands to reverse the trend.

The Folly of Miracle Cures

Tens of millions of people profess the desire to lose weight; surprisingly few succeed. Much of this appears to have to do with trying to run a sprint when we ought to be running a marathon. A week-long bout of absolute fasting can easily rid someone of 5 to 10 pounds, but it's going to be a miserable experience followed by a rapid rebound. To be successful, you need a sustainable method that doesn't amount to torture and doesn't leave you craving familiar foods.

Alas, most of the popular diets make this task hard. They force adherents to abandon a lifetime of dietary habits, taste preferences, and eating schedules—and stuff themselves full of kale, turnips, quinoa, açaí berry, or whatever else happens to be the "fat-fighting superfood" of the week. To add insult to injury, most nutrition fads aren't backed up by reproducible science; suffice to say that in the '70s, table sugar was widely touted as a dieting aid.[2] Even today, a lot of weight-loss advice revolves around dubious or disproved concepts—say, the existence of negative-calorie foods, the alleged superiority of low-carb and high-fat diets, the evils of high-fructose corn syrup and aspartame, or the significance of eating on a particular schedule throughout the day.

Just as important, our innate nutritional instincts can be badly misguided too. For example, contrary to common wisdom, bananas aren't any healthier than potatoes, and the bulk nutritional qualities of a glass of apple juice are pretty close to those of a can of Sprite. Heck, good old butter has fewer calories than olive or coconut oil, so a sophisticated and "healthy" bruschetta isn't far off from a less-reputable southern delicacy: deep-fried butter on a stick. The same goes for fast-food choices. The supposedly nutritious burrito from Chipotle easily packs four times as many calories as a greasy burger from McDonald's, while a loaded coffee at Starbucks is about the same as two hot dogs with a heaping side of mashed potatoes to boot.

All this probably helps explain the abysmal track record for most weight loss regimes; the self-reported long-term success rate for people who try to slim down appears to be around 20 percent.[3]

Establishing a "No Diet" Diet

Perhaps the most sustainable approach to weight loss is to make sure that our diets don't feel like diets. Ultimately, calories matter far more than anything else. The maintenance calorie intake for most individuals who don't perform hard physical labor hovers around 2,000 kcal a day, and to safely lose about five pounds a month, the number needs to be brought down to about 1,400 to 1,500 kcal.

One potential trick is to start the day with foods that are tasty and have a well-established satiating effect. One notable example are mashed or boiled potatoes, with an empirical satiety index three times that of bread. Other contenders include oatmeal, apples, and oranges.[4] Insoluble dietary fiber supplements or protein shakes in the morning are sometimes reported to help too.

Beyond this, it's probably best to stick to favorite foods and not feel pressured to skip regular meals—but to cut all portions in half, even if it means throwing out a half-eaten burger. The method may seem nonsensical, but it works because portion control is almost entirely psychological. Our blood hormone and nutrient levels go up only some time after we've cleaned our plate, so we habitually eat more than our body needs to feel full.[5]

For routine snacking, finding lower-calorie options is essential and can be easier than it sounds. For example, salted popcorn or Lipton noodle soup are two easy, extremely lean options that are well liked by most; peanuts, on the other hand, pack a ton of calories despite having a reputation as a healthy snack. Some less trendy veggies, such as carrots, raw sauerkraut, or pickles, make for guilt-free choices too. And for soda addicts, artificially sweetened variants are almost certainly a better alternative to sugary versions, despite some lingering controversy.

When buying food, it's best not to fall for "diet," "reduced fat," "low sugar," or "low carb" ice cream, yogurt, cake, pizza, pasta, and so on. The differences are so minor that we might as well have the real thing and stop fooling ourselves. It's also important to watch out for deceptive portion sizes. For example, Cheetos are labeled as 150 calories per serving, but a regular bag contains almost 10 servings. Frozen fries are another sneaky example. They look pretty low-cal until you realize that a serving is only around 10 to 15 pieces.

Calorie Restriction vs. Exercise

Calorie restriction is one way to force the body to burn some of the fat; another well-known method is exercise. This is the source of a rift in the weight-loss community. Some believe in diets, and others swear by hitting the gym.

I don't think one approach fits all, but it needs to be said that exercise takes a lot of time. For an effect comparable to the calorie-restriction goals outlined earlier in the chapter, one would need to sprint for an hour a day, every single day. In the long haul, such demanding exercise regimes tend to be difficult to maintain, especially for people with children or taxing jobs. On top of that, drastic increases in physical activity can trigger cravings or upend nutritional needs, causing paradoxical weight gain unless calorie intake is closely monitored.

This is not to say that exercise is harmful. It's just that it's probably a more difficult way to achieve weight loss, or to sustain it in later years.

The Importance of the Long Haul

As with the task of building a rainy-day fund, the key to success in dieting is to set realistic, long-term goals. Effortlessly losing one or two pounds a week while slowly developing better eating habits is far more meaningful than pulling off a bold but unsustainable feat. It helps to get an accurate bathroom scale, take daily measurements first thing in the morning, and put the data in a spreadsheet to monitor the results. For most overweight or obese people, it may take six to nine months to achieve the desired outcome. Daily fluctuations are almost completely meaningless; the trend to look for is a consistent and predictable biweekly drop.

Of course, it goes without saying that readers with existing health conditions should talk to a doctor first. In such situations, aggressive dieting can carry additional risks that call for routine blood or heart monitoring along the way. Similarly, if any diet makes you feel listless or sick, it's definitely time to give it a break.

12

BUILDING A COMMUNITY

In some of the more radical flavors of survivalist lore, no sin is as grave as letting others know that you prep. The thinking is that the unwashed masses are irredeemable and destined to perish in the wake of The Event, so there's no need to trouble yourself with helping them; as for survivalists who spill the beans, they'll undoubtedly have to fend off angry mobs clamoring for a share of their supplies. Moved by such visions, many newcomers to the community go to great lengths to conceal their hobby—not just from neighbors or relatives, but also from delivery people, banks, and other perceived prying eyes.

I don't buy this philosophy. Of course, restraint has merit: nothing good can come of posting selfies with gold bars or wads of cash, and in a widespread and profound downturn, the number of souls a single person can help is limited. But in trying times, people almost always come together and find strength in local communities. It's much better to be a part of a resilient group than a lone warrior trying to take on the world. Given the localized nature of most disasters, it's also better if your group consists of neighbors, coworkers, and relatives, rather than a scattered collection of internet strangers who live hundreds of miles apart.

Further, most disasters aren't the end of the world. A week-long power outage is a fantastic opportunity to make friends and support neighbors in small ways; it would be a shame to barricade the door the moment the lights go out, anticipating that they might never come back on. It's also good to remember that most disasters don't unfold precisely as planned. If you break a leg in the midst of the commotion, or if your supplies are damaged or spoiled, having self-sufficient kindred spirits you can turn to can make all the difference in the world.

I suspect the reason some members of the prepping community are so insular is that they don't feel taken seriously by the outside world. The obligatory and harmless joke uttered by many outsiders—"Oh, you're a prepper. I know where to go if I need anything!"—is taken as a genuine threat. Some of the difficulties the prepared encounter have to do with the lingering toxic influence of TV series such as *Doomsday Preppers*, but some of the pain is clearly self-inflicted: when survivalists unload fringe critiques of fractional reserve banking or their theories of nuclear warfare onto an uninitiated audience, it's hard to blame the other party if all they can come back with is a blank stare or an off-the-cuff joke.

My favorite approach to getting folks interested in emergency preparedness isn't to school them on how they should be living their lives or to bury them in data, but to casually bring up a perilous experience lived by a common friend, or to mention a regional disaster that happened some weeks back. Then, rather than giving my conversation partner unsolicited advice, I ask them how they feel about it, and if there's anything we could conceivably do to protect our families. If they laugh it off, I might try once more some time later, perhaps bringing up one of the simple steps I decided to take, but then leave it at that. The goal isn't to convert; it's to plant the seed of rational doubt about their current approach to managing risk. It can be months before the seed takes hold, and if it never does, that's fine. Not prepping is a rational choice too.

Beyond building a network of like-minded individuals interested in disaster preparedness, cultivating neighborly relationships throughout your community in a more basic way is also worthwhile. In a crisis that overwhelms hospitals, for instance, being on good terms with a veterinarian or a physician can help avoid misery or even save a life. For introverts and extroverts alike, it pays to say hi to neighbors, engage in small talk, and offer to help with minor hurdles every now and then; finding common interests is a powerful bonding method too. I figure that even if the zombie apocalypse never comes, such gestures can't be a waste of time.

13

HATCHING A PLAN

The ultimate marker of the prepared lifestyle is having a plan: a personalized playbook with simple, practical steps you intend to follow if faced with any of the consequential hardships you can reasonably anticipate. Now that you've evaluated the risks and considered possible lifestyle adaptations to limit your exposure to some of them, you're ready to put pen to paper and start mapping out strategies for handling the hazards you can't so neatly contain or evade.

At first blush, the idea of creating such a document may sound odd. The future is uncertain, so it would seem more useful to formulate a precise action plan in the moment, once you know exactly what you're dealing with. This, indeed, would keep things simple—but as highlighted in Chapter 10, you should never underestimate the difficulty of making good decisions hurriedly and under intense stress. A checklist written ahead of time is essentially a letter to your anxious and tired future self, helping you collect your thoughts and make sure you don't miss anything. Checklists are the lifeblood of many critical professions; they feature prominently in aviation and in medicine, and they're common in my own field when responding to data breaches and other computer incidents. If they're useful for pilots and brain surgeons, they'll be useful for you too.

Another reason to sketch out a plan, to paraphrase noted author Joan Didion, is that writing helps you find out what you think. The concepts in your head can be nebulous and ever shifting, and the mental shortcuts you take may not be obvious until it's too late. Organizing your thoughts on paper captures a better-defined snapshot that can be refined over time and pressure-tested for flaws.

As you start writing your playbook, it's okay to leave some gaps. At this stage, you might be undecided about some of the disasters outlined in Chapters 2 through 4 or still mulling over the financial choices of Chapters 6 and 7. You may also have doubts about supplies, such as whether you should be buying bottled water or self-defense gear. All of this is fine; capture the open questions and make the playbook a living document. Some of these topics will be addressed later in the book. Others may warrant independent research down the line.

Jotting Down Scenarios of Concern

The best way to organize a playbook is to begin with the set of general scenarios you're hoping to address, heeding the advice from Chapter 1: broad outcomes matter more than the precise causative events. Simple keywords and phrases—*recession, wildfire,* and so on—can serve as chapter titles for the document, followed by blank pages to be populated with additional notes later on.

No prescribed set of issues must be included in a plan, but the basic hardships captured in Chapter 2 are probably a good starting point, along with any considerations unique to your family situation, occupation, and so forth. Some of the regional calamities outlined in Chapter 3 may be worth incorporating, but this should be done with care; for example, residents of Florida probably don't have to worry too much about volcanic activity in the state. As for the existential cataclysms of Chapter 4, most can probably be left out of the document, unless any of them strikes a particular chord.

Modeling Sequences of Events

With key scenarios locked in place, the next step is to capture a short narrative for each of the crises outlined in the document, imagining how the situation could unfold, how long it might last, and what impacts it could have. The narrative you develop doesn't need to be perfect. Writing something that seems plausible based on what you know today suffices, taking note of any matters you want to study further at a later date.

On this assignment, it's easy to get drawn to the worst possible outcome: a recession that progresses to a global financial collapse, a local territorial dispute that ends in nuclear war. A simple way to counter this bias is to split each scenario into three separate stories that can merrily coexist in the document. The first one should deal with the most optimistic prediction, a mild variant of the crisis where the impacts are modest and the duration of any hardships is reasonably short. A middle-of-the road narrative should follow, marked by significant hardships that align with reasonably recent historical precedent. The final story is the severe variant, a believable but pessimistic prophecy in which the situation spirals out of control and almost all bets are off.

Once you have these three short narratives written, annotate each with a gut-feel estimate of the probability that it might come true. Both the optimistic and the pessimistic variants probably hinge on multiple events unfolding in a particularly fortuitous or a particularly disastrous way. In light of this, the middle-of-the-road variant might very well be the best way to model the consequences of a particular calamity.

Defining Basic Strategies

With the narratives in place, you can now draft the first, half-baked iteration of the action plan for each scenario in the document. I recommend structuring the plans as simple numbered lists, each divided into two parts. The first part should deal with helpful measures you can take care of ahead of time, such as getting your finances in order or stockpiling gear. The second part should focus on the steps you must follow as the disaster unfolds, such as loading specific items into the car and evacuating from a wildfire to stay with a friend or relative. "Before the disaster" and "during the disaster" work as simple monikers to organize the list.

The plans don't need to be elaborate but should be reasonably precise; for example, without a list of the belongings you want to save from a wildfire, there's no way of knowing whether the items would even fit into a car. Similarly, if your plan doesn't pick a specific destination to evacuate to, you may end up sleeping in the car or staying at a noisy and crowded shelter for weeks.

Identifying Indicators and Decision Points

If there's one metaphor that comes to mind when reading almost every single firsthand account of a slow-simmering crisis, it's the parable of the boiling frog: when every hour, every day, or every week is only a tiny bit worse than the one before it, humans find it extremely difficult to draw the line and take decisive action before it's too late. The desire to "wait and see" is how people perish in wildfires, end up on on the roofs of submerged homes, or fall prey to murderous regimes that, after years of dehumanizing their enemies, finally progress to genocide.

Knowing about that peril, it's wise to annotate your plans with a set of *crisis indicators* that would signal when things are no longer normal and you need to switch gears. For a pandemic, the indicator could be a particular number of cases diagnosed in your town; for impending genocide, it could be the exclusion of certain groups from political or economic life. The point of these criteria isn't that they need to be perfect and immutable. It's that revising them is a deliberate and conscious step, taking the place of a gradual cognitive drift.

An important extension of crisis indicators are *critical decision points*: in essence, an estimate of how long you can wait and still escape serious harm. For example, if the floodwaters are rising, safely leaving the neighborhood after a particular street is partly submerged might be impossible; similarly, with a wildfire, you will need a certain minimum distance to the fire front to still give you enough time to pack your belongings and reach the interstate.

Planning to Fail

When disaster preparedness strategies collide with reality, some bruising is hard to avoid. The plans you hatch can be derailed in countless ways, from flawed intelligence to malfunctioning equipment, unexpected guests, or incidental injury. To avoid unpleasant surprises, it's important to stress-test your assumptions by asking what could go wrong every step along the way. For example, what if you're someplace other than home? What if some of your supplies are misplaced or spoiled? Or, what if it's unsafe to travel in the direction you wanted to go?

You don't need to obsess over implausible corner cases. For instance, considering what would happen if you were caught away from home is certainly worthwhile, but that doesn't mean it makes sense to haul 50 pounds of survival gear on your short, once-in-a-blue-moon vacation getaway. The probability that something disastrous will happen that particular week is infinitesimally low.

On the other hand, if you spend much of your waking hours at work or at school, the wisdom of keeping a bag of supplies locked in the bedroom closet should be called into question; putting some items in the trunk of the car may be a better bet. Unnecessary complexity in your plans should be called out too. For example, for short-term emergencies, ready-to-eat foods are far better than an elaborate off-the-grid cooking plan.

Facing the Final Contingency

As hinted in Chapter 2, you simply can't cheat fate in some situations—and in such circumstances, a will is a natural extension of your "living" contingency plans. This is particularly important if your spouse, children, or other loved ones depend on you for support.

Jurisdictions differ, but in most places, a will doesn't have to be written by a lawyer or follow any special template; it just has to be written clearly and witnessed by two other people or formally notarized. The document essentially prescribes a set of steps to follow in a variety of scenarios, depending on who survives you or on any other factors you want to take into account. The will should also name an *executor*: a person who would tend to the estate, settle any enforceable debts, and faithfully carry out the instructions in the document. Naming a backup executor in case the primary one is unable or unwilling to serve is a good plan; otherwise, the court may appoint a stranger who's going to collect a hefty fee or make the process more burdensome than it needs to be.

For families with children, it also makes sense to include instructions for the custody of minors and for how their portion of the inheritance should be managed until they reach legal adulthood. This can be particularly important for first-generation immigrants, as the court may have a hard time locating and communicating with the surviving relatives of the child.

Finally, it may be best to keep some assets out of probate, either to make the transfer speedier or to keep family finances out of public view. As noted in Chapter 2, the simplest method is to set up any new accounts as *joint tenancy* or *community property*. This way, if you die, the other owner on the record lawfully retains full control of the funds. Another nearly seamless approach is to leave *transfer-on-death* directives with your financial institution, usually requiring nothing more than a simple online form. More complex strategies may involve setting up a closely held LLC or a living trust with a prescribed method of divvying up the assets if a member dies. The tax consequences for each of these arrangements differ; some research should be done to avoid saddling others with unnecessary bills.

A common challenge faced by heirs is tracking down all the assets of the deceased. This can be particularly tricky if some of the property is distributed across several financial institutions or stashed away in storage units, safe deposit boxes, and so forth. The will should provide hints, and must itself be discoverable too: most lawyers would advise against preparing multiple copies to avoid potential confusion, but from the point of view of disaster planning, it can be a good move. One copy can be stored with your own vital documents, while the other can be deposited with a close family member or a trusted friend.

From Plans to Supplies

A robust financial safety net, a sense of job security, and a series of contingency plans work together to let you rest easier and enjoy your everyday life. But plans can only go so far: it helps to know that you have food to put on the table when the grocery stores are closed, or water to drink when the taps are running dry. On the next pages of the book, we'll have a look at such basic necessities—and then some more.

PART III

THE ESSENTIALS

Exploring survival supplies and their uses

14

THE DISCREET CHARM
OF THE BULLETPROOF VEST

Supplies are essential to any preparedness
plan. Keeping some extra water and shelf-
stable food in the kitchen is far more sensible
than walking for miles to a nearby reservoir or
trapping squirrels and raccoons in a community park.

Emergency gear can help you stay comfortable and informed too: for
example, in the middle of a prolonged power outage, a small generator or a
battery bank can get you back online so you can get a sense of what's going
on in other parts of town. At the same time, however, shopping for gear can
easily turn into a habit: the thrill of unboxing new gadgets becomes an end
unto itself and one can always find a way to justify adding another item to
the towering pile of high-tech toys.

Perhaps my favorite example of equipment excess is the ballistic vest. In a
way, this accessory is just cool: we imagine ourselves strolling through a post-
apocalyptic war zone, carrying out acts of valor with not a worry in mind. In
reality, this costly gadget offers limited protection against an unlikely threat
and is bulky and uncomfortable enough to preclude almost any casual use.
Alas, in more than a decade in the prepping community, I must have tried to

talk sense into at least a hundred people who were contemplating buying one, yet I don't think I've ever managed to dissuade a single person from the plan.

To me, the key to equipping yourself is simplicity. Ideally, every purchase you make should be subordinate to an entry in a well-researched response plan—and it should be the simplest and most effective way of solving the problem at hand. A bizarre fire-starting protocol that involves 9V batteries, steel wool, and taxidermied squirrels is probably not nearly as good as a disposable lighter or two.

Getting practice with the equipment you buy is equally important. This isn't just to avoid frantically flipping through the manuals by candlelight, and it's not just because mastering certain tools takes a fair amount of practice and muscle memory. More simply, it's because quality assurance mishaps happen pretty often; if you have several dozen items in your survival stash, chances are at least one of them isn't working correctly. Camping trips can be a fantastic way to test some of the gear, but so can a drill where you don't use running water or electricity for a couple of days, or you don't buy any groceries for a while and cook with what you have.

Maintaining an inventory is important too. Food items expire, batteries need to be replaced every now and then, and a year or two down the line, you might not remember how many cans of cheese or throwing stars are in your kit. An up-to-date spreadsheet with item names, descriptions, counts, and expiration dates is what sets prepping apart from simply hoarding junk.

Lastly, every gadget should be a component of a well-defined, purpose-built kit, and the kits shouldn't be allowed to grow with no end in sight. For example, a small tote in the trunk of your car, meant to help with roadside emergencies or workplace accidents, probably doesn't require weeks' worth of food or a camping stove. Similarly, a larger selection of boxed supplies meant for evacuating from natural disasters may not require tents and hunting gear, at least not in regions where motels and grocery stores are plentiful.

With these principles in mind, the next several chapters will look at some of the main categories of gear that may play a role in a balanced emergency response plan.

15

WATER

Second only to air, water is the most fundamental human necessity. Without it, death comes in a matter of days. This somber biological truth makes hydration a pressing, nonnegotiable priority in almost every preparedness plan.

It can be argued that water is never far away. Most human settlements have been built on the banks of rivers or other natural water sources, and even if municipal pumps or rural wells grind to a halt, relatively little infrastructure is needed for water trucks to get on the road. But this sentiment lacks nuance. Nowadays, tens of millions of people live in arid regions where water needs to be hauled from hundreds of miles away, and even in temperate climates, suburban sprawl puts many families far from the nearest river or lake. Some disasters—ranging from nuclear accidents to storms that overwhelm sewage treatment plants—can spoil surface water too. As for water trucks, their ability to reach all families in need depends on the condition of area roads and bridges, both of which can be rendered impassable by earthquakes and other natural cataclysms.

For all these reasons and more, keeping enough water to get through at least 72 hours is strongly recommended—not just by wacky doomsayers on the internet, but by most authorities. In the United States, this guidance comes from both FEMA and many local governments.[1] Water is cheap and shelf-stable, so there's little reason not to heed their advice. On the flip side, because it's a bulky and heavy good, a principled examination of our needs is of essence to avoid coming up short or wasting precious space.

Estimating Water Needs

When it comes to drinking, it's generally believed that about 1 quart of water per day is the safe minimum for survival, provided that exertion and perspiration are kept in check. For comfort, most people settle for around 1.5 to 2 quarts a day.[2] That said, under extreme conditions, such as for soldiers involved in strenuous physical labor in desert climates, the required daily intake may increase quite dramatically, all the way to a gallon or two.[3]

Of course, this statistic doesn't tell the full story. The average person in the United States uses about 80 to 100 gallons per day—most of it not for drinking, but for other domestic needs.[4] Some water uses are discretionary; long showers, dishwashing, or watering the lawn can easily be curtailed for a couple of days or weeks, for example. But the most water-intensive activity around the home is flushing the toilet, and giving that up is a much tougher sell. Less dignified sanitation options, such as bagging waste or digging out a latrine, may be integrated into some emergency plans—more about that in Chapter 17—but such solutions don't work everywhere or might not be sustainable in the long haul.

For short-term outages that last a day or two, most household uses can be put on hold, and hydration can remain the only priority. Under such assumptions, storing about 2 quarts per person per day might be a defensible choice, but this leaves little room for error. A child or a pet with a hygiene accident, a nasty heat wave, or an unexpected guest could throw a wrench in the works. With this in mind, I would aim a bit higher, and store about a gallon per household member per day; this happens to be the quantity recommended by FEMA too.

When considering longer-term disasters—those that span a week or longer—sanitation, hygiene, laundry, and cooking can no longer be ignored, although you can manage your water use through careful planning. Cooking-related waste can be minimized by avoiding pasta and other water-intensive meals, for instance, while the frequency of laundry can be reduced with a small stash of antiperspirant, wet wipes, and clean undergarments reserved for the dark days. That said, even with such measures in place, it's safer to budget perhaps two to three gallons per day when preparing for the longer haul.

How many days' worth of water you should actually keep on hand varies based on where you live. A generous margin of safety is wise in hot and dry regions that get minimal rainfall during the summer months. For example, a resident of Los Angeles or Las Vegas may be best served by a water plan that gets them through two to three weeks; such a prolonged outage is unlikely, but the stakes are extremely high. On the flip side, a far more relaxed approach can be taken in regions less prone to drought; in the Northeast, around five to seven days might be a sensible baseline for most. A larger stockpile of water can have some utility, but the returns are diminishing, so you should carefully consider the trade-offs.

Household Storage Options

One week's worth of water for a family of four tips the scales at a bit over 200 pounds and takes up roughly 4 cubic feet—a rather imposing presence in any bedroom closet or kitchen cabinet. It follows that in many urban and suburban homes, your available space will dictate your approach to water storage. In some situations, you might need to get creative; for example, it might be useful to browse for odd-shaped water jugs that can slide neatly under the frame of a raised bed.

In households with a storage situation that isn't particularly dire, there's a temptation to take the path of least resistance and stock up on one-gallon jugs of spring water picked up at the grocery store. At first blush, this is a sensible choice, but I can't in good conscience recommend this approach. The paper-thin plastics used to make these containers often develop pinhole leaks at the creases and have ruined more than their fair share of cabinets and floors. If cost is of the essence, a better option may be to recycle two-liter soda bottles. Because such containers must withstand significant pressures, they're made out of sturdy plastics that are unlikely to leak. In contrast, reusing milk or juice jugs is not advisable, even if they appear to be made sturdily. The containers are difficult to clean properly, and the residues of organic matter can lead to unpleasant smells or worse.

When convenience is more important than cost, five-gallon Scepter brand cans are a good option. Available online and at many outdoor outfitters for about $20 apiece, these containers are labeled for water and made out of food-safe plastics for added peace of mind. For unusually shaped or stackable jugs, it pays to check out WaterBrick and Aqua-Tainer products too.

For readers with large families and backyard space, bulk containers may be an economical solution. Perhaps the most common choice is a 55-gallon drum, normally available for around $70 and taking up about as much room as a typical curbside trash bin. On the decidedly extreme side of the spectrum, one can also procure pallet-sized 275-gallon industrial IBC totes, or towering 500-gallon storage tanks from companies such as Poly-Mart.

But before going off the deep end, it's worth noting that most suburban households have existing stores of water within reach. For example, water-heating tanks in many US homes hold between 50 and 100 gallons and can be drained by opening a tap at the bottom of the tank; despite some sediment that may come out at first, the water should be safe to drink. Hot tubs, pools, ponds, and rainwater catchment systems can provide non-potable water for assorted domestic uses too—although drinking it would be a dicey proposition due to a variety of possible contaminants.

For any water kept outside the home, it's important to consider the risk of freezing. Ice is about 10 percent less dense than water, so any closed container filled to the brim is likely to rupture at the seams. A simple workaround is to leave 15 percent of headspace when filling any barrel, can, or jug that may be exposed to prolonged temperatures below 32°F.

Hydration on the Road

For those evacuating from a wildfire or hurricane, a barrel of water sitting in the backyard is of little use. Regardless of how you store the bulk of your water, at least some of it must be packed into sensibly sized containers that can be loaded into a vehicle or stashed in a backpack before you hit the road.

The precise amount of water to pack should be dictated by your travel plans, but typically wouldn't need to exceed three to four days' worth: a bit more than needed to reach a family member, a friend, or a motel of your choice in a place less affected by the event. Remember to decide on a destination or a set of possible destinations ahead of the time. Driving off into the unknown isn't a sound plan, and neither is pitching a tent in the wilderness in the middle of a snowstorm or in freezing rain.

In rare situations, there might be no alternative to leaving home on foot; in such cases, water management involves some difficult and uncomfortable trade-offs. It's usually impractical to carry more than two to four quarts as a part of a balanced "bug out" kit, so your plan should be to reach a hospitable location within a day. When this is impossible, filtering or chemically treating surface water can be an option, but it isn't an ideal one. Some regions might have a dearth of sources of fresh water to begin with, and then, not all pollutants can be reliably eliminated by a simple gravity filter or a disinfecting tablet stirred into a cup.

That's not to blow the problem out of proportion. Given the choice between dehydration and drinking from a scummy pond, drinking from the pond makes sense. In temperate climates, water that looks and smells fine is usually safe, and deadly waterborne diseases are few and far between. By far the most common ailment is giardiasis, which, while unpleasant, generally resolves on its own. Every year, the media dwells on the horror stories of toxic algae or brain-eating amoebas, but serious injuries and deaths caused by such pathogens are extremely rare.

Still, even if it's just giardiasis, a bout of violent diarrhea is not a welcome addition to any plan, so water-treatment tools are a worthy addition to every basic survival kit. Although many options exist, perhaps the simplest and most portable choice is sodium dichloroisocyanurate (NaDCC) tablets, commonly sold under the name of Aquatabs. Their mechanism of action is similar to water chlorination. The tablets are shelf-stable, available cheaply in bulk, and take up much less space in the backpack than LifeStraw or Katadyn filters and other solutions that are sometimes promoted on the internet.

Long-Term Storage Tips

Water as such doesn't go bad. It's been around for billions of years, its cosmic origins on our planet shrouded in some mystery. Of course, bottled water purchased at the grocery store will sometimes have an expiration date printed on the bottle, but in the United States, this isn't driven by legal requirements or health concerns; it has to do with the possibility of cosmetic defects with the packaging (such as faded inks) and the risk of plastic containers gradually imparting an undesirable smell.[5]

That's not to say that nothing can spoil your water stores. For one, any container exposed to sunlight and air will probably sooner or later grow photosynthetic algae. Most algae are harmless, but the resulting biomass may eventually begin to harbor pathogenic organisms too. For this reason, properly closing containers and keeping them out of direct sunlight is important; regular monitoring is also a good plan.

Even in the absence of algae, organic contaminants can cause serious problems down the road. It's important to thoroughly rinse your containers and let the water run for a while before filling them, especially when using a garden hose that harbors all kinds of microflora when not in use. Municipal tap water usually doesn't require any further treatment, but for well water, it may be good to add about four to eight drops of regular, unscented chlorine bleach per gallon. Although this sounds wacky, it's a safe and proven method of disinfecting potable water, endorsed for emergency use by the Centers for Disease Control.[6]

In principle, properly stored water should last forever. But to minimize taste issues and other surprises, it's advisable to rotate it every couple of years, or annually if it's stored in a very warm place (such as the trunk of a car). To stay on the safe side, it pays to have some point-of-use treatment options too. This can be Aquatabs, a countertop water filter such as Berkey, or a way to boil several quarts a day. A repeated treatment with several drops of bleach is possible, but bleach isn't shelf-stable—so setting some aside specifically for this purpose and then pulling it out several years later may not have the intended result.

16

NOURISHMENT

It's a fascinating and little-known fact that about half of all the nitrogen in our bodies comes not from biological sources, but from the industrial Haber-Bosch process, which combines atmospheric gases with hydrogen to produce ammonia; the ammonia, in turn, serves as the feedstock for synthetic fertilizers used to grow much of our food.[1]

Because nitrogen-containing molecules are essential to all life, and because the element can't be absorbed from air by plants or animals, the Haber-Bosch process can be seen as one of humanity's greatest triumphs: it removed a fundamental agricultural bottleneck and allowed us to significantly expand food production while making efficient use of arable land. Yet, to some prognosticators, Haber-Bosch is a sign that we strayed from the path. They juxtapose the simple beauty of subsistence farming with the complexity—and by implication, the fragility—of chemical engineering and modern-day food supply chains. Their prediction is simple: one day, big agriculture is bound to fall apart, and our society will crumble with it.

The yearning for a bygone era of small-scale farming is lunacy; in agrarian societies, regional crop failures routinely condemned millions to death. Today, food is cheaper, more abundant, and available more dependably than ever before. If a new potato blight wipes out the crops in Idaho, America can eat more corn or pay five cents extra for taters grown in another part of the world. Compared to some other industries, farming and the associated transportation infrastructure have relatively few choke points too. In the developed world, as long as the oil is flowing and politicians don't interfere, not much else gets in the way of having a fully stocked fridge.

That's not to say that worries about food security lack any merit. Transient supply issues can happen for many of the reasons discussed earlier in the book: hurricanes and earthquakes can temporarily block roads, deadly pandemics can make frequent grocery trips unwise, and so on. Political considerations shouldn't be downplayed either. The Great Chinese Famine of 1959 to 1961 claimed 30 million lives, and did so primarily because of the deranged policies of Mao Zedong's communist regime.[2] More recently, the irresponsible fiscal practices of Nicolás Maduro coupled with sanctions imposed by the United States have led to widespread food shortages in oil-rich Venezuela.[3] A scenario that depresses global agricultural output is also within the realm of reason. As discussed in Chapter 4, for instance, a major spike in volcanic activity could bring about several years of harsh winters and significantly shortened growing seasons in many parts of the world.

Some argue that keeping a stash of rainy-day meals is a waste of space, since money can solve many food security problems as they unfold. But cash won't necessarily get you groceries when half the city is flooded—and just as important, in a widespread crisis, trying to outcompete others for vital resources won't feel right. You can build a food stockpile to last two to four weeks on a reasonable budget and with little effort. Further, when food is available but rations are inadequate, the same stash can supplement a calorie- or nutrient-deficient diet for many months to come.

Estimating Bulk Calorie Needs

The amount of calories needed to maintain constant weight is affected by many factors, but for sedentary adults, the baseline is usually around 1,800 kcal per day for women and 2,200 for men. Moderate physical activity adds about 200 kcal, while substantial and regular exertion may translate to an extra 500 kcal, and rarely more. The variability in children is surprisingly modest: toddlers may need as little as 1,200 kcal, but by the time children reach their early teens, they eat about as much as adults and can be accounted for as such. In other words, for a typical family, little can go wrong if you size your emergency stash by multiplying the number of people in the household by about 2,000 kcal per person, and then by the number of days you want the stockpile to last.

One school of thought says that emergency planning must involve a careful examination of one's actual food consumption, recording every meal and crunching the numbers to get a personalized tally. But this can be both unnecessary and misleading. Our bodies are quite adaptable, and the only short-term difference between eating 1,800 kcal and 2,500 kcal a day may be an increase in body temperature and metabolic rate. Overeaters may be tempted to crank up the AC in the summer, while undereaters may start looking for warm mittens as soon as the temperatures drop below 50°F. It doesn't follow that somebody who habitually eats 2,500 kcal a day will suffer if allotted 2,000 kcal instead.

Some survivalists argue that the calorie estimates used in disaster planning must be higher than normal, under the theory that the survivors may have to engage in hard physical labor day after day. This is possible, but looking at most of the crises in the 20th century, it seems an unlikely fate. Most of us have fairly robust safety margins too. With mean BMI figures hovering between 26 and 29 in much of Europe and in the Americas, careful weight maintenance is not a particularly pressing need for all but the most skinny of our friends.

Finally, some preparedness advocates try to apply the principles of healthy eating to their emergency plans. In the short term—up to perhaps a month—this makes relatively little sense. Calories are by far the most important need. It doesn't matter much if the energy is coming from fats, which pack up to 4,000 kcal per pound, or from sugar and protein (both around 1,800 kcal/lb). Logistics and comfort are more important than nutritional details, and so is the ability to pace yourself. It follows that familiar flavors and simple, satiating meals are often the best starting point for a plan.

Nutrition in the Long Haul

A short-term stash lasting two to four weeks should be more than enough for most emergencies discussed in this book, but an exception must be made for some less probable and longer-term crises outlined in Chapter 4, ranging from climate disasters to wars. Because of the long duration of such emergencies, some preppers eventually upgrade to a food stockpile that can hold them two to four months without groceries—or supplement a deficient diet for a year or two.

Alas, what works brilliantly for a couple of weeks may not hold up on a longer time frame. To stay healthy, humans need a range of vitamins and minerals, along with complete protein and several specific fatty acids, and on a deficient diet, the stores within our bodies run out after a while. Of course, the list of food ingredients with known or purported health benefits is long, but the aforementioned four classes of substances are the bottom line. Without them, vital biological processes in our body eventually grind to a halt.

It must be said that even when contemplating long-term disasters, there's no need to preoccupy yourself with every single essential nutrient. For example, serious chloride, copper, or fatty acid deficiencies are exceedingly rare in healthy individuals, even among those living off Cheetos and Mountain Dew. But some problems can set in surprisingly quickly and bite hard. Scurvy, once the scourge of sailors embarking on long voyages, can rear its ugly head after a month of a diet lacking any vitamin C. Other nutrient deficiencies take hold more slowly or have less gruesome symptoms, but are nevertheless of significant concern. Children are also known to be affected more profoundly and more irreversibly than adults.

It's possible to spend hours perusing nutrition labels on every item that goes into your emergency stash, mulling over the quantities of iodine, iron, vitamin B12, and so forth. But this painstaking process doesn't guarantee success. Disaster diets are inevitably constrained and poor in fresh produce, so some imbalances will probably persist no matter what. In light of this, it can be less frustrating to eyeball a reasonably varied diet, throw in a bottle of multivitamin pills to correct for any potential issues, and then promptly move on to the next task at hand.

Micronutrients aside, protein intake is another potential concern with some rainy-day diets. Protein deficiency is uncommon in the developed world but rears its head in poor countries with some regularity. Nutrition plans rich in meat or dairy almost certainly hit the recommended intake of about 50 grams of protein per day; on the flip side, fruit- or vegetable-heavy regimens may fall quite a bit short. In such cases, supplementing the stash with whey or soy protein powders may compensate for the potential shortfall without the need to make more radical revisions to the plan.

In contrast to vitamins, minerals, and protein, worrying about sodium or cholesterol in emergency rations is probably a waste of time even for the long-term stash. Lifelong excess consumption may lead to undesirable health outcomes, but two or three months of salty foods are unlikely to be your doom. Of course, this is different for folks trying to manage more acute health conditions. Diabetics, for example, may need to watch their sugar intake with zeal.

Picking a Storage Strategy

There are two basic schools of building a food stockpile. One proposes the creation of a *segregated cache* of extremely shelf-stable goods, such as canned fruit or meat—and then leaving it undisturbed for years, until it's time to replace the entire stash. Another approach is to build a *first-in, first-out buffer* in the pantry, keeping an excess of everyday goods and consuming the ones that approach the expiration date, then buying more to replenish the cache.

The buffer approach has its charm. For one, it creates no waste and ensures freshness throughout the stash. But it has downsides too. For folks who don't cook often, or who get most of their calories or flavor from perishables, the method simply doesn't scale. A stockpile created this way also isn't necessarily conducive to conserving cooking water or fuel, or to optimizing storage space. Last but not least, the approach may not play well with evacuation scenarios down the line; for example, a bag of raw potatoes grabbed from the pantry is a poor snack on the road.

Both strategies are sensible, but in the end, the segregated reserve approach may be more versatile. It allows for a varied diet optimized for ease of preparation, cost, or any other attributes that make sense in the context of your plans. The occasional waste of food is regrettable but ultimately inconsequential: a well-designed stockpile needs to be rotated only once in a blue moon. The negative impact can be minimized by donating nonperishables approaching their expiration date to local food banks; many food banks will also gladly take expired cans.

Keeping Stockpiled Foods Fresh

Food poisoning is feared but commonly misunderstood. It rarely stems from commercial canned goods or other shelf-stable merchandise. Instead, food-borne illness is almost always associated with contaminated or improperly handled perishables such as meat, milk, and eggs.[4] By contrast, about the most significant danger of eating, say, a box of crackers past their "best by" date is the possibility of choking on a poorly chewed piece. Sloppy home canning is sometimes implicated in deadly botulism cases, but the condition is far less common than believed. Fewer than 20 food-borne cases are reported in the United States in a typical year.[5]

Low-moisture, shelf-stable foods that are stored properly are very unlikely to cause issues, and as with bottled water, the dates printed on the packaging exist more for inventory management and quality assurance purposes than as a sign of mortal peril awaiting those foolish enough to take a bite a few days too late. Old crackers might still taste stale, of course, but that's caused by the oxidation of fats in contact with ambient air, as well as the loss of volatile substances that account for the flavor of freshly baked goods.

With proper precautions and a dose of common sense, all kinds of goods in rainy-day pantries can be stored much longer than their "best by" dates imply—and many will not lose flavor or texture to any appreciable extent. In particular, most factory-canned produce keeps for a decade or more.[6] Similarly, almost all dry staples—from rice to powdered milk—can be stored for years when oxygen and moisture are properly excluded from the packaging. An exception needs to be made for select higher-moisture products, such as spongy cakes; for example, despite their reputation, Twinkies don't last very long.[7]

For the storage of dry staples and cooking oil, oxygen tends to be the most significant foe. Oils should keep well in original glass packaging. When it comes to dry goods, the best defense is using bags made from metallized foil (Mylar); unlike regular plastic, the material is largely impermeable to gas. The bags are available cheaply online and can be sealed with an inexpensive tool called an *impulse sealer*—or in a pinch, with an ordinary clothes iron set to Cotton (about 400°F). It's also good to throw an oxygen absorber pouch into the bag to scavenge the air trapped inside.

For dry and canned foods alike, heat and sunlight should be avoided as much as possible. The rate of many undesirable chemical reactions roughly doubles with every 20°F, so any supplies stored in the attic or in a hot car will need to be rotated much more frequently than if kept at 70°F year-round. For foods stored in basements, backyard sheds, or other potentially damp environments, moisture is also a concern. In such a case, even ingredients that are notionally unaffected by oxygen, such as table sugar, should be bagged to prevent clumping or mold. In fact, care should be exercised even with canned goods. Although moisture has no direct effect on the contents, cans stored in damp environments can rust through and lose seal.

The final considerations for food storage are insects, rodents, and curious pets. Emergency stashes aren't any more vulnerable to critters than a regular pantry, but problems may go unnoticed for months or even years. In rural regions, preemptively placing mouse traps, and keeping bagged items off the ground or inside buckets with screw-on lids (sold as Gamma Seal), is a good plan.

Of course, especially when experimenting with unfamiliar storage and packaging techniques, it's best to examine the supplies every now and then and to perform taste tests. Many variables are at play, and—just as with regular groceries—survival provisions carry no absolute guarantees.

Stocking the Doomsday Pantry

Everyday cooking ingredients can serve as the foundation of a competent "bug-in" emergency stash: pasta, rice, beans, flour, cooking oil, vegetable shortening, sugar, salt, and most herbs and spices are just some examples of products that keep for years in original airtight packaging or in sealed Mylar bags, and that can be put to a good use whenever a trip to the grocery store isn't in the cards. As a bonus, sugar and rice are unrivaled sources of cheap sustenance—providing as many as 3,000 kcal per dollar spent.

At first blush, wrapping up the discussion right here would be fair— but then, cooking and the associated expenditure of fuel and water adds complexity to your plans. This complexity is unwelcome even when bugging in, but imagine hitting the road with a bag of flour and an Easy-Bake oven in tow. To avoid such silliness, it's good to explore shelf-stable alternatives that require only minimal preparation or are outright ready to eat—for use both in household stashes and as part of evacuation kits.

Perhaps the most familiar picks in this category are the sugary snacks that litter the aisles of every grocery store: energy bars, tea biscuits, and hard candy are cheap and calorie-dense, typically providing about 1,500 kcal per pound. Along with jams and honey, such sugar-packed goods are a handy option when you need a quick jolt. On the flip side, they make for a lousy foundation of a longer-term diet, as it's common to experience discomfort after eating nothing but sugar for a day or two. Fat-rich snacks tend to be easier on the stomach and can deliver up to 3,000 kcal per pound. On that front, peanut butter and roasted peanuts are two excellent picks. As with cooking oil, rancidity is a concern—but if kept in sealed containers, both products should stay fresh for a good while.

For more substantial low-hassle meals, canned goods are the go-to choice. The high-temperature processing method results in a distinctive texture and some flavor changes, so not all products are universally loved—but given the variety available on the shelves, almost everybody can find something to like. The relatively low cost of canned goods makes them a reasonable foundation of a bug-in stash. Unfortunately, the low-calorie density of fruit, veggies, and most soups—about 350 kcal/lb—also makes them inefficient on the go. Meats, such as SPAM or sardines in oil, fare better and provide around 1,000 kcal per pound.

On the topic of cans, it may be surprising that canned cheese and butter are available too—and don't taste half bad. Butter, imported from New Zealand and marketed under the Red Feather brand, tastes pretty normal and packs about 3,000 kcal per pound. Australian Bega cheese, resembling any number of generic processed cheese products, has about half as many calories. A little-known gem comes from the creamery at Washington State University: its unique Cougar Gold has a substantial following among non-survivalists and easily beats most store-bought cheddar cheese. It comes in massive two-pound cans and can be purchased straight from the university at *https://creamery.wsu.edu/*.

Many other grocery store picks, although not particularly calorie-dense, can add variety to a doomsday diet. Some of the most useful options include pilot crackers, powdered milk in metal cans, and various flavors of instant mashed potatoes, instant oatmeal, or instant soups. Hot cocoa and other powdered drink mixes can be a hit with children too.

Specialty Survival Foods

The products discussed so far come with one undeniable perk: they can be kept in the pantry without inviting quips from friends and relatives. That said, another selection of foods is marketed specifically to the survivalist crowd—and at least some of them are interesting enough to make it worth putting up with witty remarks every now and then.

The most utilitarian choice in this category is *emergency ration bars*, originally developed to be carried on planes and boats. These small, calorie-dense bricks have an unoffensive, moderately sweet taste somewhat reminiscent of shortcake. Available under several brands, most notably Datrex and SOS, they pack about 2,300 kcal per pound, and are an excellent choice for bug-out kits and for other emergencies away from home. The cost is fairly manageable—a single case of 20 bricks costs about $100 and will sustain one person for well over a month.

The next option of note is *freeze-dried meals*: fairly expensive products that, owing to their unique processing method, manage to near flawlessly preserve the taste and texture of meats, fruit, and vegetables, while keeping fresh for 20 to 30 years or more. All that's needed to reconstitute the meal is a cup or two of hot water and a brief wait. Not every freeze-dried entree hits the mark—for example, eggs don't feel quite right—but many could pass for restaurant made. Plenty of manufacturers are out there, but it's probably best to stick to the most reputable and best-liked duo: the Mountain House brand (produced in Oregon by OFD Foods) and the Utah-based Augason Farms.

The final contender are *MREs*, short for *meals ready to eat*. Packed in plastic pouches and processed using a method similar to canning, the entrees usually include chunks of meat or pasta in thick sauce as the main dish, and then crackers, applesauce, or pudding on the side; a chemical heater is typically provided too. MREs are popular with militaries around the world because of the solid, if uninspiring, balance of relatively long shelf life and convenience in the field. That said, they offer neither the flavor of freeze-dried meals nor the energy density of some of the simpler and cheaper choices discussed earlier—and as such, are strictly a matter of taste.

Backyard Gardens as a Source of Food

Some enthusiasts reject the idea of rainy-day food storage. To them, the answer to survival is self-sufficiency, usually practiced through small-scale farming or backyard gardening.

Farming, of course, can't be just a weekend hobby and isn't a serious proposition for all but the most determined few. Suburban backyard gardening is a far more accessible pastime, but the math doesn't quite check out. Feeding a family of three for a year requires about 2,200,000 calories. The humble potato, one of the most calorie-dense crops that can be cultivated and harvested with ease, packs about 160 kcal and weighs 7.5 ounces on average; it follows that about three tons of potatoes would need to be harvested each year to meet the family's needs. Supplanting even just 20 percent of total calorie intake from a backyard potato patch would be a rather extraordinary feat.

What *is* possible, of course, is using garden crops to gradually build a stash of pickled or dehydrated foods. But then, the result isn't fundamentally different from a store-assembled stockpile. In a crisis, the supplies would be consumed far faster than they can be replenished and are bound to run out before long.

17

SANITATION, HYGIENE, AND HEALTH

Sanitation is a curious topic. It's an essential part of our lives but also a bit taboo, politely glossed over in disaster fiction and in most discussions of emergency preparedness.

Naturally, matters such as waste disposal can be left to the imagination when an author weaves a tale of a lone survivor traversing the pristine wilderness. But during a water outage in an urban high-rise, you might end up with a pressing problem in the blink of an eye. Many other household tasks, such as doing laundry or bathing, also get complicated when the taps are dry—and especially for families with young children, can't be postponed forever.

Waste Disposal

Although ubiquitous indoor plumbing is a fairly recent development, sustainable methods of sanitary waste disposal have been with us for thousands of years. The solutions varied in complexity and elegance, ranging from regularly emptied communal cesspits to the sophisticated sewer systems of the ancient Greeks—but whatever the method, almost every permanent human settlement went to considerable lengths to keep the problem in check. Even in medieval Europe, the situation wasn't nearly as dire as commonly portrayed in fiction. Some cities occasionally experienced issues, but the popular tropes of grime-covered peasants and human excrement piling up in the streets are more a matter of artistic license than of demonstrable fact.[1]

Today, municipal sewers and flush toilets do away with all the ickiness of storing or treating waste in the vicinity of our homes. On the flip side, our reliance on such technologies means that if the water stops flowing, we find ourselves not in the shoes of mid-19th century Londoners, but in a far more perilous spot. Of course, small-scale disasters pose little concern. If only a block or two are affected by a water outage, it's easy to swing by a nearby gas station or rent a porta-potty for a couple of days. But during large-scale crises, the options aren't clear-cut—and while rural families with septic tanks may have little to worry about, many suburbanites and city dwellers may be forced to take decidedly unsanitary steps.

In principle, a water outage needn't stop you from using your toilet. You can manually refill a freestanding unit by removing the top cover of the tank, and even in systems with the tank built into the wall, flushing can be achieved with less precision but good results by rapidly dumping two to three gallons of water into the bowl. That said, the sheer amount of water needed to keep a toilet working is a significant issue for most families, except—as noted in Chapter 15—for those with backyard pools or ponds. Collecting and using rainwater can be an option, but only in some climates and in certain months of the year. Another possible solution is to recycle household gray water. Ignoring the slight yuck factor, the toilet tank can be refilled with whatever's left after cooking, dishwashing, or doing the laundry.

Still, even with these creative water-use methods, most households simply won't have enough water to regularly operate their toilets in the long haul. What's more, your own efforts won't necessarily forestall the possibility of issues arising downstream. Although municipal sewers rely chiefly on gravity, pumps—known as *lift stations*—must be added every now and then to help navigate terrain. Many lift stations have backup power, but typically just for a couple of hours. Once the fuel runs out, nearby customers may experience difficulties flushing, or even see sewage flowing back into their homes—especially during the periods of heavy rain.*

When flushing the toilet is impractical or inadvisable, the simplest solution is bagging solid waste. The task can be accomplished by opening a trash bag, taping it to a toilet seat, and then closing the bag after use and

---

* To evaluate the risk of sewer backflow, it might be useful to obtain system maps from your municipality to figure out the location of the nearest lift station and the overall architecture of the sewer system. At-risk homes can be fitted with backflow valves to reduce the likelihood of accidents. This can cost about $1,500, although some cities offer homeowner subsidies.

discarding it in a curbside collection bin or other lidded container of sufficient size. In the winter, this method can be quite sustainable, but on hot summer days, it can quickly create a foul mess. In such a case, chemical treatment can help. Using a scoop of hydrated lime (calcium hydroxide), a common gardening supply, is a cost-effective solution that creates a highly alkaline environment inhospitable to microbes. Another route is to dehydrate the waste with bentonite-based kitty litter, thus preventing decay. If you choose one of these approaches, maintaining an ample supply of trash bags and treatment materials will be an important part of your plans.

If the outage continues for days or weeks, a more sustainable alternative is to start digging out a *pit latrine*—a deep hole with some sort of a cover, where you can dump waste and let it naturally decompose. A depth of at least five to six feet is preferable, and the pit should be placed far from any household wells or ponds. To mitigate odors, you can then regularly cover the contents with a layer of soil. The main challenge is just digging the pit in the first place; rocky or clay soils are formidable foes. In high-density apartment complexes, coordinating with neighbors would be crucial too; it doesn't matter what *you* do if everybody else is resorting to stinky and unsanitary measures.

In addition to stockpiling trash bags and digging tools, toilet paper is an oft-overlooked necessity in many preparedness plans. Having a carton set aside, and a roll or two packed with evacuation supplies, is almost always a good plan. The same goes for feminine hygiene products, diapers, kitty litter, and so forth—depending on your family's specific needs.

Containment of Flooding and Leaks

Water is essential around the house, but it's a disaster when it ends up somewhere it's not supposed to go. Whether it's a faulty appliance, a damaged fixture, a leaky roof, or backed-up sewage, five-figure losses can mount in a matter of minutes if you don't have a way to stop or divert the leak. During severe storms, groundwater and surface water can become a problem too. Drainage issues are so common that millions of homes in the United States are fitted with sump pumps permanently hooked up in the basement to keep the structure dry, but such a pump is of no use when the power is out.

For plumbing leaks, the first step is clear: shut off the water, and then possibly open low-lying taps to drain the system as quickly as possible. But if the source of water can't be eliminated, containment is the backup plan. Perhaps the most expedient solution are long "socks" filled with naturally absorbent material or compact hydrogel that expands on contact with water; PIG Sock and Quick Dam are two well-known brands. The socks are usually around five feet long and can hold back around one inch of water. This is often enough to allow the spill to be pumped out, collected into a bucket, or directed toward a point where the mess can safely drain.

When storm drains are overflowing and water is coming down the street, protecting the entire home from the elements is a more daunting task. Sandbags are a popular choice that can be stored easily and then filled as needed, but they require a source of sand; as noted before, clay-based or rocky soils can make it difficult to fill the bags in time. A more robust alternative are plastic water diversion barriers that can be filled with water from a garden hose. One popular brand is HydraBarrier, with several models that can hold back anywhere from 4 to 12 inches of water without floating away. The barriers are available in lengths all the way to 100 feet.

Owners of single-family homes may also find it useful to have a portable submersible pump that connects to a garden hose, useful for expediently removing water from basements, crawl spaces, or other locations of this sort. Two popular US brands are Little Giant and Superior Pump. Such a pump won't hold off the surge from a violent storm or a burst water main, but it can prevent many lesser problems from spiraling out of control.

Dishwashing, Laundry, and Other Chores

A crisis may offer little leeway on matters of flooding or personal waste, but many other sanitation tasks can be put on hold for days or even weeks. Don't let that lull you into inaction, however: thinking about less urgent household chores can still pay off. For example, you can greatly cut down on dirty dishes if you opt for ready-to-eat meals that can be enjoyed straight out of the bag or can. In the same vein, keeping a stock of disposable plates and cutlery, along with several rolls of paper towels to wipe down plates and kitchenware, can help conserve water and time whenever one or both are in short supply.

When it comes to general cleaning, grime can be allowed to accumulate for a while, but it pays to remember Murphy's law and expect an untimely accident or two; this is especially true if you have kids or pets. The prepper community is obsessed with recipes for oddball DIY cleaning agents—often involving vinegar, hydrogen peroxide, or baking soda—but it's simpler to have an extra bottle of your favorite surface cleaner squirreled away, along with some clean rags. Even when preparing for long-term emergencies, DIY cleaners are seldom a necessity. It's better to look into concentrated products marketed to restaurants, hotels, or other commercial establishments. For example, a small bottle of Diversey PERdiem, normally diluted to 1 part cleaner per 64 parts water, would last in a typical household for a year or two.

On the topic of laundry, some argue that clean clothes wouldn't be a priority, but that's an overly simplistic view. A spectrum of emergencies lie between "business as usual" and "back to the Stone Age," and in many circumstances, you may still want to feel fresh. In the short term, the simplest approach may be just to have clean underwear in your emergency stash, but when laundry can no longer be avoided, undergarments can be soaked for a couple of hours in the sink with a small amount of water and detergent and agitated vigorously every now and then. The clothing can be then wrung out, rinsed, and hung to dry; with a bit of practice, it's possible to make do with two to three gallons of water per batch. Regular dish soap can work just as well as a laundry detergent, but if you plan on storing laundry products, the longest shelf life can be expected of powdered formulations sold in plastic tubs. Popular brands to look for include Arm & Hammer and Charlie's Soap.

Personal Hygiene

Anytime laundry is important, so is keeping bodily odors in check. The time-tested approach to bathing without running water is to fill a small bowl and then use a wet rag plus a touch of soap to wipe down all the areas of concern. But this method isn't without problems. For one, it produces dirty linens and can be uncomfortable in the winter if the water is ice-cold. The approach is also cumbersome on the road.

A more expedient alternative is to use store-bought wet wipes, ideally sealed in Mylar to prevent the contents of the original pouch from drying out. No-rinse shampoos and body washes deserve a mention too. These products, commonly used in healthcare settings for bedridden patients, are designed to lift dirt without leaving any irritating or unsightly residues.

Another sustainable approach to emergency hygiene is to control the bacteria that cause bodily odors in the first place. Although there are limits to what's possible, good antiperspirant can save the day. Products containing aluminum complexes—such as aluminum zirconium tetrachlorohydrex gly— are hard to beat, so even if you prefer more natural-sounding formulations, it might be a compromise worth making in the time of need. Of course, because antiperspirant dries out skin and can be irritating, it shouldn't be used on your intimate parts; benzalkonium chloride (BZK) wipes, available from companies such as Dynarex, are a better choice on that front. Such medicated wet wipes contain a substance that is both a detergent and a potent but gentle antiseptic, and work wonders when alternatives are out of reach.

Antiperspirant aside, a close look at your everyday bathroom routine may reveal other supplies worth including in an emergency kit. Most people would probably want to keep an extra tube of toothpaste, for example, and many may want to include safety razors and shaving cream.

Medication and Medical Supplies

In a disaster, well-being depends not only on staying fresh and fabulous, but also on the ability to deal with any incidental illness or injury that arises along the way. That said, medical care during emergencies shouldn't be confused with emergency medicine. The problems to account for in a disaster plan are for the most part no different from the ailments we experience on normal days. Many survivalists imagine treating gunshot wounds or performing field amputations, but in most circumstances, good tweezers and cough medicine are worth more than a bone saw.

It's important to remember that seemingly prosaic health conditions can turn life-threatening when circumstances deteriorate; for example, preventable and treatable diarrheal diseases kill more than a million people annually in some of the poorest countries of the world.[2] On the flip side, many of the worries inspired by survival fiction, such as gruesome infections, are overblown. It's unusual for gunshot injuries or knife wounds to get seriously infected; in one study of major hand lacerations, the overall infection rate hovered around 5 percent.[3] The one type of routine injury that is prone to getting infected is animal bites, but on that front, prevention is worth more than a cure.

For readers who are critically dependent on prescription medication to treat chronic health conditions, the first step of building an emergency healthcare plan is to ensure the uninterrupted supply of the necessary drugs. This should start with a frank conversation with your doctor—but because of the pop-cultural stigma of prepping, broaching the topic in a less inflammatory way may be useful. In rural places, it may be enough to discuss a previous incident of getting snowed in for a couple of weeks and express a desire to have a safety margin if the prescription can't be refilled in time. In urban settings, upcoming travel may be a reasonable motivation.

The conversations around scheduled drugs, such as most pain medication, will be more difficult. Doctors are subject to strict regulations and often skeptical of the stories their patients tell, so success is unlikely unless the doctor knows you well. Perishable medications, such as insulin or epinephrine, pose some challenges too. They aren't difficult to obtain but may need to be replenished fairly regularly, possibly at a nontrivial cost. Maintaining a first-in, first-out stockpile, as discussed in Chapter 16, may reduce waste. Refrigeration can help too but isn't suitable for all meds.

Prescriptions aside, quite a few common over-the-counter (OTC) medications are worth having at home and on the road, unless specific contraindications preclude their use. Common examples include meclizine (to treat vomiting, vertigo, and motion sickness), loperamide (for diarrhea), cetirizine (for allergies), ibuprofen (for fever and headaches), and dextromethorphan (for cough). Sufferers of serious hay fever may benefit from nasal glucocorticoids (such as triamcinolone acetonide or fluticasone propionate); those prone to asthma may also want to add Primatene, an OTC epinephrine inhaler available in the United States. Rehydration salts can help with recovery from electrolyte imbalance; caffeine pills can be of use when you need to stay alert longer than usual; and extra contraceptives may be valuable to couples who don't want to conceive.

When it comes to skin conditions, topical lidocaine cream (anesthetic), miconazole nitrate (antifungal), and hydrocortisone (anti-itch) come in handy sooner or later, and are probably worth including in almost every kit. For dealing with serious cuts and other injuries, plenty of options are available, but it's important to be realistic. Without practice, for instance, few of us would be able to properly suture wounds, so skin staplers and elastic bandages (such as 3M Vetrap) tend to be much more practical. Clean water can be used to rinse dirty wounds; despite their popularity, the merits of antiseptic rinses and ointments aren't clear-cut.

For many respiratory diseases, it's good to have a dependable thermometer and a clip-on pulse oximeter, along with spare batteries for both. Although these devices don't really aid in treatment, they're a good way to decide when it's essential to seek urgent medical care, and in that capacity, they're particularly useful with small children who can't express themselves well.

Oral antibiotics are controversial in the prepper community. It's true that their frivolous use contributes to the emergence of antibiotic-resistant strains of diseases—but this is an argument against casual self-medication, not against keeping an emergency stash of last resort. The need to match antibiotics to a specific ailment, or the health risks of taking the wrong one, are often overstated too. Popular choices, such as amoxicillin, have broad-spectrum activity and are unlikely to cause serious harm (except to those with specific and generally well-understood allergies). In some parts of the world, the substances are available over the counter, and can be stockpiled easily. In other places, preppers resort to stashing away leftovers or purchasing pills labeled for veterinary use.

Another topic worth considering in an emergency plan is dental care. Although most dental issues develop slowly, some—such as a chipped tooth—can arise suddenly and cause debilitating pain. Topical anesthetics, including benzocaine ointments and eugenol, can be the first line of defense, while temporary cement may be used to protect the exposed area for a couple of days. Dental picks and floss for removing stuck pieces of food can be useful in any evacuation kit as well.

Of course, in a now-familiar mantra, it should be said that the list of supplies outlined in this section isn't exhaustive. Other OTC medications may be valuable to people prone to certain ailments, and various surgical and wound care implements—from hemostats to chest seals—may be of interest to readers hoping to build more comprehensive kits. That said, as with anything else, going overboard has diminishing returns—and there are very real risks of using such tools improperly and causing serious harm.

Medical Skills

Medical knowledge is worth more than trauma gear, and a lot of this knowledge relies on muscle memory. Few people can properly perform the Heimlich maneuver or administer CPR simply because they read a pamphlet several years back. Signing up for basic first-aid training is therefore a vital part of any preparedness strategy.

The Stop the Bleed program (*https://www.stopthebleed.org/*) is of particular note. It covers injuries that happen to all age groups and in situations where the initial response—before the paramedics arrive—can make the difference between death and swift recovery. Knowing when and how to apply a makeshift tourniquet, or how to stop the bleeding from a torso wound (applying substantial pressure with your hands or even with an elbow or a knee should help), can save a life.

In contrast, the more commonly taught CPR procedure is actually far less beneficial than perceived, perhaps because of its entirely unrealistic portrayal in film. When surveyed, people believe that CPR is successful in 75 percent of all cases; the true survival rate for the sufferers of cardiac arrest given CPR is perhaps 10 percent—often with vastly reduced quality of life.[4] To be sure, this isn't an argument against learning or performing CPR; rather, it means that you shouldn't simply settle for a knowledge of this procedure and nothing more.

For folks who can't be persuaded to take a course, a good family health handbook is valuable to have at hand; the *Mayo Clinic Family Health Book* by Scott C. Litin (Mayo Clinic, 2018) is a solid pick. As for dealing with medical emergencies with makeshift tools, *Wilderness Medicine: Beyond First Aid* by William W. Forgey (Falcon Guides, 2017) is a fantastic choice.

18

FUEL AND ELECTRICITY

Energy may be important to our lives, but compared to water, food, and sanitation, it's not urgent. In the short haul, we can typically make do just fine without electricity, gasoline, or natural gas. Shielding yourself from the occasional inconvenience caused by temporary outages or fuel crises is possible, but hatching elaborate plans of this nature usually doesn't make much sense. It costs far more to keep the appliances humming along through a week-long power outage than it would to throw out the spoiled contents of the fridge once in a blue moon.

In some situations, this assertion doesn't hold true, of course. Fridges filled to the brim with fine caviar notwithstanding, a more solemn example is a family that depends on lifesaving medical equipment that must remain plugged in at all times, or that needs to preserve perishable medications for everyday use. But in the general case, the payoff for whole-house generators or off-the-grid energy storage just isn't there, making the pursuit of energy independence an interesting hobby for the affluent but an ill-advised expense for the average Joe.

With the prices of batteries and solar panels coming down every year, this will eventually change. Until then, let's have a look some of the more cost-efficient ways of dealing with a disruption to discretionary energy needs while stuck at home.

Keeping the Lights On

During power outages, illumination tends to be the most pressing need. We're used to staying up well past sunset, and it's hard to change habits at the drop of a hat. Just as important, even during the day, many homes lack sufficient natural light in areas such as bathrooms, closets, attics, or basements.

Some families still take the traditional route of keeping candles in case of an emergency, but in this day and age, it's an unnecessary fire risk. Battery-powered flashlights are a much more practical choice; alkaline batteries cost as little as 20 cents apiece in bulk, can be stored for 5 to 10 years, and a pair of AAs can deliver 100 hours of illumination with ease. Without delicate lightbulbs to burn out or shatter, modern flashlights are also a lot more durable than the technologies of old.

When buying flashlights for emergencies, it's important to note that more lumens don't automatically mean a better purchase. In most situations, there's no need for retina-searing beacons that light up the sky and chew through a crate of batteries a day. Indoors, as little as 10 to 20 lumens is enough for most household work. Outside, around 200 lumens is sufficient to scout the backyard or go on a night hike. Only the owners of larger rural properties may benefit from 1,000 lumens or more—and that's only for investigating disturbances hundreds of yards away.

It should also be noted that the traditional handheld form factor isn't always the right choice. Carrying a flashlight ties up one of your hands and gets in the way of many household chores. For reading, dining, or cooking, omnidirectional lanterns that can be set on the table or on the counter are more convenient. Headlights are fantastic too, although they have the disadvantage of blinding whoever is standing right in front of you—so while they're well liked by their users, they might not always win acclaim from other family members or friends.

Spare batteries for flashlights and other electronics should be stored in a dark, cool, and dry place to maximize their shelf life. It's preferable to keep alkaline cells out of any electronics that don't need to be operational at a moment's notice; this is because, no matter what the manufacturers promise, the batteries occasionally spring corrosive leaks of potassium hydroxide, damaging metal contacts and printed circuit boards in the device. If the equipment must be stored with batteries, it's best to rely on somewhat more expensive but leak-proof lithium cells. These are available in a variety of specialized sizes, such as 18650 or CR123, but also as retro-fits for alkaline AA, AAA, and 9V (look for the Energizer Ultimate brand). Another option is to inspect and replace installed batteries regularly, as the likelihood of leaks increases with age. In this model, tossing out old batteries after one year in the device is best.

Powering Small Electronics

In the midst of an outage, it helps to be able to connect with friends or relatives, to follow local headlines, and to get timely updates from the utility company. In Chapter 22, we'll look at what to do if conventional communication networks fail, but in most cases, the obstacles to staying in touch with the rest of the world aren't as profound. The nearest cell tower or the telco office may have backup power, or may be outside the outage area to begin with. Under such circumstances, having a way to recharge a phone or a laptop, or a method to power a router, may be all you need to get online for your daily fix of funny cat videos and people getting angry at each other on Twitter or Facebook.

As might be expected, countless power-generation solutions are marketed to survivalists. From hand-crank generators to folding solar cells, the reliability and performance of these products tends to be poor. Instead of spending money on gimmicks, for those who own a vehicle, the most straightforward option is to recharge any battery-powered equipment from the accessory socket in the car. The method isn't particularly efficient, but in most cases, it's perfectly adequate: the vehicle's battery alone has enough juice to keep a typical phone charged for weeks. Turning on the engine can extend the run time considerably too, depending on how much fuel you have in the tank.

Of course, a quick recharge session is one thing, but idling the car for days to power a router becomes a wasteful affair. For devices that need to be plugged in continuously, a popular alternative is lithium-ion power stations, invariably made in China and available on the US market under at least a dozen ephemeral brands. But this technology has a gotcha: the affordable units usually pack very little juice—maybe 200 watt-hours, barely enough to power a typical laptop for one afternoon, or a microwave for about 10 minutes or so.

High-capacity units are better, but can cost south of $1,000, so for avid DIYers, a more economical option is to buy a regular car battery, charge it fully, and then pair it with a basic 120V inverter whenever the need arises. Such a rig should provide around 800 watt-hours for under $200; it also can be trivially extended by adding more batteries. The only real disadvantage is that lead-acid car batteries weigh a ton, so it's not an option on the go.

Still, there are limits to what can be done by stashing batteries around the home, no matter if they're alkaline, lead-acid, or lithium-ion. For more substantial or longer-term needs, a small gasoline-powered generator is the best choice; such generators can provide around 5,000 to 6,000 watt-hours per gallon of gas. As with power stations, countless options are available on the market, but because a generator is a fairly complex and somewhat dangerous piece of equipment, it's probably best to stick to reputable brands. Honda EU2200i and Yamaha EF2000iS are considered to be the best of the best. Cheaper generators branded by Champion, Westinghouse, and Generac have a good reputation for their quality assurance as well.

If you decide to buy a portable generator, fuel storage deserves some thought. In most situations, keeping around 10 to 15 gallons is the sensible maximum that's unlikely to attract the wrath of authorities* or cause serious problems in the event of a leak. But even with this modest quantity, you should take care not to create undue fire risks. Gasoline vapors are heavy and can travel considerable distances, so the fuel needs to be stored in suitable containers, in a place with good airflow, and far from any sources of ignition—including water heaters, washers and dryers, and other appliances commonly found in or near the garage. Where possible, it's best to investigate outdoor storage in a backyard shed or other detached structure; proper metal cans are preferable to cheap plastic jugs too.

Gasoline does deteriorate over time but does so mostly when in contact with oxygen and moisture. This is why it's important to follow the manufacturer's instructions for draining a generator after every use (and why small gas-powered lawn tools, such as weed wackers, are notoriously unreliable when pulled out of storage after a couple of months).

On the other hand, gasoline that's stored in properly closed, full containers tends to stay good longer than urban legends dictate. To avoid problems caused by moisture, it's best to use ethanol-free gas in states where this option is available at the pump. Oxidation can be limited with fuel stabilization preservatives such as STA-BIL or PRI-G. With these precautions taken, fuel can easily be stored for a year or more—although it's still wise to rotate it every now and then, most simply by putting it in your car's fuel tank. It's best to do this when the tank isn't completely empty; mixing it with fresh gas minimizes the chance of any hiccups on the road, however unlikely that may be.

Staying Warm

When the power is out, your usual way of heating the home may stop working. This may sound worse than it is. Cold weather can be a serious hazard to people stranded outdoors, but in the safety of your abode, serious harm due to the loss of heating is rather unlikely—provided you have adequate food and clothing on hand. Even in extreme situations, covering windows with some insulating material and then huddling in a single room tends to be enough. Thermal underwear, a warm hat, and a bunch of extra blankets may be about the most important winter preps to have.

---

* Most cities have surprisingly elaborate, if obscure, regulations on the kinds of materials you can keep in your home or the hobbies you can engage in. This can include limits on the amount of gasoline you can keep outside the tank of a car.

On the flip side, braving the cold isn't the only concern when the utilities are out. If the temperature inside the house drops below freezing for a longer while, the water in the pipes may freeze and cause the piping to burst. A simple work-around is to leave the taps slightly open, allowing somewhat warmer water from the main to continuously flow through the pipes. Even if the liquid eventually freezes, the slow trickle may relieve some of the pressure and disrupt crystal formation. In single-family homes, it's also possible to preemptively shut off the water and drain the system by opening a low-lying tap, although losing running water is seldom a good deal.

The water used in certain types of closed-loop heating systems can be a bit more of a nuisance. To avoid trouble, some homeowners opt to add inhibited glycol to their hydronic systems or indirect water heaters. The glycol depresses the freezing temperature of the mix, making this a worthwhile endeavor in some settings, especially in regions where outdoor temperatures frequently drop below 10°F. Draining the system during prolonged outages may be a last-resort option too—although this takes the heating out of commission until refilled and properly purged of air.

Because of the risk to indoor plumbing posed by subfreezing temperatures, it's good to have alternative sources of heat. Some houses, especially in cold climates, may be equipped with two or more independent heat sources, such as a gas fireplace and electric baseboards. For homes without an adequate backup, inexpensive indoor-safe units, such as the propane-powered Mr. Heater, can bridge the gap. These heaters can be operated from disposable 1-pound camping cylinders—or, with the correct hose, from a standard 15- to 20-pound propane tank commonly used for backyard grills (although bringing such a cylinder indoors should be a measure of last resort). Of course, any portable heater needs to be used with the utmost care and kept well clear of flammable items. Adding a battery-powered carbon-monoxide detector is wise too.

Staying Cool

The loss of air-conditioning during a power outage may seem like a less serious worry, but surprisingly, heat waves kill far more people than the cold. This is because in most situations, managing heat exhaustion is more difficult than staying warm. The warning signs of a heat stroke are also far less obvious. To avoid trouble on exceptionally hot days, hydration should be watched closely. As noted in Chapter 15, as many as four to eight quarts of water a day may be needed to offset losses due to sweating, and we don't always have a strong instinct to drink more. Eating much less than usual is beneficial too, as it tends to slow metabolism and gives our bodies more headroom to regulate body temperature.

When we're hot, we usually enjoy standing in a light breeze or in front of a fan. What's less understood is that the principal cooling mechanism in this situation isn't the motion of air, but the evaporation of sweat from our skin. Water takes a surprising amount of energy to evaporate, and the process can cool surfaces by 20°F or more. It follows that carrying a spray bottle filled with water to mist your skin, hair, or clothes can go a long way toward keeping you cool.

When the humidity is sufficiently low, the same principle makes it possible to operate a *swamp cooler*: a simple electrical device consisting primarily of a fan and a water-soaked mat. Compared to real air conditioning, swamp coolers require little power and can be easily operated from a small generator or a larger power bank. But the gotcha is that they work well only if the humidity is below 40 percent or so; in humid climates, they do very little or even make the situation worse.

Cooking

Your cooktop may be another casualty in a power outage—but in many cases, it may be wise to let it go. Cooking is a welcome addition to any preparedness plan, but only when it brings joy and simplicity, not when it's an added constraint. In other words, your survival plans shouldn't hinge on the ability to cook pasta or slow-simmer a steak, but might incorporate such activities as a way to brighten an otherwise dull and stressful day.

With this in mind, the simplest way to cook during outages is to have a backup option that uses an energy source different from your regular stove. For owners of gas ranges, the solution may be a portable electric hot plate; for those with electric cooktops, the answer could be a propane- or butane-operated camping stove.

As with power generation, many other alternatives are promoted by survivalists, but the pursuit of novelty usually makes little sense. Sterno cans, for example, are far less energy-dense than propane, while portable wood stoves are patently unsafe to use indoors—in part because of the amounts of smoke and carbon monoxide they produce.

For many families, cooking outside is another option, but the drawbacks need to be carefully evaluated before settling on that plan. For one, outages often go hand in hand with unfavorable weather, so the merits of solar ovens should be called into question—and the same may go for fiddling with a grill in the middle of a storm. The efficiency of grills or campfires is much lower too, requiring that far more fuel be stored to achieve the same effect as a camping stove. In rural settings, firewood may be abundant, although it can be laborious to collect; in a typical suburb, on the other hand, trying to chop down a public tree may land you in jail, so being realistic about the available fuel sources is key.

Getting Around

It doesn't take a global fuel crisis for gas stations to shutter. A simple power outage is enough to stop the pumps, with no practical way to move gasoline from the underground holding tanks. Alas, when it comes to transportation woes, there are no quick fixes. Especially in sparsely populated locales such as much of the United States, few alternatives to driving exist—and, as discussed earlier, building a substantial stockpile of fuel carries pronounced legal and environmental risks. Having an off-the-grid, solar-charged electric vehicle is a common prepper dream that's becoming more and more of a possibility for well-off families—but with a high five-figure price tag, it's still a tough sell for most.

For owners of gasoline-powered vehicles, the most pragmatic way to maintain mobility in a crisis is to get in the habit of always keeping the tank at least half full. Although this doubles the frequency of gas station visits, it's a minor hurdle—especially given that the stops get shorter with less fuel to pump. The range afforded by this reserve of fuel can be safely incorporated into any evacuation plan.

When driving isn't an option—whether it's because you don't own a car, or are planning for a time when fuel might run out or roads may be impassable—a bicycle may be a worthwhile and inexpensive prep, at least on days when the weather is nice. Kick scooters or electric scooters can also work, provided that you live in a place without too many hills and with well-maintained roads. If you choose to go somewhere on foot, a beach cart can make it easier to haul any bulky items. For the most part, however, it's best to assume that in a major disaster or fuel crisis, you won't be able to travel much or go very far—and plan accordingly.

Looking Beyond Short-Term Outages

The approaches proposed in this chapter make sense in situations that are fairly transient and localized. In effect, we're devising an approach for a week-long regional power outage, rather than a solar flare that takes out the entire power grid for months. This bias isn't merely a reflection on probabilities; it stems from the observation that during a more profound cataclysm, energy challenges would no longer boil down to business-as-usual tasks such as keeping the lights on or reheating a meal.

In a prolonged and global crisis, the widespread disruption to industrial production, municipal utilities, and food distribution would put other, more basic needs—like food and water—at the forefront of your strategy. Such needs wouldn't be remedied by a solar panel or a tarp-covered barrel of gas. Instead, you'd have to go back to the basics, and rely on the supplies and strategies discussed in other parts of this book.

19

HOUSEHOLD AND VEHICLE TOOLS

Most of the supplies discussed in this book so far have one thing in common: they wouldn't look out of place in any normal home. There's nothing odd about owning a first-aid kit or keeping a well-stocked pantry, and this holds true whether you're a young urban techie or the proprietor of a sprawling rural homestead.

That's not to say that on several occasions I didn't bring up choices that could attract some scrutiny. A barrel of water in the backyard or a portable generator in the garage might be unremarkable in some parts of the country, but in some times and places, these items would stand out like a sore thumb. But then, the worst-case outcome is having to acknowledge in passing that you're prepared for snowstorms, earthquakes, or hurricanes; there's no need to go off the deep end and bring up monetary system collapses or EMPs.

In the next couple of chapters, we'll start crossing the line between household items and survival gear with a bit more courage, examining a wider selection of supplies that may come in handy during disasters but that could invite probing questions if kept in plain view. Your chances of getting grilled by friends or relatives will vary: a pry bar in your garage may make perfect sense if you just finished remodeling a deck, but will look out of place if your proudest DIY accomplishment is hanging a picture on the wall. The bottom line is that as you accumulate more equipment, you might eventually have to come out as a full-fledged survivalist—and if you want to keep your friendships, you'll need to be careful not to bring up extraterrestrials or zombies on day one.

Even when delving into proper survival gear, it still pays to keep our feet on the ground. The market for prepper tools is chock-full of bizarre inventions, from bracelets made out of parachute cord, to credit card–sized fishing kits, to razor-sharp "self-defense" pens. It's best not to be distracted by such knock-off spy gadgets. Let's start small: the first stop on the journey to becoming a certified weirdo is the local hardware store.

Storm Cleanup Equipment

A wide range of disasters may culminate with broken windows, damaged roofs, or tree limbs blocking the way. Under normal circumstances, it's possible to call a pro, but if the damage is more widespread—such as in the wake of a severe storm—wait times for roofers or city services may be measured in days or weeks. In the meantime, it may be up to you and your neighbors to keep your surroundings habitable and safe.

For apartment-dwellers, an emergency repair kit can be simple, perhaps focusing just on expedient repairs to damaged windows and doors: a heavy-duty tarp, construction nails or screws, and a couple of planks should do the trick. For owners of single-family homes, especially in areas with tall trees, another worthwhile purchase may be a good chainsaw, along with the requisite protective wear, chain oil and sharpener, and a modicum of safety knowledge to avoid gruesome injuries.

For a complete set of chainsaw precautions, it's best to turn to the manual or to the safety videos published by the manufacturer. That said, when dealing with trees, one of the most important points is that wood is surprisingly elastic and that limbs can be under considerable tension—especially if propped against vehicles, nearby structures, or other trees. Many chainsaw incidents involve people getting knocked off ladders, whacked on the head, or pinned down when a tree snaps back or shifts unexpectedly during a cut.

Another significant danger is the kickback from the saw itself, common when the tip of the chain bar makes contact with uncut material at an angle of 90° or less. This can cause the chainsaw to be propelled toward the operator with considerable force, sometimes producing gnarly cuts on the forehead or the extremities. Finally, it's also possible to carelessly lower the chainsaw before the chain comes to a complete stop, potentially causing leg injury.

A somewhat safer and less-known suburban cleanup tool is a *power puller*, also known as a *come-along*: a simple ratcheting mechanism that, when coupled with tow straps and a sturdy anchor point, can be used to effortlessly move very heavy objects such as uprooted trees or disabled cars. Power pullers come in several varieties, typically rated between two and five tons; in most situations, a two-ton model should do.

Another hardware store purchase to consider is a full-size pry bar, useful for dismantling partly collapsed wooden structures or forcing open windows and doors to get to people in need. Finally, a lightweight extension ladder, a pair of sturdy shoes, and some cut-resistant gloves are almost always good to have on hand—not just for disasters, but for all-around home maintenance work.

Dealing with Car Malfunctions

Every car owner will sooner or later get stuck on the road—and in some situations, it can be difficult to get help. Skidding off the road in a major blizzard or hitting road debris and getting a flat tire in the wake of a hurricane may mean waiting for hours, if not more, before a tow truck shows up. On a rural road with little or no traffic and with spotty cell coverage, getting timely assistance may be quite a feat even on a good day.

Not all car issues can be solved easily, so especially on long drives through sparsely populated areas, it's a good plan to carry the essentials needed to spend the night in the car. That said, in many other situations, getting back on the road is possible if you carry the right tools. The most familiar roadside problem is a flat tire. In some cases, this can be dealt with by using tire plugs, a portable compressor, or a Fix-a-Flat type of product containing a sealant in a can—but such solutions don't work for blowouts or major damage to the sidewalls. A more reliable solution is to pull out the spare tire, along with a lug wrench and a scissor jack. Unfortunately, about a third of new vehicles no longer come with a spare, at least not unless you pay extra;[1] it's also not uncommon for secondhand cars to miss some of the accessories or come with a spare that's in poor shape. It pays to check.

Another common class of problems are battery issues, usually manifesting when trying to start the car. At times, getting stranded after a brief stop would be unpleasant or even dangerous, and on such trips, it makes sense to carry jumper cables or a battery-powered jump starter, especially if the car is several years old. That said, I'd advise against keeping a jump starter in the car at all times: vehicles parked on the street get extremely hot in the summer, and this doesn't bode well for the lithium-ion chemistry inside.

In cold climates, carrying chains in the winter months is a good plan. Even if the roads are well maintained in your part of the woods, the chains come in handy if the car skids off the road. For the same reason, carrying a tow strap and road flares may be advisable. To deal with electrical malfunctions, it's also good to carry a selection of fuses and spare lamps; once again, these are often supplied with the vehicle, but it's best to double-check. Older vehicles can be more temperamental, so some drivers carry everything from extra motor oil, to radiator sealants, to replacement serpentine belts. This isn't always necessary, but if you know of any recurring issues with your car, it's smart to plan ahead.

Many drivers fear that they could find themselves in a slowly submerging car, unable to open the doors or operate the power windows. Such accidents aren't common in real life—and when they do happen, the casualties tend to involve people who are unconscious or pinned down. That said, if having a way to break tempered glass would give you some peace of mind, one of the cheapest and most reliable choices is an *automatic center punch*: a simple spring-loaded device that, if pressed against side windows, should shatter them without fail.

Other Household Gear

Car repair and storm cleanup are two excellent examples of activities that are aided by the purchase of specialized tools, but as before, it pays to think about any other equipment that may be needed to round out your emergency plan. For example, a quick walk-through of your home may identify a need for spare fuses, filter cartridges, or other consumables required to operate furnaces, well pumps, and other critical machinery.

More broadly, almost every household can benefit from a robust selection of small hand tools, including screwdrivers, hammers, pliers, adjustable wrenches, and so forth. Although such gear isn't necessarily essential during life-and-death emergencies, it can help investigate or rectify many smaller-scale problems, from leaky faucets, to poorly adjusted doors, to stubborn water shutoff valves.

If the task of mapping out all possible repair tasks feels overwhelming, don't panic: the knowledge comes with time. The initial goal doesn't need to be to get everything perfect. It suffices to reduce the odds of having to deal with nasty problems at inopportune times by keenly taking notes every time you have to fix something around the home.

20

EVACUATION GEAR

Wilderness survival has an undeniable allure. It's tempting to imagine being capable of fashioning a shelter out of sticks and leaves, or hunting game with a makeshift spear. In nearly all emergencies, however, staying in built-up areas is better than running for the woods. Putting yourself in unfamiliar surroundings and at the mercy of the elements, possibly without a way to turn back or call for help, is simply not a good self-preservation strategy—not when sensible alternatives exist.

That's not to say that you need to remain in your home come hell or high water. In some scenarios, prompt evacuation is the right move. The point is that when you have to hit the road, the road should ideally lead somewhere familiar and safe. There's no shame in renting a motel room or crashing with a coworker or a friend, and the supplies needed for this eventuality are simple: some cash and a change of clothing will be worth more than a machete and a set of fishing lures.

Of course, not all trips go precisely as planned. For one, mass evacuations may leave you stranded in endless traffic jams for hours or days. Worse, your destination may prove inaccessible, overcrowded, or unsafe in some other way. In other words, although wilderness survival should almost certainly not be your primary plan in all but the most extreme situations, it still pays to be ready to spend a night or two under the stars.

General Preparations

Planning for evacuations is all about making tough choices: no matter the mode of transportation, you can never take as much as you'd like. There's always another keepsake, another ration, or another tool that might come handy—but the only way to take it with you is to leave something else behind.

Such limitations are by far the most painful when leaving on foot. If there's no guarantee of being able to replenish water or food, your safe range may be limited to the distance you can easily cover within a day or two; for most people, that is about 30 miles. Beyond that point, the extra rations needed for the trip begin to weigh you down, offering rapidly diminishing returns. The constraints may be less severe in places where clean water is plentiful year-round, but you should beware of unreasonable optimism: not every route is teeming with pristine mountain creeks, and a squiggly blue line on a map may turn out to be nothing more than a dusty storm drain or an abandoned irrigation ditch.

Compared to walking, a bicycle can usually get you farther, thanks to the increased travel speed and the greatly improved carrying capacity. Distances of around 100 miles should be attainable for any person in good health. At the same time, a bicycle is a seasonal mode of transportation, easily thwarted by snow or ice. Its range is also greatly diminished in areas with steep terrain or poorly maintained roads.

The outlook is best for those leaving by car. The safe range on half a tank of gas is typically 100 to 200 miles, depending on the vehicle and the conditions on the road. If this doesn't get you out of Dodge, you can typically bring enough camping supplies to keep a family of three content for at least a week.

No matter how you're traveling, the essentials to pack are roughly the same: cash, clothing, and a selection of the items discussed earlier in this book—food, water, a range of health and hygiene products, a flashlight with some spare batteries, and a charger for your phone. Another indispensable addition are paper maps of the region you live in, along with a good compass. These will help you orient yourself if the phone malfunctions or runs out of juice.

It's a common recommendation to pack the copies (or originals) of essential documents too—birth certificates, IDs, property deeds, or the insurance policy for your home. Although we live in an era when almost all this information is digitally recorded and backed up, a physical copy can come in handy if the records are damaged or lost. That said, paperwork is seldom needed on the go, so for the sake of simplicity and safety, it may be better to keep the documents with a trusted friend or in a bank deposit box. Alternatively, digital copies on a thumb drive should work.

Setting Up a Camp

In principle, camping requires no special introduction. More than 40 million Americans practice it every year,[1] and even those who prefer five-star resorts to mosquitoes usually have a pretty good command of the concepts at play. At the same time, given that camping is most often undertaken in good weather and by driving to a developed campsite, some of the nuance may be lost.

For one, setting up a proper camp while bugging out on foot is a tall order. Although many hikers carry tents and sleeping bags with them for tens of miles, this is because they can carefully plan the route and take just the gear they need for that hike and for the weather they reasonably expect. In bug-out situations, that kind of precision is a pipe dream. It may be more practical to seek shelter along the way, either knocking on strangers' doors or taking a nap under a found or improvised canopy.

When traveling by car or by bike rather than walking, carrying a tent, a sleeping bag, and a pad is usually not difficult. On the flip side, the car itself offers superior shelter against rain, snow, and wind, so the need for such gear is diminished. Still, a tent may provide more room for family members to get a good night's rest. It's also possible for the vehicle to be stuck in a dangerous location, making it desirable to camp some distance away.

Your choice of tent isn't hugely consequential. Tents from reputable manufacturers tend to have better quality assurance and may be made from more durable materials, so it's probably best not to go for the bargain bin. It's good to remember that tent sizing is a bit wonky too: a model advertised as suitable for five people would likely fit only three adults comfortably. Huddling can be desirable in extreme cold, but most of the time, the party would probably prefer a bit more space.

In addition to the tent itself, it's good to carry a heavy-duty tarp and rope. The tarp can be suspended to provide shade or to protect the tent from wind or rain, or it can be placed on the ground to act as a moisture barrier if the soil is very damp.

More so than tents, the choice of sleeping bags and pads is key to staying warm. Inflatable pads have excellent insulating properties and take up little space compared to foam-type products, so they're an excellent choice—provided that you also carry a kit to patch any holes. As for sleeping bags, they should be chosen with local climate in mind, and ideally tested in the backyard on a cold night. Manufacturers provide ballpark temperature ratings, but you might end up freezing your butt off in a bag that's toasty for somebody else.

It's possible to buy disposable sleeping bags sewn out of Mylar foil. Their advantage is that they're small and lightweight, fitting in the palm of your hand and easily squeezed into even the tiniest bug-out kit. Their main disadvantage, aside from being fairly fragile, is that they're incredibly crinkly and quickly get damp because of poor breathability. In other words, they're a choice of last resort but not a particularly good alternative to the real deal. They're an extremely valuable survival item on day hikes through the wilderness gone wrong, though—and for this reason, are worth having on hand.

Bad Weather Preps

Human bodies exhibit two interesting adaptations that are probably related to each other. First, unlike most other animals, we can sweat profusely, allowing us to endure heat with relative ease—at least when we have enough to drink. But then, unlike most of our mammalian buddies, we lack fur—and without the right clothes, we're extremely vulnerable to cold.

The art of dressing warmly in the winter isn't taught in schools. Instead, we rely on our instincts, and for millennia, they served us rather well. Yet, people in the developed world increasingly spend their lives indoors, with only fairly brief shuffles between warm offices, stores, and homes. In such a reality, the instincts sometimes get dull.

If there's one maxim to memorize, it's that you get far more out of tight-fitting base layers, such as thermal underwear, than out of fluffy jackets or pants. It follows that carrying such lightweight garments in your emergency kit, along with warm socks, a beanie or a balaclava, and a pair of winter gloves, should get you through a major snowpocalypse even if you absent-mindedly head to the office in a bomber jacket and dress pants.

Other than the cold itself, getting your clothes wet is the most significant winter survival risk. Disposable raincoats are worth keeping within reach; the same goes for a change of socks. Shoes can get soggy when trudging through the snow, and frostbite is never far behind.

In the summer, needs are simpler: sunglasses and a flap hat can greatly improve comfort; sunscreen to avoid unpleasant burns can be valuable too. But as hinted in Chapter 15, the most important summer prep is adequate hydration and a plan to stay in the shade when it gets too hot. In some climates, this may mean traveling before dawn or after dusk. If that's your plan, be sure to make the proper accommodations—such as carrying extra batteries for flashlights or headlights.

Food and Water in the Wild

The topics of foraging and hunting dominate survivalist lore. In my view, it's a folly to think one would be able to live off the land when bugging out. In populated areas, wild sources of food are scarce—that is, unless we consider dumpster diving to be a foraging technique. In the wilderness, the story is messy too. In some parts of the world, wild fruit or nuts can provide reasonable nourishment, but only for a brief portion of the year. Otherwise, munching on leaves, bark, or grass is mostly a waste of time: just because a plant is edible doesn't meant that it packs any calories. Hunting may be a more viable source of energy, but inexperienced hunters will probably have little success stalking squirrels with an AR-15; not to mention, in any disaster that doesn't involve a complete collapse of civilization, poachers still face steep fines and jail. Having said that, for those dead set on squirrel stew, trapping varmints with snares is more likely to succeed than shooting—and small wire snares can be purchased or handcrafted on the cheap.

The procurement of water is a more realistic endeavor, and if your evacuation plans fall through, it may become a pressing issue long before the food runs out. We explored the topic of water treatment in Chapter 15, but briefly: if you find a creek or a pond, Aquatabs and a lightweight one-quart cup should get you pretty close to safety.

In wooded areas, campfires can provide comfort and warmth, and can be used to boil water or cook food. It follows that along with a lightweight aluminum or titanium pot and utensils, it makes sense to bring what's needed to build a fire on the go. The prepper community is fascinated with unorthodox fire-starting techniques, but the reliability of several BIC lighters is hard to beat.

Lighters or not, the difficulty of starting a fire on a rainy day shouldn't be underestimated. To help with this, it's good to also bring some easily ignited fuel, such as paraffin-based fire bricks (for example, Weber 7417 or WetFire); homemade solutions, such as dryer lint impregnated with petroleum jelly, should also work fine. When bugging out by car, bringing a small, collapsible butane stove might be a good idea too—although, as with lithium-ion batteries and aerosol sprays, gas cylinders shouldn't be left inside cars that are parked in the searing sun.

Knives and Other Camping Tools

A knife is by far the most versatile camping implement—and one that invariably evokes passionate responses from gadget nerds around the globe. Many enthusiasts spend untold hours comparing grades of steel and debating the merits of different blade grinds. Fierce brand loyalty is common too, making it difficult to decide who to listen to. But for all their occasional beauty and craftsmanship, knives are also some of the simplest tools out there, facing some stiff competition from the wheel and the pointed stick. For most intents and purposes, a trashy knife from the dollar store works as well as a $5,000 heirloom with grips carved out of fossilized mammoth ivory.

That's not to say that all knives are the same; it's just that the differences have relatively little effect on their short-term utility. Higher-grade models may be made from exotic steels that hold a sharp edge for longer or are less prone to rust. They may feature smoother opening mechanisms and a superior look and feel, or they may have more robust construction, allowing the spine of the knife to be hammered to split wood. All fine qualities, to be sure—but seldom a matter of life and death on a brief camping trip.

For all these reasons, recommending a knife is difficult. Tastes are subjective, emotions tend to run high, and relatively few choices are truly wrong. It's also easy to get distracted by form over function. Many low-quality knives have aggressive styling that tricks customers into thinking they're buying not a tool for cutting rope and slicing steaks, but a mythical weapon forged deep in the bowels of Mount Doom.

For folding knives, I'd start with a simple but functional drop point blade, around three inches long. A well-regarded and popular choice under $50 is the Kershaw Leek, with the company's famous one-handed opening mechanism. On the upper end, my personal favorite is MKM Terzuola Clap, a traditional-looking Italian-made knife with a blade forged out of premium M390 steel, combining excellent rust resistance with superb edge retention. The price to pay for this pleasure is about $200.

Although fixed-blade knives tend to be less versatile, they're commonly associated with hiking and come in handy for tasks such as preparing firewood, so they aren't an entirely frivolous addition to an emergency stash. In this category, drop point or clip point blades around five inches are probably the sweet spot; shorter blades offer little advantage over folding knives, while longer ones tend to weigh a ton and get in the way when strapped to a belt. My favorite ultra-lightweight option is the plain-blade version of the SOG Seal Pup Elite (product code E37SN-CP), selling for about $80. On the higher end, I'm partial to MKM Terzuola Jouf, made with well-regarded N690 steel and retailing for about twice as much.

Although a knife is a tool far more than it is a worthwhile weapon, special care should be taken to understand the law. Knife regulations around the world tend to be remarkably boneheaded, with obscure rules rooted in long-forgotten moral panics. For example, the government of California bans the citizenry from possessing ninja throwing stars and lipstick-shaped knives.* More practically, many localities put confusing restrictions on certain blade shapes, opening mechanisms, and so forth. Picking on California again: a folding knife of any length can be carried concealed (for example, inside your pocket), but any fixed-blade knife must always be in plain view. If you've ever purchased any pointy cutlery and carried it to the car in a shopping bag, you might be a violator of Penal Code 21310, eligible for up to a year in county jail.

Knives aside, I'm unconvinced that any other basic tools deserve to be included in a camping kit. An ax or a saw is useful for bushcraft, but in most cases, there would be no need to chop down larger trees. Shovels can be useful for waste disposal, but on short timescales, it's not a pressing need—and on balance, it may be better to pack light. Breaking-and-entering tools, such as crowbars or lockpicks, seem like a sure way to get arrested or shot. Finally, knife sharpeners, although commonly recommended, are probably overkill. A knife should stay sharp for a while, and even if it doesn't, it can be sharpened reasonably well against any smooth rock.

---

* California Penal Codes 22410 and 20610.

Wildlife Management and Physical Security

Right after hunting and foraging, campsite security is a major topic in survivalist circles. Many enthusiasts daydream about complex trip-wire systems or elaborate patrol routines to spot vagrants and deter bloodthirsty grizzly bears.

In reality, not much ever happens at campsites. Bear attacks are rare, and so are visits from ax murderers. The most significant wilderness foes are insects, especially mosquitoes; carrying high-potency insect repellents (containing at least 40 percent DEET or 20 percent picaridin) is a good plan, particularly in the South. As for aggressive wildlife, dogs kill and maim far more people than bears,[2] but bear spray is a fairly universal and reliable remedy for all kinds of furry woodland predators, so it should be included either way.

Knives, as hinted earlier, aren't a weapon to depend on. Although a blade may tip the scales in your favor in a tussle with a mountain lion, it won't keep sharp claws or angry teeth sufficiently far from your fragile human flesh. As for firearms, we'll discuss them in more detail in Part IV, but for now, it suffices to say that despite persistent misinformation, handguns appear to work reliably against belligerent wildlife, perhaps a bit better than bear spray.[3] That said, compared to bear spray, they also have two marked disadvantages. One is the regulatory burden placed on them in many localities; another is that they just weigh more. Ultimately, I'm not saying guns should be outright shunned or blindly embraced—it's just that in bug-out situations, they have some cons.

21

PROTECTION AGAINST POLLUTANTS AND DISEASE

We have a primal fear of beasts such as mountain lions, wolves, and bears, but there's no doubt that in almost all circumstances, we're the ones calling the shots. When a predator steps out of line, we deal with the problem with ruthless efficiency—whether it's with a round of buckshot or a tranquilizer dart. In the end, far more people are killed in the United States by lawnmowers than by animals of prey.

The enemies we can't corral with such ease tend to be of the microscopic kind: a toxic cloud floating through the air or a deadly disease carried by mosquitoes or fleas. Against such adversaries, guns are of little use. The surest survival strategy is to isolate and wait until the danger passes on its own, or until a treatment is developed and made available to those in need. But this is easier said than done. Sooner or later, we might need to venture out or let others into our homes. Worse yet, animal-borne diseases may come to us no matter where we are; when basic services such as trash collection get flaky, rodents and insects may show up in force—and usually find a way to get indoors.

In this chapter, we'll look at supplies that provide some degree of protection from the environment when we can't simply get away from the risk.

Human-to-Human Transmission of Diseases

The emergence of COVID-19 gave most of us a crash course in the control of respiratory diseases, but the quality of the lessons wasn't always up to snuff. In March of 2020, in a now-deleted tweet, the US Surgeon General scolded Americans who were buying N95 respirators, proclaiming that the masks weren't effective in preventing the spread of respiratory diseases—and that wearing one may even somehow leave you worse off.[1] The early advice from the CDC was similarly unambiguous: if you wear a respirator on a trip to the grocery store, you might be an anti-science nut.

Several weeks later, mask mandates rolled out across the nation, but the continued shortages of specially designed N95 respirators (made out of electrostatically charged plastic fibers) led to the use of loosely fitting face coverings fashioned out of ordinary cloth and offering considerably less protection to most.[2] Confusingly, many health authorities prohibited the use of common N95 respirators with exhalation valves, even though they almost certainly did more to protect the populace than a piece of cotton with ear loops. Other poorly substantiated promulgations followed: California designated recreational marijuana dispensaries as essential businesses and advised people to sing or chant only "below the volume of a normal speaking voice,"[3] while in Michigan, big box stores were allowed to stay open, but only if they cordoned off the sections with garden supplies and paint.[4] In coastal regions around the world, police sometimes chased and arrested lone surfers and beachgoers[5]—seemingly to crack down on insubordination, not to manage any well-articulated health risk.

It takes a profound suspension of disbelief to see such silliness as a matter of evolving science. It was well understood, long before COVID-19, that viral respiratory diseases spread most rapidly in crowded indoor settings, including mass transit, offices, grocery stores, churches, and so forth—and that outdoor recreation posed negligible risk. It was also known that N95 masks, common in healthcare settings, captured respiratory viruses and bacteria with remarkable efficiency.

The untold story of the crisis is that instead of stockpiling low-cost masks and drafting common-sense plans in anticipation of a likely crisis, local governments spent billions in federal emergency preparedness funds on more whimsical pursuits, such as armored vehicles, drones, and grenade launchers for local cops.[6] The leadership failures in Washington, DC, mounted for years, too, culminating in a dizzying display of finger-pointing, wishful thinking, and outright denial. The most painful lesson of the pandemic is that the science in the news isn't always sound, and that a plan to respond to a disaster can't be wholly deferential to the authorities. The line between independent thought and conspiracy theories can be thin, but sometimes the best course of action is the one that bucks the trend and earns you funny looks on the street.

For respiratory diseases, because the risk of transmission is highest in crowded quarters where unrelated strangers interact every day, the best prep is a familiar one: a robust financial safety net and a balanced stockpile of essentials that allows you to cut down on shopping trips—at least until the disease is better understood and it's possible to make informed decisions about the odds. Setting clear and objective criteria for any potentially disruptive actions is important too. For example, ask yourself if a certain threshold of cases within 25 miles of where you live would prompt you to take some time off or pull your kids out of school, even if the government is advising otherwise.

When exposure can't be avoided, disposable N95 or P95 masks from reputable manufacturers do offer protection. Fit testing is often mandated in healthcare settings but, contrary to some internet lore, isn't a categorical requirement. Shaving facial hair, following the instructions provided by the manufacturer when putting on the mask, and then checking for obvious gaps is typically enough.

Make sure to buy more masks than you think you'll need. Although the respirator will stay effective for many weeks of use under clean-air conditions, the masks do get gross over time; small children are also prone to losing them or dropping them into the mud. My favorite compact respirator available on the US market is the 3M Aura 1870+. A more comfortable but bulkier option with a valve and a robust face seal is the 3M 8271. For children, 3M 1860S and 8110S respirators are two nearly identical picks.

Masks aside, some diseases are transmitted through high-touch communal surfaces, such as door handles, grocery carts, and more. Although the skin on our hands provides a robust barrier, it's what we do with our hands that becomes an issue. For one, we tend to touch our faces quite a bit, and from there, viruses and bacteria can make it onto mucous membranes through the mouth, eyes, or nose. Frequent handwashing, a good idea even when there isn't a pandemic going on, curbs the spread of mundane but annoying diseases such as norovirus or pinworms too. When handwashing isn't practical, carrying alcohol-based hand sanitizer can be worthwhile, although this habit was less socially acceptable before 2020.

Hazmat suits and heavy-duty respirators, despite being featured prominently in pandemic-themed fiction, are much less useful in real life. That said, in the event of an exceptionally deadly or virulent disease, a simple protective suit, along with disposable gloves, a respirator, and goggles, could theoretically reduce the likelihood of tracking the pathogen all over the place. Positive-pressure suits seen in the movies are expensive and extremely unwieldy, but rubberized coveralls, such as DuPont Tychem, are available on the cheap and, in addition to potentially protecting against pathogens, can be used around the home for all kinds of messy jobs, especially when dealing with spray paint or glass wool.

If you choose this option, having a way to spray the suit with diluted plastic-safe disinfectant upon exiting any high-risk area would be a good plan to avoid cross-contamination. Although it's difficult to make blanket statements, Diversey Oxivir Five 16, Expose, and Virex II 256 are three commercial sanitization products with very different chemistries—peroxide, quaternary ammonium salt, and phenolic—that would probably do the trick.

Zoonotic Disease Vector Control

Respiratory ailments have gotten the lion's share of public attention in the last 20 years, but illnesses transmitted by animals have a remarkably grim track record too: even if we forget the Black Death, malaria still kills around 2.5 million people a year. Malaria may seem like a distant problem confined to the developing world, but it was common in the United States until the early 1950s, when the government undertook a large-scale eradication campaign and sprayed more than 5 million homes with dichlorodiphenyltrichloroethane (also known as DDT).[7] I find it conceivable that a new zoonotic disease could make inroads in wealthy nations, or that one of the old hits could make a comeback—especially if economic trouble or political unrest mounts down the line.

For the control of disease-carrying flying insects, malaria provides a solid playbook. Some of the simplest control techniques include window screens, bed nets, head nets, and the removal of breeding grounds such as stagnant water around the home. Insecticides can work wonders too. One popular choice is deltamethrin, a long-lasting synthetic compound derived from pyrethrin, a natural substance produced by chrysanthemums. This extremely potent neurotoxin for insects is poorly absorbed and rapidly metabolized in most mammals, thus posing relatively little risk if used properly. Other modern insecticides include a family of tobacco-derived neonicotinoids such as imidacloprid, a bacteria-produced bug neurotoxin known as spinosad, and insect hormone look-alikes such as (S)-hydroprene or pyriproxyfen. That last category doesn't kill on contact; instead, the substances—also known as *insect growth regulators*—disrupt the normal life cycle of a bug, for example by preventing it from progressing past the larval stage.

Insecticides can be purchased as ready-to-use consumer formulations or as concentrated liquids that need to be diluted with water. The latter option, labeled chiefly for agricultural and garden use, is considerably cheaper and can cover far more ground, but has higher potential for misuse. Although modern insecticides are fairly safe compared to their predecessors from 50 years ago, they certainly aren't harmless—and some people who mishandled them have suffered lasting harm. In the end, the choice is yours; just be aware of the trade-offs.

Besides insects, rodent control is worth considering. Such critters haven't been directly implicated in a whole lot of devastating pandemics, but they can carry disease-spreading fleas—and even when healthy, they wreak havoc around the home, making their arrival a plague of its own. When dealing with such unwelcome guests, it pays to pursue multiple strategies. Rodents are somewhat clever and may wise up to certain trap designs or certain types of bait. Various spring-loaded mechanical traps are the simplest choice and usually work fine; peanut butter is well-liked and tends to work better than cheese, but it's good to try out multiple foods.

For rodent poison, there are two popular choices: anticoagulants such as bromethalin or bromadiolone, which cause uncontrolled bleeding, and cholecalciferol (vitamin D3), which causes severe hypercalcemia culminating in death. The former class of substances is used in products such as Tomcat and Just One Bite, and the latter is the active ingredient of d-CON. Poisons have the benefit of working continuously, whereas a mechanical trap needs to be reset after every kill; this can matter for vacation homes or for some hard-to-reach spots. On the flip side, the poisons can be dangerous to dogs and small children, so they shouldn't be placed within easy reach—not unless contained in a tamper-proof bait station of some sort. A rodent that eats some poison and then dies in the wall or in the ductwork can be a stinky problem too—although it tends to resolve on its own.

Chemicals and traps aside, there's also the time-tested solution of getting a cat or two. Although pets have their own personalities and the outcomes can be a bit hit-or-miss, most cats—no matter how well-fed and pampered—are ruthless rodent killers who murder for sport. In other words, when mice show up, Mr. Binx will probably earn his upkeep.

Smoke and Industrial Accidents

When smoke from distant wildfires or a noxious cloud from a nearby chemical plant blankets the town, the best response is usually not to bring out the hazmat gear, but to stay home with the windows closed. In particularly serious situations, it may also be appropriate to seal any major inlets of air, including fireplaces, bathroom vents, and so forth—and for that, trash bags and duct tape may be all you need. Particulates such as soot can be trapped with higher-grade HVAC filters or stand-alone air purifiers, or can be taken care of with an N95 respirator—but this method won't work for anything in the gaseous phase.

To protect against gases that find their way indoors, it would be necessary to purchase more substantial gear. The most versatile and affordable solution short of a military gas mask is a 3M 6500 series half facepiece coupled with a 3M 60926 multi-gas cartridge, possibly paired with sealed goggles if eye irritation is also a concern. (Full facepieces, such as the 3M FF-402, are also available—but cost a lot more.) Wearing a large respirator for hours would be unpleasant, but in some unlikely disasters—for example, an overturned chemical tanker on a nearby thoroughfare—it could perhaps save the day. A more portable but shorter-term option is an escape respirator, such as the 3M 5512. Meant only for temporary use, it's small enough to easily fit into the car or an office kit and may allow you to make a hasty retreat to safety.

It's also worth noting that many common and harmful industrial gases are highly water-soluble. This means that breathing through a wet towel, or draping a wet cloth to form a tent over a stroller or an infant car seat, might conceivably offer some short-term protection when all other options fail.

Nuclear Disaster Preps

As discussed in Chapter 4, the popular perception of nuclear disasters is quite wrong. Atom bombs produce intense but fairly short-lived fallout, and for anyone who can survive a couple of weeks in a moderately sheltered location with adequate provisions, the outlook should be relatively good. Reactor meltdowns can spew out longer-lasting pollution over vast expanses of land—but except for the vicinity of the damaged reactor, the contamination is fairly low-grade, somewhat increasing the incidence of certain diseases but having no marked and immediate impact on most residents. In other words, the exposure is more of a large-scale health policy concern than a grave individual risk.

The cinematic portrayal of the health effects of radiation exposure is fairly lopsided too. Receiving a lethal dose would be a terrible way to go, but developing radiation sickness—with its hallmark symptoms such as vomiting and hair loss—isn't a sure sign of impending death. The received dose of radiation is often measured in units called *sieverts (Sv)*;* an acute dose of around 1 Sv is enough to cause all the usual symptoms, but the vast majority of individuals would be back on their feet in a matter of days. It's true that their odds of dying of cancer later in life would go up by several percentage points,[8] but that's hardly a life-altering prospect, given that our lifetime odds of getting cancer already hover around 40 percent.[9]

Of course, even if the danger is overblown, the best approach is to get out of harm's way. But when evacuation is impractical or unsafe, the next best strategy is to shelter in a sealed home or other structure where you can stay for a longer while. In anticipation of nuclear fallout, the priority is to put as much distance and mass as possible between yourself and the outside world—especially lawns, roofs, and other horizontal surfaces where highly radioactive dust may accumulate.

Regrettably, most wooden-frame single-family homes offer fairly meager protection in this regard. Hiding in the basement or moving to the middle floor of a multistory structure may be the best bet. If this isn't an option, any dense material can offer shielding. In a pinch, a fort made out of mattresses or heavy furniture, and positioned far from the outer walls of the house, should do the trick. The goal is simple: maximize the odds that the photons of penetrating gamma radiation will collide with other matter before reaching you.

As with other scenarios discussed in this chapter, relatively little can be gained from donning hazmat suits or gas masks while indoors. These articles are essentially transparent to gamma radiation, and their main utility is that they can be used to prevent you from inhaling radioactive dust or tracking it into the home after venturing outside. Ideally, such excursions should be avoided for as long as possible. Having said that, when it's time to

---

* Some literature uses another popular unit called the *roentgen (R)*. For gamma radiation, which is usually the most significant concern and the primary type of radiation measured in the wake of a nuclear disaster, the conversion rate is 100 R = 1 Sv.

head out, this protective gear can help, along with a sensible decontamination protocol upon your return.

The radioactivity of the fallout should decrease fairly quickly to levels that pose no immediate hazard when walking around. The lingering radionuclides would still be dangerous to ingest or inhale, however, so care would need to be exercised when drinking, eating, or disturbing dirt. Therefore, it's best to live off existing supplies for as long as possible; past that point, simple precautions can minimize harm. For example, streams and rivers should become safe fairly quickly, but bodies of standing, shallow water would best be avoided for a while. As for agriculture, cultivation of crops can resume, but in more contaminated regions, it would be desirable to remove several inches of topsoil first.

A *Geiger counter* is the quintessential element of post-apocalyptic chic—and in principle, these meters can offer valuable insights when communications are shot. The problem is that most of the low-cost units available on the internet are toys. Their detectors quickly become saturated and begin returning deceptively low readings past a certain very modest threshold. The wide-range models useful in life-and-death situations are more expensive. Thankfully, many fire departments and other local government agencies stocked up on such gear in the wake of 9/11 and are now liquidating their inventories on the cheap. With a bit of patience, high-quality units such as an NRC ADM-300 or a Canberra MRAD113 can be found on eBay for a good price. Analog Civil Defense units from the 1960s are popular too, but they're fairly ancient; without careful testing and calibration, their performance is hard to predict.

The most basic measurement mode of a Geiger counter is to display the dose rate, measured in sieverts per hour (Sv/hr); as noted earlier, roentgens per hour (R/hr) may be encountered too. It's believed that the effects of radiation are roughly cumulative, so the dose rate is telling you the speed with which your body might be accumulating radiation injury. To illustrate, you can reach the symptomatic dose of 1 Sv by being subjected to 200 mSv/hr for five hours, or to 500 mSv/hr for two hours. For comparison, the normal background dose rate is about six orders of magnitude lower—typically somewhere between 0.1 and 0.5 µSv/hr, depending on factors such as soil composition and altitude.

The first threshold for a cumulative dose resulting in apparent health effects is about 100 mSv. At that point, your lifetime risk of developing cancer ticks up about one-half of a percentage point; a handful of Fukushima residents are believed to have reached this point. As mentioned earlier, at a dose of about 1 Sv, mild radiation sickness is often present, and the lifetime cancer odds go up about 6 percentage points; some residents of Chernobyl are believed to have received this much. At the considerably higher dose of 5 Sv, the odds of death are around 50 percent, and the survivors typically get all kinds of tumors down the line. Finally, doses over 10 Sv are almost invariably lethal; they have been seen among some of the first responders at Chernobyl.

As for treating radiation sickness, there doesn't appear to be much that can be done. The treatment is mostly symptomatic and supportive, and the body of available medical knowledge is fairly modest. There's little in the way of preemptive treatment options ahead of exposure too—about the most valuable intervention is iodine pills that can block the uptake of radioactive iodine-131 by the thyroid. Such pills are available over the counter under brand names such as iOSAT and can be cheaply included in a survival kit. Far less convincingly, several dietary supplements have shown some radioprotective benefits in preliminary or low-quality animal studies; these include pyrroloquinoline quinone (PQQ),[10] N-acetylcysteine (NAC),[11] diindolylmethane (DIM),[12] vitamin C,[13] and melatonin.[14] If there's one thing that can be said, it's that while the benefits of these substances are dubious in the event of a nuclear apocalypse, they're also pretty unlikely to cause harm—so if you're swayed by the claims, purchase away.

22

EMERGENCY COMMUNICATIONS

Many families spend a good portion of the day away from each other—perhaps with kids shipped off to school and one or both parents at work. If anything unsettling happens during that time, the universal instinct is to grab a cell phone, check in on each other, and decide what to do. But if at that very moment, all your cell phone can muster is "no service" or "call failed," you might find yourself in a tough spot. After all, we no longer have phone booths on every corner, and most homes don't have a landline to try.

There's no doubt that wireless telecommunications infrastructure is prone to disruption too. The simplest observation is that a typical cell tower can handle a fairly modest number of concurrent transmissions, far fewer than there are handsets in range. It follows that in the wake of major terror attacks or other high-profile calamities that prompt everyone to check in on their loved ones, the networks inevitably get overloaded and croak. Such problems can persist for hours. Worse yet, power outages, earthquakes, and hurricanes can take the local communications backbone offline for days, until physical repairs are made.

The consequences of losing communications aren't particularly serious when all family members can travel on their own and safely make it back home. At worst, some anxious thumb-twiddling lies ahead. But more gut-wrenching outcomes are possible: imagine a natural disaster that has two parents racing to pick up a young kid from a distant school, only to get stuck in traffic for hours because of road closures and detours. When they finally arrive at their destination, they find the classroom vacant amid chaos, suggesting the kid must've left with somebody else—or perhaps wandered off. Scenarios like this are why having some form of backup communications isn't just a luxury, but can be a very real need.

The Lost Art of Pen and Paper

When contemplating emergency communications schemes, we tend to gravitate toward high-tech solutions: two-way radios, satellite phones, or experimental technologies such as goTenna, a peer-to-peer mesh networking platform marketed by a startup based in New York. Alas, most of these approaches aren't nearly as versatile as they may seem. Handheld radios suffer from abysmal range in densely populated cities; satellite technology can be prohibitively expensive; and mesh networking isn't popular enough to work reliably in most communities under normal circumstances, let alone when the power goes out.

Given these obstacles, instead of trying to replicate the convenience of instantaneous communications, it may be better to develop a strategy that helps your family collect its bearings without immediately touching base. For a young child, this plan could involve telling them where and for how long to wait for pickup, and then where to seek shelter after dark. For adolescents and adults, the plan may consist of a prioritized list of meeting points—such as a friend's place or a nearby motel—along with suggestions about how long to wait at each location and where to leave a note if you need to hit the road again. Because such instructions are hard to recall, it's best to print them on a laminated card, and then make sure that every household member carries it in their wallet, backpack, or purse. Adding paper and writing implements is important too.

Satellite Communications

After pen and paper, satellite communications are probably the most dependable way of staying in touch—and indeed, the technology is commonly relied on by those responding to natural disasters or traveling to the farthest reaches of the world. That said, satellite *phones* aren't a good choice for most preppers, simply because the devices and the plans are expensive. The unit itself costs around $1,000, and the subscription adds about $70 a month—and most families would need at least a pair. Battery life is fairly poor as well, usually lasting only about two to three days on standby before needing a boost.

A better alternative are satellite *messengers*, sold by Garmin under the brand inReach. The basic inReach SE+ device operates on the global Iridium network and costs around $400. The monthly subscription is about $12, making it a far more sensible expense, especially for those who also occasionally go on hikes or travel through rural areas with no cell phone coverage. The battery in these units lasts up to several weeks on standby, and around three years in storage, so recharging isn't an immediate need.

Satellite messengers allow two-way communications similar to mobile texting, although the latency is considerably higher, around five minutes or so. Messages can be delivered to other inReach devices, to email addresses, or to regular phones outside the outage area; GPS coordinates of the sender are included too. It's also possible to request emergency help from the authorities, which may not accomplish much in a large-scale disaster, but could prove invaluable when injured or lost on a remote hike.

Some aspects of the messaging service depend on terrestrial infrastructure; the satellites merely relay the signal between the subscriber and the hub. After some sleuthing, I believe that the primary Iridium communications gateway is located in Tempe, Arizona, while their satellite control facility is in Leesburg, Virginia. The location of Garmin inReach servers is more difficult to divine because of the way they're set up, but the company does have some data-center technician jobs in Olathe, Kansas. Several of their other job listings also mention Azure, a cloud-based environment run by Microsoft; the Azure data center nearest to Garmin headquarters is in West Des Moines, Iowa, so it could be a natural pick. While making definite pronouncements is hard without insider knowledge about how these companies operate, I'd wager that unless a regional disaster occurs in one of the aforementioned locations, your inReach has a good chance of working just fine.

Two-Way Radios

Two-way radios are sort of like bulletproof vests: weirdly difficult to resist for any techie, yet of very little use to most. To be fair, handheld radios *are* more practical than Kevlar. It's just that neither of these tools works as neatly as we imagine they would.

In the event of a prolonged power outage, handheld radios can be a wonderful way to connect with friends or relatives who live nearby or to stay in touch with family members running errands close to home. But they're severely constrained by their range. In high-rise environments, direct handheld-to-handheld communications are possible within perhaps two to five blocks; in densely populated suburbs, you seldom get more than a mile. There are ways to extend the coverage—we'll talk about them a bit later—but they all come at a cost.

Staying apprised of emergencies by listening to first responders with low-cost handhelds is tough too. Many urban and suburban agencies have moved onto frequency-hopping digital radio systems, and a growing percentage of the traffic is encrypted to keep nosy peasants out. A dedicated $500 scanner from Uniden may be able to follow the unencrypted traffic, but all you're going to hear on a low-cost BaoFeng radio are angry modem noises, and perhaps bits and pieces of conversations every now and then. Older, single-frequency systems may still be in use in your region—for example, the California Highway Patrol still relies on old-school FM—but I wouldn't expect this to last. The chatter on amateur frequencies can be more accessible but is seldom particularly worthwhile. In a major disaster, most strangers won't be able or inclined to help, and the airwaves turn into rumor mills not different from what you often see on Facebook or Nextdoor—except with no way to quickly fact-check the claims. In the end, for almost all intents and purposes, a battery-operated AM/FM radio receiver that lets you receive official broadcasts may offer more bang for your buck.

If you're still interested in two-way radio communications, ask yourself if you and your potential contacts have a genuine interest in mastering the craft. Especially for licensed amateur radio bands, the radios can be finicky and there's a fairly steep learning curve, so it probably isn't realistic to just buy a pair of handhelds, stow them away, and hope for the best.

Understanding the Range of Handhelds

The manufacturers of two-way radios are notorious for making extraordinary claims about the capabilities of their products, but in urban high-rise environments, the range of handheld radios is modest. Vertically, you might be able to clear anywhere from 5 to 20 floors in a building; horizontally, as noted earlier, you can typically get two to five city blocks if you're standing on the street. In suburban areas, the outlook is a bit better. Direct handheld-to-handheld communications are typically feasible within a mile, depending on housing density and terrain (hills and commercial buildings can get in the way). Finally, in sparsely populated rural regions, a range of three to four miles is usually attainable—although again, this can be less if the circumstances aren't right.

Newcomers to radio communications often assume that the range of their gadgets can be significantly extended by cranking up the transmit power or installing a larger antenna, but for handhelds, the upper limit is a matter of basic physics. The problem is simple: for the most part, radio waves propagate in straight lines. The usual distance to the horizon from the vantage point of a person of average height is around three miles; past that point, the scenery ends up in the largely impenetrable radio shadow of the planet we call Earth.

Of course, in urban and suburban environments, the horizon isn't your only worry. The signal from your radio is attenuated every time it has to cross through drywall or masonry, but more important, the longer it has to travel, the more likely it is to eventually encounter a far less permeable obstacle—say, a metal garage door or a major appliance in somebody else's home. There's also the ever-growing chance that the increasingly faint transmission will be drowned out by a source of interference closer to the recipient; motors, light dimmers, motion sensors, fluorescent and LED fixtures, TVs, computers, and car ignition systems are just some of the things to worry about.

In other words, while transmit power or antenna choice can make a difference, the payoff tends to be disappointing; for example, switching from a 2-watt (W) handheld to a 5 W one is unlikely to increase your range in the suburbs by more than 30 percent, and going from 5 W to 8 W is just a way to more quickly discharge your battery.

What *does* work for extending the range of a radio is getting to a higher vantage point. When you do this, your horizon moves farther away: you can see almost 7 miles out by the time you climb to 30 feet. Just as important, the straight-line propagation path between you and other people no longer hugs the ground, so the signal travels mostly through free space, avoiding many of the low obstacles along the way.

For extending your range in this fashion, sometimes nature does all the hard work. If your home is perched on a hill that overlooks a rural valley, you might be able to communicate across vast distances without breaking a sweat. For everybody else, the simplest way to gain ground may be to climb to the top of a parking structure or tall building. The solution isn't always convenient or practical, but it's a solid life hack if other methods fail. Another approach is to erect a base station at home, mounting an antenna on a tall pole or on your roof; that said, this solution isn't always compatible with apartment living or with HOAs from hell.

A natural extension of transmitting from a higher vantage point is to use a specialized relay, also known as a *repeater*. Repeaters are present in most populated areas in the United States (see *https://repeaterbook.com/repeaters/*) and are often installed on mountaintops or on tall buildings. The repeater simply listens to traffic on its input frequency and then broadcasts it on an output frequency. Because the path from your handheld to the repeater (and vice versa) doesn't hug the ground, the reach of two street-level handhelds communicating through a repeater can increase tenfold or more. On the flip side, repeaters can be damaged by storms, hurricanes, earthquakes, and so on, and while some have emergency power, others don't. In other words, a repeater adds new failure modes to your plan.

When transmitting from high ground or using a base station or repeater, the practical upper limit to your range probably peaks at around 20 to 30 miles in densely populated areas, or 40 to 60 miles in rural valleys. More might be sporadically possible, and sometimes you can find a network of linked repeaters that can carry your voice 200 miles or more—but such systems are few and far between.

In the absence of dependable long-distance comms, manually relayed radio messages can be a work-around. If you befriend other operators in your vicinity, they may be willing to retransmit information on your behalf, helping you reach faraway places in a couple of hops. The odds of pulling that off increase if you learn your radio, find out where the regulars meet, and master the on-air etiquette beforehand.

Radio Bands and Types of Service

Any person looking to acquire a two-way radio will have to choose between a variety of bands and services. There's CB, GMRS, FRS, MURS, ham radio, and more—each designated its own portion of the electromagnetic spectrum, and each governed by its own rules. Some of these options work well for emergency preparedness; others can derail an otherwise sound survival plan.

For handhelds, the frequency the radio operates on has relatively little impact on its range and reliability. It's true that different parts of the electromagnetic spectrum have very different propagation characteristics: Wi-Fi signals pass through drywall, visible light shines through glass, and far infrared can travel unimpeded through a metallic germanium lens. Similarly, on some radio frequencies, signals can pass through oceans or bounce off the ionosphere and reach faraway lands, while on other wavelengths, line-of-sight propagation reigns supreme, and a little bit of rain can get in the way. But while this may point to the importance of choosing the right wavelength for the task at hand, virtually all the frequencies that offer beyond-horizon signal propagation require bulky antennas that can't realistically be mounted on a handheld device.

In practice, modern handhelds usually operate in two short-range frequency bands: the 144 MHz band (aka 2m) and 420/430 MHz (70cm); you can also sometimes bump into 222 MHz (1.25m), but it's comparatively rare. All these frequencies behave fairly similarly; a little bit of range may be gained with 2m compared to 70cm in rural settings, but the differences are small. What matters more is the exact type of radio service you pick. Depending on the device you purchase and the licensing you secure, you might have different privileges and different types of radio infrastructure at your disposal in the time of need.

The first service worth mentioning is *citizens band (CB)* radio, an ancient but well-known band available to the general public. In the United States, transmitting here doesn't require an explicit license, outside of the manufacturer's certification for the transceiver itself. Operators are limited to 4 W, with no repeaters allowed. CB uses 40 designated channels centered around 27 MHz; astute readers will note that this is well below the common frequencies used by handheld radios today. The low frequency theoretically offers better propagation, but also means that most CB handhelds with small antennas won't be transmitting efficiently. The technology is much better suited for vehicles and homes, and the handhelds are just a poorly performing afterthought.

In any case, once popular in all kinds of settings, CB is now mostly extinct, except for some long-haul truckers, who use it as a sort of roadside chat room. A distinctive culture surrounds CB, with its own lingo and a set of recurring conversation topics. If you call for help on these frequencies near a major road, you'll probably get help; but beyond that, it's not an environment to everybody's liking and probably not a service to embrace.

Another class of radios that require no special licensing is *Family Radio Service (FRS)*. The equipment operates on a set of 22 designated channels between 462 and 467 MHz, with a power limit of 2 W. Many of the cheapest "blister pack" walkie-talkies are FRS. There are no bells and whistles: you won't find any repeaters, the radios don't support digital communications, and there's no FRS community to speak of. The frequencies are typically quiet in most parts of the country, except for the occasional kids messing around with the walkie-talkies they found under the Christmas tree (an increasingly uncommon gift). FRS can be a good choice for short-range emergency communications when your conversation partner isn't particularly tech-savvy and is uninterested in paying for a license. The low cost of the radios is also a perk.

Next, we have *General Mobile Radio Service (GMRS)*, an upgrade to FRS that allows more transmit power and permits the use of repeaters. Curiously, although most of the GMRS channels are shared with FRS, to use GMRS radios, you still need to get "licensed" in the United States. The license is really just another tax: you pay $35 to the Federal Communications Commission (FCC) and get a piece of paper for your effort, good for you and other members of the household.

With this requirement satisfied, the maximum transmit power you can use is 50 W, although handhelds generally stick to around 2 W. There's no discernible GMRS culture that I know of. The service appears to be used mostly for private communications between people who know each other, much like FRS. It's fairly popular on farms and in other rural settings, but is largely displaced by cell phones in places where network coverage is robust. Still, in an emergency, GMRS can be a solid bet. GMRS repeaters can be found in some metro areas; to see if there are any nearby, you can visit *https://mygmrs.com/browse/*.

The last category of service—*ham radio*—is a bit of a different animal. At its core, it's a license to build almost any equipment you please and transmit in almost any way you please, on a wide range of frequencies dedicated specifically for hobbyist use. The license requires passing an exam, and that exam requires you to spend a day or two memorizing a bunch of answers—some useful and some silly. It's pretty straightforward, but you need to do the work; you can study and schedule a volunteer-administered exam at *https://hamstudy.org/*.

Ham culture is comparatively sophisticated, with a number of clubs maintaining repeaters, drafting regional frequency plans, building emergency response plans, and so forth. The service also has a well-developed, if at times goofy, on-the-air etiquette, and a culture of experimenting with basic digital technologies, including packet networks and keyboard-to-keyboard comms. The frequencies used by ham operators generally aren't crowded, given that the use of the spectrum has been declining since the 1990s, but you can still hear a fair amount of chatter in any major metro area if you scan the frequencies for a while. In a crisis, ham radio bands are where you're most likely to encounter other preppers in your town.

At the same time, *ham radio* is also shorthand for something more tangible: a range of more complex handheld transceivers, generally operating on 144 to 148 MHz or 420/430 to 450 MHz, meant for licensed amateurs who don't want to be confined to the realm of consumer technologies such as CB, FRS, or GMRS. Traditionally, the equipment came from a handful of Japanese manufacturers—Yaesu, Icom, Alinco, and Kenwood—but in recent years, the sales of ham handhelds are dominated by newer bands from China, notably including the ubiquitous BaoFeng: a cheap $25 radio that has gained notoriety as a fashion accessory of the far-right and far-left militias in the United States. Depending on the manufacturer and on how much you want to spend, the units available in this category range from basic products supporting analog voice transmissions, to sophisticated devices capable of sending digital audio, text messages, GPS beacons, and much more. The usual maximum transmit power is 5 W.

Before we move on, it must be said that several other niche types of non-commercial radio systems exist, but they are more restricted or far less appealing than the options already outlined. The *Multi-Use Radio Service (MURS)*, for instance, offers just five channels and a dearth of consumer radios to choose from.

Digital Radios and Data Transmission

Digital communications can be worthwhile in a disaster, just as they are day-to-day. When your favorite mobile app is no longer working, for example, a computer-connected radio could run a neighborhood bulletin board or automatically display the GPS coordinates received from family members on the go.

Alas, most consumer and amateur radios are stuck in the past. They use analog signals to encode voice, with the frequency or the amplitude of a carrier signal continuously adjusted to transmit sound waves. This is a rare anachronism in a world that has moved to digital in almost all other domains. Compared to analog voice, modern digital protocols require less bandwidth, less transmit power, and offer far better sound quality. Digital modes also offer support for reliable, high-speed data, with all the benefits noted earlier—and more.

But today, betting on digital amateur radio is still risky. In addition to old-school amateurs being largely a recalcitrant bunch, a bit of a "system war" is going on: the three completely incompatible contenders are D-STAR, backed by Kenwood and Icom; System Fusion, backed by Yaesu; and Digital Mobile Radio (DMR), an offshoot of technologies developed for commercial use. It's difficult to say who is winning. For example, there are plenty of Fusion-capable repeaters, but this is largely because the manufacturer is handing them out on the cheap to local clubs; the actual use of the system seems far lower than the repeater counts imply. Taking this into consideration, D-STAR and DMR are probably in the lead when it comes to organic use, and DMR is growing more rapidly, in part owing to the availability of sub-$100 radios from China. But the winner is still far from clear. If you decide to go digital today, there's some risk of betting on the wrong horse and then having to switch to a completely different system down the line if you want to be able to talk to other folks.

In addition to modern digital voice and data, the *Automatic Packet Reporting System (APRS)* deserves a mention. This comparatively ancient but still widely used digital protocol is used to send all sorts of short messages between radios. The messages can range from automated GPS beacons, to weather station reports, to hand-typed text. The huge perk of APRS is that many regions have substantial APRS infrastructure that automatically rebroadcasts and routes messages, possibly reaching destinations hundreds of miles away. In effect, APRS is an example of a decentralized mesh network that actually works today. Few radios support stand-alone APRS messaging between handhelds, but many can be tethered to a laptop or a phone, so tinkerers may find it an interesting piece of tech to experiment with. To check out the APRS repeaters and activity in your neighborhood, go to *https://aprs.fi/*.

Licensing Requirements

Many preppers make the argument that in situations where a radio would be necessary, nobody's gonna bother to enforce licensing rules. There might be some truth to that. But if they refrain from unlicensed use of their radio today out of the fear that the FCC is going to come busting through the door, they won't know which repeaters they can reach or what the practical range of the radio may be in their neighborhood when a disaster strikes.

Heck, with bargain-bin radios, it's not uncommon to find out that they don't properly transmit at all. Ham radio transceivers are also easy to put in an unexpected mode by pressing the wrong button, and recovery may be difficult. The manual assumes you already know what *SSB*, *squelch tones*, *notch filters*, and *VFO* mean. The problems aren't insurmountable, but not fun when you're working by flashlight without an internet connection to turn to for help.

For all these reasons and more, those interested in ham radio should get the basic license: *technician class*. The test is simple. Some of the questions are perplexing and pointless, but they can be memorized with ease (and you don't need a perfect score to earn a passing grade). If you really dislike the idea of exams, a solid GMRS handheld is probably a better plan; the Midland GXT1030VP4 seems like a good pick, with the added benefit of taking regular AA batteries in a pinch.

For those taking the amateur radio route, the ham community can be a bit crotchety, with many clubs being rather protective of the things they're familiar with and suspicious of newfangled tech. This is in part explained by the demographics: many of the most active members are retirees, and they're more interested in discussing prostate exams than quadrature amplitude modulation digital modes. That said, you don't really need to integrate. The frequencies aren't crowded, and you're unlikely to step on any toes as long as you aren't being a jerk.

Looking Beyond Handhelds

Some seasoned amateur radio operators may be taken aback by this chapter's singular focus on handheld radios. After all, they'd protest, stationary gear that transmits in the HF band (3 to 30 MHz) and uses skywave propagation can easily reach destinations hundreds of miles away!

This is true, but the emphasis on handhelds is intentional. Spending $50 or $200 on a pair of portable radios to maintain street-level communications may be easy to defend even if the ultimate benefits of the technology are limited. In contrast, investing thousands into stationary transceivers, antenna masts, and emergency power is a far tougher sell, especially if it needs to be done on both sides of the call.

Serious ham radio enthusiasts will have an edge in some disasters, and preppers with a knack for electronics might be inclined to pursue the hobby for its own sake. But for most others, the benefits probably don't justify taking the plunge—especially when, as noted earlier, satellite communicators offer a credible alternative.

23

ENTERTAINMENT AND MORE

Most emergencies are slow and boring, a far cry from what we see in action-packed disaster films: everybody is stuck at home, the internet is out, and you can't even turn on the stereo, cook anything fancy, or run any power tools. At the same time, the lingering uncertainty and the transitional nature of the event make it difficult to focus on profound creative endeavors. In other words, that novel you have in the works probably isn't getting finished any time soon.

It follows that having a way to pass the time can be an important component of a survival strategy, even if it sounds frivolous compared to the consequential matters discussed before. For groups of people, classic board games such as Risk, Monopoly, or Scrabble tend to work well—and are sometimes available in travel-sized varieties. A deck of cards, along with a pocket rule book, can be a source of old-fashioned fun too. For small children, a new plush toy or two is worth including in any evacuation kit; for adolescents and adults alike, an interesting book or a mechanical puzzle game can do the trick.

Of course, there's no need to go low-tech. Handheld gaming consoles, ebook readers, and portable media players are all great options, provided that they work reliably without a network connection and that you have a way to recharge them every now and then. The precise choices are a matter of personal preference, but in the end, a small library of games, books, or fun electronics has a place in every preparedness plan.

Another discretionary prep I like is keeping a small cache of doomsday "party favors": inexpensive but useful goods that can be handed out to neighbors or relatives in need. These may include cheap dollar-store flashlights, AM/FM radios, or wristwatches—or indeed, a travel-sized board game or a deck of cards. Other low-cost examples are travel-size oral hygiene kits, antiperspirant, energy bars, or water treatment pills.

Handing out such practical items during a power outage or other minor calamity leaves the entire neighborhood better off, earns you goodwill, and can make others reflect on the merits of prepping after the crisis ends. Just as important, it can set clear boundaries with those who know you prep. When you're proactive and offer every person the same modest but valuable deal, you're less likely to be suspected of playing favorites or hoarding more.

PART IV

ACTIVE SELF-DEFENSE

Responding to threats to property, life, and limb

24

THE POLITICS OF
PUTTING UP A FIGHT

In this fourth and final part of the book, we'll end on a topic that many other survivalist publications begin with: actively defending yourself, your loved ones, and the property you own.

The reason I decided to break ranks and save this matter for later is simple: despite what we pick up from 24-hour news and the grainy CCTV footage occasionally shared on YouTube or Facebook, active self-defense isn't a common need. Events such as mass shootings or kidnappings are rare. As for everyday crime, as noted in Chapter 10, most burglaries happen when the occupants are away—and in such situations, a gun kept under the pillow isn't of much use, except as an easy picking for whoever ransacks your home.

On the streets, many unwelcome encounters start off ambiguously and don't escalate to deadly force. In such circumstances, being too eager to pull out a knife or a firearm to make a person back off could land you in legal trouble; even the use of pepper spray may count as assault. Naturally, violent confrontations can and do happen, and when a shadowy figure is closing in on you in a dark and empty parking lot, a weapon within reach can be worth the peace of mind. It's just that the ultra-militaristic focus of many survivalist scholars goes too far.

It also bears repeating that although the right to fight for your life is enshrined in most legal systems around the world, the realities of self-defense can be murky. This is especially true in places where the letter of the law no longer aligns with prevailing social attitudes. Take California, for example: the bestselling primer on the state's labyrinthine gun regulations is the aptly titled *California Gun Laws*, a 560-page opus by C. D. Michel and Matthew D. Cubeiro (Coldaw Publishing, 2020). The book is updated every single year, and on quite a few key questions, it simply states that the regulations are indecipherable and that it's anyone's guess as to how they might be interpreted by the prosecutors or the courts. In London, meanwhile, where guns are out of reach for most folks, the government would like a word about your pocket knife: in a 2018 tweet, the mayor said that there is "never a reason to carry a knife" and that those who do "will feel the full force of the law."[1]

Once again, that's not to say that actively defending oneself is a folly and that nothing but trouble awaits those who try. In certain times and places, having options is worth the price. It's just that boisterous online slogans (say, "Better judged by twelve than carried by six") are best set aside in favor of a measured evaluation of the trade-offs. At the same time, I urge equal caution against the politically tinged misinformation meant to dissuade you from considering the full spectrum of choices you might have.

In the United States, the gun debate is a particular minefield of bad-faith arguments and sketchy science. We can disagree about policy, but from an individualistic point of view, the math seems simple: in a society where firearms are ubiquitous and commonly available to criminals, refusing to own a gun doesn't appear to confer an obvious advantage in a confrontation with a perp. Yet, the allure of this argument is precisely what makes it anathema to some proponents of stricter gun control—and so, they strive to cast firearms not as normal tools, but as a unique menace that, if invited into your home, inevitably puts you in harm's way. The argument is commonly backed by studies that count fragmentary reports of lawful self-defense killings, and then contrast them with comprehensive medical statistics of firearm-related suicides, accidental injuries, or even all gun homicides. The conclusion is simple: if you have a gun, you're supposedly an order of magnitude more likely to harm yourself than save a loved one with it.

Of course, that comparison is apples to oranges. For one, although robust statistics on defensive gun uses in the United States are hard to come by, both sides contend the incidents probably exceed 100,000 a year—and most don't involve firing a single shot, let alone killing anyone.[2] In other words, lawful killings are an intentionally terrible proxy for "beneficial" outcomes of gun ownership.

The other side of the equation is lopsided too, although in a less obvious way. To illustrate the problem, let's go with the somber example of suicides as a risk attributed to firearms. In countries with easy access to them, guns can be a common choice for suicidal individuals, and in the United States, they account for about 24,000 out of 47,500 annual deaths.[3] No rational person would disagree that removing firearms would cause *firearm* suicides to plummet. What doesn't necessarily follow, yet what is implied in most analyses, is that doing so would also drastically reduce *total* suicides—in other words, that guns are an important causative factor, not just an implement of choice.

This question is more complex than intuition may dictate. Consider that for many decades, the US per capita suicide rate trailed that of many developed countries with strict gun regimes, including much of Europe.[4] It's true that the US rate started climbing rapidly around the time of the housing crisis of 2007 to 2009, and continues its upward trajectory to this day,[5] but this particular trend is more readily explained by economic shifts than by the proliferation of guns. Lastly, while the recent increases have put the United States ahead of some of its wealthy peers, its overall suicide rate is still in the same ballpark as that of Finland, Belgium, Latvia, or Japan.[6]

In the end, knives, nunchucks, pepper spray, and firearms should be thought of as dangerous tools. Much like the car in your garage or the drugs in your medicine cabinet, they can cause terrible accidents and must be treated with care. Nothing good comes of approaching such tools with unconditional love—or with irrational fear—but when handled in a balanced way, a weapon can be a small building block of a comprehensive preparedness plan.

25

STANDING UP FOR YOUR BELONGINGS

The intense attachment we have to our possessions tends to blur the line between the sanctity of the backyard tool shed and the sanctity of life—but as far as the law goes, the two are nothing alike. So, before we go further into this last section of the book, let's talk about something that technically *isn't* self-defense: safeguarding one's property from destruction or theft.

To the best of my knowledge, in most of the world, people have the right to use a degree of force to protect their belongings. But almost everywhere, this force is more limited than what can be used to defend yourself or your loved ones, or to protect the lives of strangers on the street. Given the legal peril and inherent risk of injury that comes with trying to be a hero, one school of thought instructs victims of property crime to simply avoid confrontation and accept their fate.

This advice has some merit, of course, but is also rather myopic: submissive victims may fare better in the short haul, but over time, their behavior emboldens the crooks. The decision to pursue, detain, or fight a thief is never as simple as a blog post or a book makes it out to be, but it's best to make the call with a clarity of purpose and a solid understanding of the risk.

What You Aren't Allowed to Do

Broadly speaking, the force you can use in the protection of your possessions must be reasonable. You might be able to push a mugger aside, forcibly grab what they're holding, or detain them until the cops arrive—but if you intentionally or recklessly cause great bodily injury, you would almost certainly be crossing the line. In a handful of jurisdictions, deadly force may be permissible to stop the commission of certain specifically enumerated property crimes, but about the only universally sound defense for causing death or severe injury is that you reasonably feared for your own or somebody else's life—and that the perceived threat was imminent and not of your own doing.[1]

The same holds true when it comes to defending your land. Contrary to urban legends, it's unlawful to shoot trespassers in the absence of serious aggravating factors, and this holds true in Texas as much as it does in California or in Japan. In fact, as noted earlier, in many jurisdictions even pointing a weapon at a stranger or displaying it in a menacing way may be a big legal faux pas if you aren't protecting a life.

Of course, sometimes property-related confrontations spiral out of control. If a trespasser starts beating you to a pulp or pulls out a knife, you're now in a self-defense situation and might be justified in using any force necessary to stop the assault. On the flip side, if you chase down a fleeing burglar and get too carried away dispensing your own brand of justice, you might find yourself in trouble—and that's no matter how big your locality is on property rights.

Another thing popular in fiction but verboten in real life is setting traps. Any covert device that causes harm to trespassers or burglars could make you liable for their injuries or even land you in jail. Some exceptions apply: when an intruder knowingly takes a stupid risk and gets hurt (say, climbing over barbed wire), or if a freak accident takes place and a burglar is injured by a device not actually meant to be a trap, you should be in the clear in most parts of the world. But the line is thin. If you build a gator-filled moat and post a sign that reads "BEWARE OF GATORS," for instance, you might still be liable if a child falls in or gets snatched by one of your reptilian friends.

Buying Some Peace of Mind

Because the right to defend your property is constrained, and because you're not always there to defend it in the first place, it's generally better to heed the advice in Chapter 10 and focus on deterrence and hassle-free outcomes, rather than let everything hinge on the outcome of a fight. Dogs, alarm systems, and properly working locks can deter many criminals. Being smart about where you keep valuables can limit the losses if burglars get in too.

Another loss-minimization strategy worth mentioning is a well-tailored homeowner's or renter's insurance policy. Many less common valuables, such as a prized Mr. Potato Head collection, may not be covered to any appreciable extent unless explicitly itemized on a so-called *floater* attached to the insurance paperwork. Mr. Potato Head memorabilia aside, more popular items such as furs, watches, jewelry, precious metals, musical instruments, cash, and firearms are frequently subject to steep coverage restrictions that will saddle you with the bulk of the loss if the valuables aren't itemized on the policy.

In general, many home insurance companies aren't particularly keen on insuring unusual or high-value items and may try to scare you away with mounds of paperwork, appraisal requirements, or exorbitant quotes. An insurance company specializing in collectibles, such as Collectibles Insurance Services (*https://collectinsure.com/*), may be a more willing partner in such pursuits.

Buying Time

It's good to know about unwanted visitors loitering on or around your property. Even if you aren't the type to grab a shotgun and chase them away, such knowledge can give you options, such as calling a friend or dialing 911, rather than being accosted when taking out the trash.

The desire to maintain an awareness of one's surroundings drives many preppers to explore all sorts of perimeter security devices. The two most common examples are passive infrared (PIR) motion sensors or cameras around the home. All too often, such solutions become a distraction; for example, in wooded areas, deer and other wildlife will cause frequent alerts, especially in the middle of the night. In the suburbs, squirrels, raccoons, dogs, and neighbors' kids are bound to give the concerned homeowner headaches as well. Achieving complete coverage and ample advance notice of a threat is difficult. That said, the technology can still work when deployed more judiciously and on a limited scale. A motion sensor overlooking a section of the driveway that's pruned of vegetation, and another device guarding a seldom-used backyard gate, will probably cause relatively few nuisance alarms.

Still, given the difficulty of reliably detecting unsavory characters who have no business in your driveway, another approach is to make their entry into the home as slow and as noticeable as possible. Simple solutions shouldn't be discounted. Keeping the doors and backyard gates locked is often enough; prickly bushes can also be surprisingly effective, especially around any street-level windows that would otherwise be easy to pry open or smash.

A final line of defense may be window security film manufactured by 3M. If installed properly, this transparent material keeps the glass in place even if the window is hit with a rock. Compared to window bars or security shutters, the film is much cheaper and less unsightly—and is probably as far as a typical household would ever need to go, given that a truly determined intruder can always cut or even simply punch a hole through the siding and the drywall of a typical stick-frame home.

26

FIGHTING FOR YOUR LIFE

In the words of Sun Tzu, the greatest victories are the ones that require no battle; or, to put it differently, the objective of most warfare isn't to destroy the enemy, but to frighten them into submitting to one's demands.

This may seem like an oddly militaristic introduction to self-defense, but what's true for large armies also holds true for individuals. Very few people who threaten to harm others actually have violence as their goal; it's a means to an end, and given the inherent risks of combat, it's one they'd often rather *not* exercise. If a mugger or a home invader brings a weapon with them, it's almost always just to make the victims turn over their belongings without too much of a fuss. It follows that to turn the tables on an assailant, the victim usually doesn't need to resort to lethal force. Displaying a reciprocal ability to cause serious harm can be enough. This demonstration can be purely visual too; for example, seeing the muzzle of a gun or the blade of a kitchen knife is sufficient to make most burglars reconsider their plans.

This should be a comforting thought to those of a pacifist demeanor: defending yourself doesn't necessarily mean engaging in a deadly fight, and choosing to arm yourself doesn't need to be driven by a dark urge to kill. It's just that sometimes, the surest way to avoid violence is to make it clear that you mean business and aren't going to be an easy mark.

However, the threat of force is always an escalation—and if the assailant calls your bluff, the situation can quickly take a turn for the worse. As such, when you signal the willingness to cause harm in self-defense, even if just to dissuade a potential attack, you should carefully evaluate the odds and be ready to follow through—and ideally, know how to do so within the bounds of the law.

Of course, no amount of diligent reading is going to prepare a person for a showdown in a dimly lit parking lot. That said, my hope is that the overview of self-defense tools in this and the following chapter will help you figure out what skills to practice or which classes to take.*

The Legalities of Self-Defense

In most situations, it's unlawful to use force, or credibly threaten to use force, to harm another person. That said, legal systems around the world recognize that the defense of life and limb is a valid excuse for taking many actions that would otherwise violate the law, possibly all the way to homicide.

At the same time, in most jurisdictions, several fairly specific conditions must be met in order for such a legal excuse to succeed. The first nearly universal requirement is *innocence*. The situation that led to the use of force must not be a consequence of your own unlawful or reckless behavior—say, deliberately starting a fight. Of course, this rule is applied with considerable nuance. For example, in some places, if you try to disengage and walk away from a brawl of your doing, those pursuing you may now be in the wrong, and you might be able to lawfully fend them off. Still, it's best not to put yourself in situations where your freedom would hinge on finer legal points of this sort.

The second component of lawful self-defense is a rational fear of *imminent harm*. You must reasonably believe that there's an immediate and serious risk of injury or death. In many jurisdictions, especially in the United States, you don't need to be objectively right. If you mistook a toy pistol for a real gun, for example, you might still be cleared in court. On the other hand, you can't beat up another person just because they voiced a vague threat ("I'll kill you!") but didn't start making good on that plan.

The third prong present in most legal systems is *proportionality*. Your actions must be commensurate with the severity of the threat and must

---

* To understand how violent encounters unfold in real life, readers with stronger stomachs may want to check out a YouTube channel called Active Self Protection (*https://www.youtube .com/c/ActiveSelfProtection/videos*). The channel provides a mesmerizing collection of narrated CCTV footage from all over the world; it's a lopsided and gritty view of reality—benign encounters don't make the cut—but also a valuable counterpoint to the improbable action sequences in Hollywood films.

cease once the immediate danger ends. A grown man can't viciously beat a small child; a fleeing robber typically can't be shot in the back. Beyond such egregious examples, in the United States, this rule is usually applied in a fairly relaxed fashion, recognizing that not every decision is perfectly measured in the heat of the moment. As a morbid example, few people get in trouble for emptying half a magazine into an armed felon, even if a single shot might have theoretically stopped the threat. In countries with a dimmer view of self-defense, such as the United Kingdom, proportionality is often dissected with much greater zeal.

The final element, found only in some judicial systems, is the *duty to retreat*. The law may compel the victim to try to get away from the assailant, allowing the use of force only if there's no safe way to escape. In the United States, such laws are fairly rare. As far as I can tell, no state requires you to run away from your own home, but a limited duty to retreat in other situations is present in several states in the Northeast, plus in Wisconsin, Minnesota, Nebraska, and Hawaii.

The Right to Arm Yourself

While the legal right to defend yourself appears to be universally recognized, the right to posses or carry weapons is a wholly different animal, with drastic differences in various parts of the world. On one end of the spectrum, some governments take the position that the desire to fight off potential attacks isn't a legitimate reason to possess *any* dangerous tools, even as benign as pepper spray.

As an illustrative example, in a FAQ published by a police organization in the United Kingdom, readers are advised that "the only fully legal self-defence product at the moment is a rape alarm" and that it would be illegal to possess "a product made or adapted to cause a person injury" in public— or even privately in some circumstances.[1] The government's intention is to reduce the number of drunken brawls or other confrontations that end in severe injury. Yet it must be noted that without access to any equalizing defensive tools such as pepper spray, the law of the street is that *might is right*: a pack of athletic males may terrorize frailer citizens with relatively few worries in mind.

In the United States, the possession of self-defense tools is tolerated better, although local laws provide plenty of gotchas and little rhyme or reason. Pepper spray appears to be allowed everywhere and subject to few practical restrictions. Stun guns, on the other hand, require firearm licenses in Massachusetts and Illinois. As hinted in Chapter 20, knife carry laws are typically permissive, but a mess of obscure municipal and state rules restrict specific blade shapes, opening mechanisms, and so forth. The American Knife & Tool Institute maintains a good catalog of the rules at *https://www.akti.org/state-knife-laws/*. It gets even more confusing when it comes to exotic arms. In California and Massachusetts, for example, the possession of nunchucks may land you in jail, but carrying a medieval maul appears to be okay.

When it comes to the right to carry firearms, the United States is rather unique. As of this writing, the vast majority of US states and counties either practice *constitutional carry* (allowing most individuals to carry a concealed or openly displayed gun without needing any kind of government-issued permit) or have permitting regimes that are by law or in practice *shall issue* (permits are swiftly granted to any unprohibited person who bothers to ask).

At the same time, some of the country's most populous regions, especially on the coasts, effectively adopt *no issue* policies: the local government maintains the pretense of having an application process, but the process is designed so that no ordinary citizen can ever meet the bar. Miraculously, prominent campaign donors and minor government dignitaries tend to qualify with more ease; pay-to-play permit issuance scandals have rocked the San Francisco Bay Area,[2] New York City,[3] and other gun control strongholds around the country.

The Merits of Unarmed Combat

In places where the government looks dimly at the possession of self-defense tools, the practice of martial arts has undeniable merit. A proficiency in hand-to-hand combat techniques offers other perks too: unlike a knife or a can of pepper spray, the muscle memory to take on assailants can be brought with you on a plane and will follow you even when you must go through metal detectors and walk past "no weapons" signs.

That said, martial arts techniques can be difficult to master. Many dabble, but most lack the multiyear commitment to truly hone their skills. It's also important to be realistic about what martial arts can and cannot do. Real life isn't an action film, and if the assailant is armed, all someone might be doing with their impressive karate moves is bringing fists to a knife fight.

Just as important, a fighting stance and a battle cry may have no practical deterrent effect coming from a petite woman or a nerdy dude with pool noodles for arms, even if they're incredibly skilled. The assailant might not be inclined to back off until the fight starts and they realize they're facing a pro. This may sound like an acceptable trade-off, except the outcome of a fight is never certain. The attacker may turn out to be quite skilled too and able to land some good blows, or perhaps they're clutching a knife just out of sight.

For all these reasons, I advise caution. Martial arts are a meritorious and rewarding pursuit, but they might not be the simplest, the safest, nor the most dependable way to get out of trouble. They can augment your strategy but probably shouldn't be the only trick up your sleeve. For those interested in pursuing hand-to-hand combat, I recommend pragmatic fighting schools over the ones designed for spectating or self-discovery; Krav Maga is perhaps the best-known utilitarian pick.

Less-Lethal Defense Tools

In situations where defensive weapons are permissible, there are clear merits to implements that are designed to repel or immobilize assailants, rather than cause them grievous harm. For one, such equipment may be safer to hand over to inexperienced users, including teenage kids. The rules for the purchase or possession of such tools may be considerably less stringent as well. Last but not least, although the legal bar for the use of force may not be very different for lethal and less-lethal weapons, the practical consequences of wrongfully shooting someone are far more serious than the consequences of making their eyes itch.*

On the note of itchy eyes, pepper spray is by far the most versatile and dependable less-lethal defense tool out there. It's inexpensive, compact, easy to use, and difficult to resist. Just as important, a single can is enough to hit multiple targets from a reasonably safe distance of about 10 feet. The final perk is that the spray also works against aggressive dogs and many other animals. About the only drawback is that the weapon becomes less effective in strong wind, with some risk of blowback toward the user or innocent bystanders. This problem is less pronounced with gel-based products that expel a narrow stream of liquid rather than a cloud.

The other well-known self-defense tool in this category, a stun gun, is a misnomer. It's not a gun, and it doesn't knock people out. It can be thought of as a pain compliance device, much like a cattle prod. When pressed against the body of the assailant, it causes an intensely unpleasant sensation. Although the current does cause some muscle contraction, almost as soon as the contact is broken, the perp is back in the game, hopefully less enthused about continuing the assault.

Because of the need to get up close, the inability to take on multiple assailants in rapid succession, and the possibility of clothing getting in the way, stun guns seem to me as vastly inferior to pepper spray. An exception can be made for actual gun-like devices, such as the Taser pistols used by the police and sometimes available to civilians. These weapons expel barb-like electrodes and long wires to deliver a continuous shock to subjects 15 feet away or more. But Tasers are rather expensive and bulky—and you get only one or two chances to hit the attacker before needing to reload.

Many other less-lethal defense options are promoted on the internet, but I've yet to find one that deserves a serious note. In the United States, you can buy plastic "firearms" that expel bits of rock salt or paintballs filled with pepper gel, supposedly with unpleasant effects if you manage to hit a delicate part. More seriously but less conveniently, a regular pump-action shotgun can be loaded with riot-control rubber slugs or bean bags. The impact is incredibly painful—but it's strictly a home defense weapon, not a gadget to carry around town.

In the parts of Europe where real firearms and many other self-defense tools are verboten, air rifles capable of firing tiny skin-piercing metal pellets seem to be the less-lethal weapon of choice. To me, that's an unconvincing approach. Getting hit by a pellet is unpleasant and occasionally dangerous,

---

* At least for the most part. Although weapons such as pepper spray and stun guns are thought of as nonlethal, *less-lethal* is a more accurate term. There's still some risk if the tool is used improperly, if the targeted person has a serious medical condition, or if they simply trip and suffer a fall injury.

but in most cases, it serves to anger the assailant, not stop them in their tracks.* In the same vein, a bizarre but persistent myth claims that wasp spray works as a stand-in for pepper spray. Any homeowner who has experienced blowback while trying to eradicate a nest will know that the spray is oily and a tad smelly, but that's where the unpleasant effects end (that is, unless you're a wasp).

Weapons That Kill

Deadly weapons serve two functions. The more obvious and definite one is to injure an assailant to the point where the attack stops. But a more common function, as discussed earlier, is to warn the aggressor of the terrible consequences that await if they don't surrender or withdraw. From that perspective, appearances matter: a machete says you mean business far more loudly than a kitchen knife can.

Knives, for all their reputation, don't actually make for a particularly good defense tool. Their sinister rep is more deserved on the offense, especially when the victim isn't expecting an attack. But in defensive situations, much like stun guns, they require close bodily contact, along with good reflexes, to cause serious harm. The consequences of a knife injury aren't instantaneous, either—so even if you mortally wound an armed assailant, you might still get stabbed or shot. Because of this, the longer, the better: anything that builds the distance between you and the attacker is a plus. In a desperate home defense situation, I'd much rather be clumsily swinging a sharp sword than expertly manipulating a paring knife.

Blunt instruments, from baseball bats to iron pipes, make for another popular home defense pick. They're especially fashionable in some of the more restrictive parts of Europe, kept with the hope of telling the authorities that you're just an avid amateur plumber or a big fan of baseball. The problem with blunt instruments is mostly that they're only as menacing as the person wielding them. Another drawback is that lacking a sharp blade, a pipe or a bat can be easily grabbed and possibly wrestled away. Solutions to this problem have been proposed, such as putting a sock or a stocking over the implement—but I'd wager that the real-world efficacy of this life hack isn't what it's cracked up to be.

The next popular defense tools are old-fashioned ranged weapons: crossbows and bows. A bow takes skill to load and aim, but a crossbow has a point-and-click interface not very different from a gun. Both weapons are deadly, especially when equipped with broadhead arrows or bolts meant for hunting. That said, the main problem with these weapons is that they're incredibly clunky. If you hear knocking on the door at 11 PM, it may be weird to greet a neighbor or a police officer while holding a cocked

---

*Although some high-pressure (PCP) air rifles are capable of expelling projectiles with tremendous force, in most of Europe, license-free air guns are limited to muzzle energies that are between 1 and 4 percent that of a typical 9mm handgun. The lightweight pellets weigh a fraction of a gram and measure about 0.18 inches in diameter; while they can pierce the skin, they usually don't travel very far.

crossbow in your hand. Another problem is the abysmal rate of fire. If you miss your first shot, or if you're dealing with multiple assailants, you're hopelessly exposed for the four to eight seconds it takes to reload.

This brings us to more modern ranged weapons: firearms. Although not as lethal as commonly imagined (for handguns, only about 20 percent of gunshot injuries treated in hospitals end in death),[4] firearms are perceived as far more intimidating than machetes, baseball bats, crossbows, and the like. For this reason, they're remarkably good at resolving conflicts without having to fire a single shot. Just as interestingly, when a shot must be fired, most assailants are stopped in their tracks even if the injury isn't immediately disabling or life-threatening. The effect may be at least partly psychological. Heavy intoxication or unusual agitation can blunt this instinct and cause assailants to keep coming at the victim despite being shot multiple times.

Of course, access to firearms is heavily regulated in much of the world. That said, even in regions customarily painted with a single brush, the permitting regimes vary quite significantly. For example, Finland, Switzerland, and Germany enjoy surprisingly high firearm-ownership rates compared to many of their neighbors. Still, the United States is unique in its recognition of the right for individuals to own firearms without the need to give a reason or otherwise actively qualify.

No matter where you live, for those who can and wish to consider a firearm in their preparedness strategy, we'll have a look at some of the options—and the essential safety considerations—in the next and final chapter of the book.

27

UNDERSTANDING FIREARMS

In a hyperpolarized world, ignorance becomes a point of pride, and there are few places where the phenomenon is more evident than in the ongoing debate about the individual right to bear arms. In the United States, which has more guns than people,[1] deliberate firearm illiteracy is the only explanation for the comical errors in big-ticket Hollywood productions or the endless stream of befuddling and contradictory gun control bills.

Meanwhile, in Europe, where the history books document centuries of near-constant conflict and conquest, the prevailing dogma is that citizens will never again have to take up arms to defend their families or land. As for the pro-gun side on the new continent, many of the movement's most devoted supporters have their own flavor of reality: feverish visions of totalitarian globalist forces coming for their freedoms, mixed with the siren song of the American Revolution, Part Deux.

In a world plagued by partisan dogma, making considered decisions about personal risk is difficult. To remedy this, my hope is that this final chapter of the book will offer those less versed in firearms a practical understanding of the capabilities and dangers of such tools—without convincing readers that gun ownership is their patriotic duty, nor that it's a symptom of a small and diseased mind.

Handguns

Handguns are a class of small, low-powered firearms that, generally speaking, can be carried without attracting attention or interfering with everyday tasks. As noted in the previous chapter, most handguns have a fairly modest stopping power: absent expert aim, multiple rounds may be required to dissuade an angry bear or a homicidal maniac from continuing an assault.

For most novices, the practical range of a handgun is about 10 yards, and even at that distance, accuracy can vary. A telling statistic is that in shootouts, police have a hit rate of perhaps 35 percent.[2] A well-recognized contributing factor to such dismal performance is the spike in adrenaline that happens in high-stress situations and tends to obliterate fine-motor skills.

When poor aim and poor stopping power conspire, capacity matters more than most gun skeptics suspect. Some regulators and gun control activists have variously floated three, five, seven, or ten rounds as the limit of what a civilian may reasonably need for self-defense; to me, this is an overly simplistic take. But no matter: whether legislators limit you to one, five, or a hundred rounds, let's have a look at some of the major types of handguns available on the market, and the pros and cons of each.

Semiautomatic Pistols

Semiautomatic pistols are a true marvel of engineering. This type of gun diverts some of the energy of the previously fired cartridge to perform a carefully choreographed sequence of operations: extracting and ejecting the spent casing, chambering a new round, and possibly cocking the spring-loaded firing mechanism to prime it for the next shot. The whole cycle takes about 50 milliseconds. When taken apart, semiautos look simple, but they're the pinnacle of hundreds of years of advances in metallurgy, propellant and cartridge design, and more.

The most important advantage of semiauto handguns is their capacity, typically ranging from 6 to 18 rounds that are housed in a removable magazine in the grip. As discussed, the challenges of handgun accuracy make this an important selling point. On the flip side, the disadvantage is the complex user interface. The firearm can be in multiple conditions—cocked or uncocked, with an empty or loaded chamber, with the safety on or off—and this can confuse less experienced users, somewhat increasing the likelihood of the gun not firing when needed or discharging when handled negligently.

The reliability of semiautos is somewhat debatable too. Compared to the intricate internals of revolvers, they may be less likely to suffer a catastrophic mechanical failure, but every semiauto pistol owner will probably sooner or later experience a jam—a failure to fully eject a spent casing or fully chamber a new round. Such problems can be resolved fairly easily, but practice is needed to build the muscle memory; without it, the operator risks standing doe-eyed, trying to understand why the gun only goes "click."

Revolvers

Revolvers are a more ancient type of a repeating firearm, typically holding five or six rounds in a nonremovable cylinder that's mechanically rotated with every pull of the trigger. Compared to semiautos, the interface of a revolver is simple and unlikely to confound a novice. On the other hand, the lower capacity of these firearms gives you fewer chances to land the decisive shot. The absence of removable magazines also means that reloading is slow and almost never attempted in the field.

Because a revolver has no metal moving back and forth to redirect and dissipate the energy of the fired cartridge, firing it may be less pleasant compared to a semiauto of the same chambering and weight. In a revolver, the bulk of the recoil is a single sharp impulse that goes straight into your wrists. That said, both revolvers and semiauto pistols can be chosen in a way that provides a comfortable shooting experience while still packing enough punch. This is done by matching the size of the weapon to the type of the cartridge and the physique of the shooter, rather than choosing the most powerful cartridge or the most compact firearm one can find.

Other Concealable Firearms

Many other handgun designs can be used for self-defense. Two classic examples are single-shot pistols and double-barrel derringers. Such guns tend to be remarkably compact. Because of this, they're often imagined as ankle-worn backup for those who expect to find themselves caught in the middle of an improbable movie plot. In real situations, the extremely limited capacity of such a weapon is probably not worth the benefit.

More bizarre designs tend to crop up with regularity too. The past several decades have seen developments ranging from two-barrel revolvers to credit-card "survival guns." Buyer beware: although such contraptions make for good internet memes and can become prized collectibles once the manufacturer inevitably goes belly up, there are darn good reasons most of these ideas don't catch on.

Deciding on Handgun Caliber and Size

As hinted earlier, new gun buyers have the tendency to go with the smallest possible weapon and the most potent cartridge available at their local gun store. That's a mistake. Such firearms deliver punishing recoil that discourages routine range practice and prevents novices from honing their skills. Accuracy tends to suffer too. Stubby barrels mean that visually aligning the front and rear sights produces far less precise aim.

For practical semiauto handguns, the gold standard of cartridges is the 9mm Luger, and this caliber works particularly well in mid- to full-sized pistols. Popular all-around options range from the budget-conscious polymer-framed Glock 19 to the sharp-looking and all-metal Sig Sauer P229.

Although subcompact pistols are also available in the 9mm caliber, they tend to be too snappy for many tastes, and this is especially true with more lightweight designs. For instance, the 16-ounce Glock 43 is far less pleasant to shoot than the 27-ounce Springfield EMP, despite both having a comparable size. In rare situations where extreme concealability is more important than stopping power, tiny pistols firing comparatively lower-powered .380 ACP rounds* may be a better choice; in this department, Ruger LCP and Kahr Arms CW380 are two fine picks.

For revolvers, the optimal cartridge is probably .38 Special, a type of ammunition that's a fairly close counterpart of the aforementioned 9mm Luger round common in the world of semiauto pistols. Many revolvers can use .38 Special interchangeably with the more powerful .357 Magnum, but in most cases, the magnum caliber is too overpowered for range practice or home defense uses. Practical and easily carried revolvers include the well-regarded Ruger SP101, the sleek-looking Kimber K6s, or the space-age Chiappa Rhino 30DS. More easily concealable options are available too; in that category, the lightweight Ruger LCR is of note.

The brands and models named here are just examples. Countless manufacturers are out there, and few truly bad firearms. Keeping in mind the size and cartridge trade-offs mentioned in this section, it's safe to pick what looks nice, fits in your budget, and feels right in your hand.

Long Guns

Although there's considerable variability among products, long guns tend to fire projectiles with much greater energy than a pistol would. For rifles, the bulk of this increase has to do with speed, with bullets commonly traveling as fast as 3,000 feet per second (compared to handgun velocities around 1,000 ft/sec). For shotguns, the gains typically come from much heavier projectiles, weighing perhaps four to eight times as much as a 9mm round.

Long barrels and high-speed projectiles produce more predictable trajectories; a longer firearm is also easier to aim. Because of these factors, even a complete novice wielding a long gun should be able to put holes on paper 50 to 100 yards away, and some high-powered rifles with expensive optics may work to 1,000 yards or more.

---

* Some readers may be scratching their heads about the meaning of these designations. The first part usually corresponds to bullet diameter, often with a mix of imperial and metric units: in particular, .38 Special, .380 ACP, and 9mm Luger all use bullets of about the same girth. The second part references the inventor or the trade name of a specific cartridge design, thus conveying information such as the precise shape of the shell or the amount of gunpowder inside. When used together, the keywords unambiguously describe a particular type of ammunition that can fit a particular gun.

On the flip side, long guns are far less versatile than handguns. They're unwieldy and impossible to carry without alerting strangers or spooking guests. For the same reasons, rifles and shotguns make for a questionable addition to a typical bug-out kit. Although they may have some uses in the wilderness, the sheer weight of a long gun and a couple boxes of ammo means that other, possibly more useful items would need to be left behind.

Rifles

In some respects, rifles can be thought of as powerful handguns with extended barrels. Just like a pistol or a revolver, they fire a single spin-stabilized projectile, typically made of copper or lead. In contrast to handguns, however, rifles vary quite considerably when it comes to mechanical operation. There are single-shot and semiautomatic varieties, but also lever-action guns familiar from westerns, bolt-action flavors commonly associated with hunting and long-range marksmanship, and more.

The ammunition-feeding devices seen on rifles are more varied too. Many modern designs, such as the ubiquitous AR-15, use detachable box magazines, but permanently built-in ammunition-feeding devices are also common. For example, a lever gun may have a tubular magazine sitting right under the barrel and extending throughout the length of the gun.

For most shooters looking for an affordable and reliable multipurpose rifle, there may be no special reason to look past an AR-15 clone designed for .223 Remington or 5.56×45mm NATO. This is the most popular rifle in America, and it enjoys this status not because of exceptional lethality, but simply because it's an inexpensive and well thought-out design that can be customized in nearly infinite ways.

The most significant drawback of the platform is just its reputation. Its aggressive styling earned it the somewhat meaningless moniker of an *assault weapon*, prompting a variety of restrictions and bans. Those who want to own an AR-15 but who live in a restrictive state may want to check out the sleek FightLite SCR, designed to accept many AR-15 accessories while staying clear of the cosmetic features banned in certain states. Meanwhile, buyers put off by any association with the AR-15 brand might want to consider a less menacing wooden-stocked rifle, such as the venerable Ruger Mini-14.

A subjective drawback of the AR-15 platform is that part of the reciprocating mechanism responsible for chambering new rounds extends in a straight line into the stock. Although this offers benefits, it makes the butt of the gun sit at a rather unnatural angle, requiring the optics to be mounted higher and the shooter to rubberneck a bit. Between the high-mounted optics and the protruding pistol grip, the AR-15 is also very tall, taking up a lot of space in any gun safe. Interestingly, this problem isn't present on the FightLite SCR, which uses an angled mechanism and a traditional stock geometry while—again—retaining most of the other features of an AR-15.

My final and still-unconvincing critique of the AR-15 platform is that it's perhaps a bit *too* customizable. Many alterations that look interesting to gun owners make the rifle more difficult or less pleasant to use in the real world. Muzzle brakes and short barrels live in special infamy: they greatly increase the likelihood of hearing damage if the gun is ever used for self-defense indoors.

For those who can't get or don't want a semiautomatic long gun, a lever-action carbine is probably the best alternative. These weapons offer a solid magazine capacity—usually 7 to 14 rounds—and can be fired far more quickly than a bolt-action firearm. Large-caliber hunting rifles may be tempting for their survivalist allure, but in home defense situations are best avoided; they suffer from excessive penetration and pack too much recoil for many novices.

On the other end of the spectrum, rifles designed to take pistol cartridges have merit. Compared to a handgun, they offer much greater accuracy and somewhat improved range. Popular pistol-caliber carbines include Henry Big Boy in .38 Special and Ruger PC and KelTec SUB2000 in 9mm Luger.

Shotguns

While a rifle may be thought of as a scaled-up handgun, shotguns are more like scaled-down cannons. They're large-bore weapons, often with smooth barrels, and are designed to propel all kinds of payloads when the delivery of a devastating force is more important than precise aim. The projectiles fired by shotguns range from massive metal slugs that can stop a grizzly to clusters of tiny lead balls that can be fired in the general direction of a flying game bird. As noted earlier, a shotgun can also fire less-lethal rubber batons and bean bags for use in crowd or animal control.

Shotguns make for a dependable home defense weapon, both because of the versatility of the loads and simply because they can appear far more fearsome than a small pistol held in a shaky hand. Another important consideration is that in some countries, shotguns are subject to fewer restrictions than other types of firearms. This is usually in recognition of their role for farmland predator control.

The most significant drawback of this class of firearms is their punishing recoil. Although many shooters like to brag about how they can take the punishment in stride, the reality is that any extended range session will leave you sore—and if you don't brace the gun perfectly, bruises are likely to follow too. Small-bore shotguns, capable of taking 20-gauge* or .410-caliber shotshells, are available on the market and are much easier to manage—but the choice of ammunition is far more constrained, and the reduction in power has obvious downsides.

The predominant shotgun bore size is 12 gauge (about 0.73 inches), and the most common design is a tube-fed pump-action—a mechanism found on the Remington 870, Mossberg 590, and countless other models from manufacturers big and small. That said, for shooters who want to take some edge off the recoil without tacking on an oversized shoulder pad, a semiautomatic shotgun can offer substantial relief; here, Remington V3 is

---

*Yep, yet another unit: this is an archaic British measure, nowadays used exclusively for shotgun barrels. No relation to the American Wire Gauge (AWG), used for sheet metal and wire.

probably the best pick in its class. The gotcha is that a semiauto may not cycle reliably with low-power shells, such as rubber baton rounds; the mechanism is factory-calibrated for conventional loads that pack far more punch.

Ammunition

For handguns and rifles, ammunition comes in two basic varieties. *Full metal jacket (FMJ)* bullets are made of solid metal and tend to pass through soft materials without deforming to a significant extent. *Jacketed hollow point (JHP)* ammunition has a small cavity in the front of the bullet, sometimes filled back with plastic. On impact, the pressure inside this cavity rapidly builds up, causing the bullet to mushroom and decelerate.

A less common in-between variant is known as *soft-point*. This ammunition has a solid core made from soft metal and a jacket made of a harder alloy, enclosing everything but the tip. At rifle velocities, such a cartridge tends to "pancake," somewhat similarly to JHP.

FMJ ammunition is commonly used for target practice, primarily because of its lower cost. Hollow-point bullets are preferred for self-defense because they deliver their energy to the intended target more efficiently and are less likely to overpenetrate and hit bystanders. At the same time, because it's reputed to cause more severe wounds, JHP ammunition is banned in some parts of the world. Still, where legal, it's the more rational pick. However morbid this sounds, you don't pull the trigger when you want to cause only a tiny bit of harm.

For shotguns, the ammo choices are different. There are three basic types of shotshells: bird shot, buckshot, and slugs. *Bird shot* consists of hundreds of tiny metal spheres, traveling independently and meant to take out waterfowl and other critters. Bird shot is common in hunting but may not pack enough punch and not offer sufficient precision in self-defense situations that involve distances of more than perhaps 10 yards. *Buckshot* is a variation of this idea, consisting of a smaller number of much larger projectiles, each delivering about as much damage as a pistol round. When fired from the distance of about 10 to 15 yards, buckshot will impact an area roughly the size of the palm of your hand and will almost certainly kill anything in its path. Finally, *slugs* are single bullets of considerable size and mass. When they hit something, they punch a rather massive hole. They're about as lethal as buckshot, but remain accurate and effective over longer distances—at the expense of requiring better aim.

Firearm Safety Rules

Although gun owners are commonly stereotyped as reckless, the gun community deserves praise for developing an impressive and simple set of safety rules that—if taken to heart—ensure that multiple things would need to go wrong at once to cause a dangerous accident.

The first rule of gun safety is simple: when picking up a gun, assume that it's loaded. Many accidents happen because people trust their memory, their habits, or the assurances of others—but mistakes happen, and with a deadly tool, it's essential to double-check. If you don't know how to clear a particular gun of ammunition, it's crucial to ask for help or check on the internet before messing with it. In semiautomatic firearms with removable magazines, always check the chamber *after* removing the mag. Removing the magazine alone isn't a guarantee of safety. Although some firearms may be designed not to fire without a magazine, this isn't universally true—and the interlock mechanism that ensures this property can malfunction too.

The second rule is rooted in the assumption that you'll eventually mess up rule 1, and it stipulates that when handling a gun, you should always keep it pointed somewhere safe. At the shooting range, this is toward the backstop. At home, the safest direction may be toward the ground. Accidentally muzzle-sweeping other people when manipulating a gun is a serious faux pas.

The third rule assumes that you might eventually break rules 1 and 2; it instructs you to keep your finger off the trigger until the gun is aimed at the target and you're ready to fire. The simplest way to accomplish this is to rest your index finger on the frame or the stock of the firearm just above the trigger guard. This quickly becomes a habit. You can often spot gun owners by looking at how people hold a cordless drill, a sprayer bottle, or a similar household tool.

The final rule is to know your target and what's behind it. This can mean several things. During outdoor target practice, you may want to place the target against a hill or other natural feature that will stop any stray rounds. In self-defense situations, it means you must positively identify your target and take note of any people nearby. You don't want to shoot a drunk family member or a confused neighbor in the middle of the night.

Firearm Storage

A carelessly stored weapon is an unnecessary risk. A gun can be taken by a burglar and used in the commission of violent crimes, or it may be grabbed by a curious toddler; even if you don't have children, friends may one day visit you with their offspring in tow. Some recalcitrant gun owners argue that when an intruder sneaks in, every moment counts, so a gun should be easily accessible. That said, with modern electronic locks, the ability to pull a gun out of a safe is just a split second away.

Gun safes are available in all shapes and sizes, from small handgun vaults that can be fitted inside a nightstand drawer to behemoths weighing 1,000 pounds or more. The cheapest products can be more accurately described as locking cabinets: they're made of thin steel and are meant to deter casual access, but many can be pried open with a bit of work. Once you get to the price tag of about $800 to $1,000, the security gets more substantial: the products are designed to withstand sustained attacks with hand tools, but may still succumb rather quickly to angle grinders or circular saws with the correct blade. Higher-security safes may be rated for power tool use—but tend to cost a lot, quite possibly more than the valuables one wants to put inside.

In contrast to safes, the merits of other safety devices marketed to gun owners are far less clear-cut. Cable locks that obstruct the action of the firearm do nothing to deter theft—and can be cut off with rudimentary tools; fiddling with keys in the middle of the night seems rather undesirable as well. Trigger locks may be marginally better but are even more frustrating to undo. Sophisticated electronic locks sound nice in theory and can be manipulated fairly quickly—but are finicky and prone to failure if the battery runs out.

If you have children, keeping the gun out of their reach is essential, but it's probably a mistake to keep the kids in the dark. A much better strategy is to explain the dangers, teach them the rules, and then allow them to examine the weapon or try it out at the range under close supervision. The less mysterious the item, the less likely they are to do something dumb if you accidentally leave it on the table some fateful day—or if they find an abandoned firearm in the grass on their way home from school.

Getting Good

Knowing how to handle and store a firearm isn't enough. For one, because the loud sound, the flash, and the force of recoil can be startling, many novice shooters quickly develop a flinch that takes time to go away. It's common for a new shooter to place the first shot perfectly on target and then subsequently drift away, with true aim not coming back until several range sessions down the line. Many other aspects of gun ownership come down to muscle memory too. For example, it takes time to get used to the force needed to pull back the slide on a semiautomatic pistol, and to learn how to grasp it firmly without pinching any skin.

The gun community tends to go overboard with complex tactical drills. Most gun owners don't need to train like US Navy SEALs, but they should get comfortable with their firearm. It's good to visit your local range every weekend or so until you build some confidence. Past that point, you should refresh your knowledge every couple of months.

Speaking of range time, it must be noted that recreational shooting is a source of exposure to lead, especially for frequent visitors to poorly ventilated indoor ranges and for those who reload ammunition at home. If you're willing to spend a bit more, reducing this risk is possible by using ammo made with fully encapsulated lead or solid copper bullets and nontoxic primers. Brands available in the United States include RUAG Copper Matrix, Magtech Clean Range, Winchester Super Clean, Federal BallistiClean, Remington Disintegrator, and Federal Power-Shok Copper. Basic hygiene, such as thoroughly scrubbing your hands after a range trip, can go a long way too.

EPILOGUE

When I set out to write this book, I envisioned it as what you might call *an optimist's guide to doomsday*: a merry stroll through the world of disaster preparedness. It would be a sharp rebuke to the endless apocalyptic mirages that slowly suffocate those glued to 24-hour cable news, but also a heartfelt suggestion to keep some cash and food on hand, just in case.

My optimism stems from a simple truth: I am here because my ancestors, generation after generation, bet that things would get better. In the face of some of the darkest moments in human history, they worked hard, raised children, and took care of each other. They persevered through unimaginable terrors and periods of uncertainty far greater than what I stand to experience today. They didn't always live happy lives, and sometimes their own anger or fear led them astray. But they never gave up. They bet on the future—and in doing so, they helped build a better world for all of us. I feel that I owe my children and grandchildren the same.

Of course, the universe is a harsh mistress; optimism may be wise, but recklessness is not. The philosophy I try to preach is the ethos of joyful resiliency: the art of looking at the world around us, in all its chaotic glory, and resolutely asking what can go wrong—but never assuming that it *must* go wrong. It's the art of not making bitter demands of others, but of reinventing ourselves to cleverly and confidently dispel the anxieties and frustrations of everyday life.

The method isn't bulletproof. Things don't always go as anticipated, no matter how hard we may try to prepare for them. But then, whatever the misfortune, the ride can be less bumpy when we have a solid backup plan— and a few extra gallons of water, too.

NOTES

Chapter 1

1. Peter Bergen et al., "Terrorism in America After 9/11," New America, *https://www.newamerica.org/in-depth/terrorism-in-america/*.

2. "Accidents or Unintentional Injuries," Centers for Disease Control and Prevention, *https://www.cdc.gov/nchs/fastats/accidental-injury.htm*; and "Drowning Facts," Centers for Disease Control and Prevention, *https://www.cdc.gov/homeandrecreationalsafety/water-safety/waterinjuries-factsheet.html*.

3. Bruce Schneier, "Why the Human Brain Is a Poor Judge of Risk," *Wired*, March 22, 2007, *https://www.wired.com/2007/03/security-matters0322/*.

4. "Crime in the United States: Burglary," Federal Bureau of Investigation (2019), *https://ucr.fbi.gov/crime-in-the-u.s/2019/crime-in-the-u.s.-2019/topic-pages/burglary*.

5. Kevin Simler, "Crony Beliefs," Melting Asphalt, November 2, 2016, *https://meltingasphalt.com/crony-beliefs/*.

6. Anthony Cilluffo and Neil G. Ruiz, "World's Population Is Projected to Nearly Stop Growing by the End of the Century," Pew Research Center, June 17, 2019, *https://www.pewresearch.org/fact-tank/2019/06/17/worlds-population-is-projected-to-nearly-stop-growing-by-the-end-of-the-century/*.

Chapter 2

1. Kimberly Amadeo, "Medical Bankruptcy and the Economy," The Balance, November 19, 2019, *https://www.thebalance.com/medical-bankruptcy-statistics-4154729/*.

2. Salvador Rizzo, "Sanders's Flawed Statistic: 500,000 Medical Bankruptcies a Year," *Washington Post*, August 28, 2019, *https://www.washingtonpost.com/politics/2019/08/28/sanderss-flawed-statistic-medical-bankruptcies-year/*.

3. Sheyna Steiner, "Survey: How Americans Contend with Unexpected Expenses," Bankrate, January 6, 2016, *https://www.bankrate.com/banking/savings/survey-how-americans-contend-with-unexpected-expenses/*.

4. Jeff Ostrowski, "Why the Coming Foreclosure Crisis Will Look Nothing Like the Last One," *Philadelphia Inquirer*, September 19, 2020, *https://www.inquirer.com/real-estate/housing/home-foreclosure-coronavirus-forebearance-20200919.html*.

5. "Home Structure Fires," National Fire Protection Association, November 2020, *https://www.nfpa.org/News-and-Research/Data-research-and-tools/Building-and-Life-Safety/Home-Structure-Fires/*.

6. Matt Kraus, "36.7 Million Affected by Power Outages in 2017, per Eaton Study," *Electrical Contractor*, March 2018, *https://www.ecmag.com/section/systems/367-million-affected-power-outages-2017-eaton-study/*.

7. "Squirrel 'Threat' to Critical Infrastructure," BBC News, January 17, 2017, *https://www.bbc.com/news/technology-38650436/*.

8. "Accidents or Unintentional Injuries," Centers for Disease Control and Prevention (2021), *https://www.cdc.gov/nchs/fastats/accidental-injury.htm*.

9. "Criminal Victimization, 2019," Bureau of Justice Statistics (2020), *https://www.bjs.gov/content/pub/pdf/cv19_sum.pdf*.

10. "Stalking in America: Findings from the National Violence Against Women Survey," Centers for Disease Control and Prevention (1998), *https://www.ojp.gov/pdffiles/169592.pdf*.

Chapter 3

1. Priyanka Boghani, "Camp Fire: By the Numbers," PBS Frontline, October 29, 2019, *https://www.pbs.org/wgbh/frontline/article/camp-fire-by-the-numbers/*.

2. "Impacts of Summer 2003 Heat Wave in Europe," United Nations Environment Programme, March 2004, *https://www.researchgate.net/publication/313059632_Impacts_of_summer_2003_heat_wave_in_Europe/*.

3. "Great Blizzard of 1888," Britannica.com, *https://www.britannica.com/event/Great-Blizzard-of-1888*.

4. "Dust Bowl," History.com, August 5, 2020, *https://www.history.com/topics/great-depression/dust-bowl/*.

5. "Bhopal Disaster," Britannica.com, *https://www.britannica.com/event/Bhopal-disaster*.

6. "Typhoon Nina–Banqiao Dam Failure," Britannica.com, *https://www.britannica.com/event/Typhoon-Nina-Banqiao-dam-failure*.

7. "Texas City Explosion of 1947," Britannica.com, *https://www.britannica.com/event/Texas-City-explosion-of-1947*.

8. "Beirut Explosion: What We Know So Far," BBC News, August 11, 2020, *https://www.bbc.com/news/world-middle-east-53668493/*.

9. Jeff Wallenfeldt, "Los Angeles Riots of 1992," Britannica.com, *https://www.britannica.com/event/Los-Angeles-Riots-of-1992*.

10. "France Sees Fall in New Year's Eve Car-Burnings," BBC News, January 1, 2015, *https://www.bbc.com/news/world-europe-30653784/*.

11. "European Court Dismisses Compensation Claim in Cyprus 2013 Deposit-Grab," Reuters, July 13, 2018, *https://www.reuters.com/article/us-cyprus-banks/european-court-dismisses-compensation-claim-in-cyprus-2013-deposit-grab-idUSKBN1K3242/*.

12. Will Kenton, "Savings and Loan Crisis," Investopedia, May 16, 2019, *https://www.investopedia.com/terms/s/sl-crisis.asp*.

13. Kai Ryssdal, "How an Oil Shortage in the 1970s Shaped Today's Economic Policy," Marketplace, May 31, 2016, *https://www.marketplace.org/2016/05/31/how-oil-shortage-1970s-shaped-todays-economic-policy/*.

14. Steve H. Hanke and Nicholas Krus, "World Hyperinflations," Cato Institute, August 15, 2012, *https://www.cato.org/sites/cato.org/files/pubs/pdf/workingpaper-8_1.pdf*.

15. "History of 1918 Flu Pandemic," Centers for Disease Control and Prevention, *https://www.cdc.gov/flu/pandemic-resources/1918-commemoration/1918-pandemic-history.htm*.

16. Leslie A. Hoffman and Joel A. Vilensky, "Encephalitis Lethargica: 100 Years After the Epidemic," *Brain* 140, no. 2 (August 2017): 2246–2251, *https://academic.oup.com/brain/article/140/8/2246/3970828/*.

17. @NYCHealthCommr, "Today Our City Is Celebrating the #Lunarnewyear Parade in Chinatown," Twitter, February 9, 2020, *https://twitter.com/NYCHealthCommr/status/1226508570646269954/*.

18. Lindsey Ellefson, "Vox Deletes January Tweet About Coronavirus That Really Has Not Aged Well," Yahoo, March 24, 2020, *https://www.yahoo.com/entertainment/vox-deletes-january-tweet-coronavirus-203359493.html*.

19. "America's Two Largest States Are Fighting COVID-19 Differently," *The Economist*, February 4, 2021, *https://www.economist.com/united-states/2021/02/06/americas-two-largest-states-are-fighting-covid-19-differently/*.

20. Mark Memmott, "Sniper Attack On Calif. Power Station Raises Terrorism Fears," National Public Radio, February 5, 2014, *https://www.npr.org/sections/thetwo-way/2014/02/05/272015606/sniper-attack-on-calif-power-station-raises-terrorism-fears/*.

Chapter 4

1. Brian Martin, "Nuclear Winter: Science and Politics," *Science and Public Policy* 15, no. 5 (October 1988): 321–334, *https://www.bmartin.cc/pubs/88spp.html*.

2. "Nuclear Weapons: Who Has What at a Glance," Arms Control Association, August 2020, *https://www.armscontrol.org/factsheets/Nuclearweaponswhohaswhat/*.

3. "The Nuclear Testing Tally," Arms Control Association, July 2020, *https://www.armscontrol.org/factsheets/nucleartesttally/*.

4. Dan Listwa, "Hiroshima and Nagasaki: The Long Term Health Effects," Columbia K=1 Project, August 9, 2012, *https://k1project.columbia.edu/news/hiroshima-and-nagasaki/*.

5. Glenn Harlan Reynolds, "The Unexpected Return of 'Duck and Cover,'" *The Atlantic*, January 4, 2011, *https://www.theatlantic.com/national/archive/2011/01/the-unexpected-return-of-duck-and-cover/68776/*.

6. Ole Benedictow, "The Black Death: The Greatest Catastrophe Ever," History Today, March 3, 2005, *https://www.historytoday.com/archive/black-death-greatest-catastrophe-ever/*.

7. David Routt, "The Economic Impact of the Black Death," Economic History Association, July 20, 2008, *https://eh.net/encyclopedia/the-economic-impact-of-the-black-death/*.

8. Sophie Ochmann and Max Roser, "Smallpox," Our World in Data (2018), *https://ourworldindata.org/smallpox/*.

9. Kelly B. Wyatt et al., "Historical Mammal Extinction on Christmas Island (Indian Ocean) Correlates with Introduced Infectious Disease," *PLoS One* 3, no. 11 (November 2008), *https://www.ncbi.nlm.nih.gov/pmc/articles/PMC2572834/*.

10. "Climate Updates," The Royal Society, November 27, 2017, *https://royalsociety.org/~/media/policy/Publications/2017/27-11-2017-Climate-change-updates-report-references-document.pdf*; Colin Goldblatt and Andrew J. Watson, "The Runaway Greenhouse: Implications for Future Climate Change, Geoengineering and Planetary Atmospheres," *Philosophical Transactions of the Royal Society* 370, no. 1974 (September 2012), *https://royalsocietypublishing.org/doi/full/10.1098/rsta.2012.0004/*.

11. "Little Ice Age," Britannica.com, *https://www.britannica.com/science/Little-Ice-Age*.

12. University of Cincinnati, "New Evidence Suggests Volcanoes Caused Biggest Mass Extinction Ever," Phys.org, April 15, 2019, *https://phys.org/news/2019-04-evidence-volcanoes-biggest-mass-extinction.html*.

13. Larry Mastin, "Forecasting Ashfall Impacts from a Yellowstone Supereruption," United States Geological Survey, May 26, 2016, *https://www.usgs.gov/media/videos/forecasting-ashfall-impacts-a-yellowstone-supereruption/*.

14. "K–T extinction," Britannica.com, *https://www.britannica.com/science/K-T-extinction*.

15. "Volcano Watch: Lessons Learned from the Armero, Colombia Tragedy," United States Geological Survey, October 29, 2009, *https://www.usgs.gov/center-news/volcano-watch-lessons-learned-armero-colombia-tragedy/*.

16. Michael Lynch, "What Ever Happened to Peak Oil?," *Forbes*, June 29, 2018, *https://www.forbes.com/sites/michaellynch/2018/06/29/what-ever-happened-to-peak-oil/*.

17. Roy E. Plotnick, "Relationship Between Biological Extinctions and Geomagnetic Reversals," *Geology* 8, no. 12 (December 1980): 578–581, *https://pubs.geoscienceworld.org/gsa/geology/article-abstract/8/12/578/187677/Relationship-between-biological-extinctions-and?redirectedFrom=PDF*.

18. Universitat Autonoma de Barcelona, "Probability of Catastrophic Geomagnetic Storm Lower Than Estimated," *ScienceDaily*, March 12, 2019, *https://www.sciencedaily.com/releases/2019/03/190312103717.htm*.

19. "Report of the Commission to Assess the Threat to the United States from Electromagnetic Pulse (EMP) Attack," April 2008, *http://www.empcommission.org/docs/A2473-EMP_Commission-7MB.pdf*.

20. Ibid.

Chapter 7

1. Chris Taylor, "A Little Honesty Might Preserve the Family Fortune," Reuters, June 28, 2016, *https://www.reuters.com/article/us-money-generations-strategies/a-little-honesty-might-preserve-the-family-fortune-idUSKBN0OX1RH20150617*.

2. Caroline Humphrey, "Barter and Economic Disintegration," *Man* 20, no. 1 (March 1985): 48–72, *https://www.jstor.org/stable/2802221*.

3. Ilana E. Strauss, "The Myth of the Barter Economy," *The Atlantic*, February 26, 2016, *https://www.theatlantic.com/business/archive/2016/02/barter-society-myth/471051/*.

4. Tim Harford, "How the World's First Accountants Counted on Cuneiform," BBC World Service, June 12, 2017, *https://www.bbc.com/news/business-39870485/*.

5. Ann M. Carlos and Frank D. Lewis, "The Economic History of the Fur Trade: 1670 to 1870," Economic History Association, March 16, 2008, *https://eh.net/encyclopedia/the-economic-history-of-the-fur-trade-1670-to-1870/*.

6. Sandra E. Gleason, "Hustling: The 'Inside' Economy of a Prison," *Federal Probation* 42, no. 2 (June 1978): 32–40, *https://www.ojp.gov/pdffiles1/Digitization/50862NCJRS.pdf*.

7. Satoshi Nakamoto, "Bitcoin: A Peer-to-Peer Electronic Cash System," Bitcoin.org (2008), *https://bitcoin.org/bitcoin.pdf*.

8. "Failed Bank List," Federal Deposit Insurance Corporation, *https://www.fdic.gov/resources/resolutions/bank-failures/failed-bank-list/*.

9. Drew Desilver, "Financial Crises Surprisingly Common, but Few Countries Close Their Banks," Pew Research Center, July 9, 2015, *https://www.pewresearch.org/fact-tank/2015/07/09/financial-crises-surprisingly-common-but-few-countries-close-their-banks/*.

10. "Marriage and Divorce," Centers for Disease Control and Prevention, *https://www.cdc.gov/nchs/fastats/marriage-divorce.htm*.

11. Joe Palazzolo, "We Won't See You in Court: The Era of Tort Lawsuits Is Waning," *Wall Street Journal*, July 24, 2017, *https://www.wsj.com/articles/we-wont-see-you-in-court-the-era-of-tort-lawsuits-is-waning-1500930572/*.

12. "Historical Inflation Rates," US Inflation Calculator, *https://www.usinflationcalculator.com/inflation/historical-inflation-rates/*.

13. "Exclusion of Jews from German Economic Life," United States Holocaust Memorial Museum, *https://www.ushmm.org/learn/timeline-of-events/1933-1938/exclusion-of-jews-from-german-economic-life*.

14. Emily Zentner, "What Happened to the Property of Sacramento's Japanese American Community Interned During World War II?," CapRadio, June 4, 2019, *https://www.capradio.org/articles/2019/06/04/what-happened-to-the-property-of-sacramentos-japanese-american-community-interned-during-world-war-ii/*.

15. Quentin Fottrell, "One in Five American Households Have 'Zero or Negative' Wealth," MarketWatch, December 29, 2017, *https://www.marketwatch.com/story/one-in-five-american-households-have-zero-or-negative-wealth-2017-11-11*.

16. "T18-0128 - Tax Units with Zero or Negative Income Tax Under Current Law, 2011-2028," Tax Policy Center, September 5, 2018, *https://www.taxpolicycenter.org/model-estimates/tax-units-zero-or-negative-income-tax-liability-september-2018/t18-0128-tax-units/*.

17. "Cash Payment Limitations," European Consumer Centre, December 15, 2020, *https://www.europe-consommateurs.eu/en/shopping-internet/cash-payment-limitations.html*.

18. "Swiss Narrowly Vote to Drop Gold Standard," *New York Times*, April 19, 1999, *https://www.nytimes.com/1999/04/19/world/swiss-narrowly-vote-to-drop-gold-standard.html*.

19. Jeff Cox, "Passive Investing Automatically Tracking Indexes Now Controls Nearly Half the US Stock Market," CNBC, March 19, 2019, *https://www.cnbc.com/2019/03/19/passive-investing-now-controls-nearly-half-the-us-stock-market.html*.

20. Annie Lowrey, "Could Index Funds Be 'Worse Than Marxism'?," *The Atlantic*, April 5, 2021, *https://www.theatlantic.com/ideas/archive/2021/04/the-autopilot-economy/618497/*.

21. "Greeks Cannot Tap Cash in Safe Deposit Boxes Under Capital Controls," Reuters, July 5, 2015, *https://www.reuters.com/article/eurozone-greece-cash/greeks-cannot-tap-cash-in-safe-deposit-boxes-under-capital-controls-idUSA8N0XO00920150705*.

22. Michael Finnegan, "After FBI Seizure of Safe Deposit Boxes in Beverly Hills, Legal Challenges Mount," *Los Angeles Times*, April 8, 2021, *https://www.latimes.com/california/story/2021-04-08/seizure-beverly-hills-safe-deposit-boxes-lawsuits/*.

Chapter 8

1. Miguel Perez-Santalla, "A Big Source of Silver Bullion Demand Has Disappeared," BullionVault, June 21, 2013, *https://www.bullionvault.com/gold-news/silver-bullion-photographic-demand-062120133/*.

Chapter 9

1. "Make Fall Safety a Top Priority," National Safety Council, *https://www.nsc.org/work-safety/safety-topics/slips-trips-falls/*.

2. Ola Svenson, "Are We All Less Risky and More Skillful Than Our Fellow Drivers?," *Acta Psychologica* 47, no. 2 (February 1981): 143–148, *https://www.sciencedirect.com/science/article/abs/pii/0001691881900056*.

3. Isabel Wagner, "Road Accidents in the United States - Statistics & Facts," Statista.com, July 24, 2020, *https://www.statista.com/topics/3708/road-accidents-in-the-us/*.

4. "Intersection Safety," Federal Highway Administration, October 27, 2020, *https://highways.dot.gov/research/research-programs/safety/intersection-safety/*.

5. David L. Strayer, Frank A. Drews, and Dennis J. Crouch, "A Comparison of the Cell Phone Driver and the Drunk Driver," *Human Factors* 48, no. 2 (Summer 2006): 381–391, *https://pubmed.ncbi.nlm.nih.gov/16884056/*.

6. "Keep on Your Feet—Preventing Older Adult Falls," Centers for Disease Control and Prevention, December 16, 2020, *https://www.cdc.gov/injury/features/older-adult-falls/index.html*.

7. Pedro Carpintero et al., "Complications of Hip Fractures: A Review," *World Journal of Orthopedics* 5, no. 4 (September 18, 2014): 402–411, *https://www.ncbi.nlm.nih.gov/pmc/articles/PMC4133447/*.

8. "Top 10 Preventable Injuries," National Safety Council, *https://injuryfacts.nsc.org/all-injuries/deaths-by-demographics/top-10-preventable-injuries/data-details/*.

9. Beth Braverman, "The 10 Most Dangerous Jobs in America," CNBC, December 28, 2019, *https://www.cnbc.com/2019/12/27/the-10-most-dangerous-jobs-in-america-according-to-bls-data.html*.

10. Dennis Thompson, "More Than 1 in 3 Americans Prescribed Opioids in 2015," CNBC, August 1, 2017, *https://www.cbsnews.com/news/more-than-one-third-americans-prescribed-opioids-in-2015/*.

11. "Opioid Crisis Statistics," Department of Health and Human Services, February 12, 2021, *https://www.hhs.gov/opioids/about-the-epidemic/opioid-crisis-statistics/index.html*.

12. "How Opioid Addiction Occurs," Mayo Clinic, February 16, 2018, *https:// www.mayoclinic.org/diseases-conditions/prescription-drug-abuse/in-depth/ how-opioid-addiction-occurs/art-20360372/.*

13. William M. Lee, "Acetaminophen and the U.S. Acute Liver Failure Study Group: Lowering the Risks of Hepatic Failure," *Hepatology* 40, no. 1 (July 2004): 6–9, *https://pubmed.ncbi.nlm.nih.gov/15239078/.*

14. "War on Drugs," History.com, December 17, 2019, *https://www.history.com/ topics/crime/the-war-on-drugs/.*

15. "Impaired Driving: Get the Facts," Centers for Disease Control and Prevention, August 24, 2020, *https://www.cdc.gov/transportationsafety/ impaired_driving/impaired-drv_factsheet.html.*

16. "CHA Announces 2010 Craft Industry Statistics," Association for Creative Industries, April 6, 2011, *https://blogafci.wordpress.com/tag/ cha-u-s-attitude-usage-study/.*

17. Myron Levin, "Saws Cut Off 4,000 Fingers a Year. This Gadget Could Fix That," *Mother Jones*, May 16, 2013, *https://www.motherjones.com/politics/ 2013/05/table-saw-sawstop-safety-finger-cut/.*

18. Marty Ahrens and Radhika Maheshwari, "Home Structure Fires," National Fire Protection Association, November 2020, *https://www.nfpa.org/ News-and-Research/Data-research-and-tools/Building-and-Life-Safety/Home -Structure-Fires/.*

19. Dennis Thompson, "Are High-Tech Baby Monitors Worth It? Even Safe?," WebMD, August 21, 2018, *https://www.webmd.com/parenting/baby/ news/20180821/are-high-tech-baby-monitors-worth-it-even-safe/.*

Chapter 10

1. "The Anatomy of a Burglary," *Washington Post*, July 5, 2007, *https://www .washingtonpost.com/wp-srv/artsandliving/homeandgarden/features/2007/ burglary-070507/graphic.html.*

2. Kyle Iboshi, "We Asked 86 Burglars How They Broke into Homes," KGW, March 8, 2019, *https://www.ktvb.com/article/news/crime/we-asked -86-burglars-how-they-broke-into-homes/277-344333696/.*

3. Eugene Volokh, "Stand Your Ground (35 States) vs. Duty to Retreat (15 States)," *Reason*, December 21, 2020, *https://reason.com/volokh/2020/ 12/21/duty-to-retreat-35-states-vs-stand-your-ground-15-states/.*

4. Joe Keohane, "The Lost Art of Pickpocketing," *Slate*, February 23, 2012, *https://slate.com/culture/2011/02/the-lost-art-of-pickpocketing-why-has-the-crime -become-so-rare-in-the-united-states.html.*

5. Sophie Henrys, "Pickpocketing Statistics," Safes International Scotland, January 2, 2019, *https://www.safesinternational.com/items/Safes-International -News/pickpocketing-statistics/.*

Chapter 11

1. K.M.V. Narayan et al., "Effect of BMI on Lifetime Risk for Diabetes in the U.S.," *Diabetes Care* 30, no. 6 (June 2007): 1562–1566, *https://care .diabetesjournals.org/content/30/6/1562/*.

2. Megan Garber, "'If Sugar Is Fattening, How Come So Many Kids Are Thin?'," *The Atlantic,* June 19, 2015, *https://www.theatlantic.com/entertainment/ archive/2015/06/if-sugar-is-fattening-how-come-so-many-kids-are-thin/396380/*.

3. Rena R. Wing and Suzanne Phelan, "Long-Term Weight Loss Maintenance," *American Journal of Clinical Nutrition* 82, no. 1 (July 2005): 222S–225S, *https://academic.oup.com/ajcn/article/82/1/222S/4863393/*.

4. Rick Mendosa and John Walsh, "Satiety Index," DiabetesNet.com, *https://www.diabetesnet.com/food-diabetes/satiety-index/*.

5. Ann MacDonald, "Why Eating Slowly May Help You Feel Full Faster," *Harvard Health,* October 19, 2010, *https://www.health.harvard.edu/blog/ why-eating-slowly-may-help-you-feel-full-faster-20101019605/*.

Chapter 15

1. "Always Have a Disaster Kit Ready for Potential Disasters," Federal Emergency Management Agency, March 19, 2018, *https://www.fema.gov/ press-release/20210318/always-have-disaster-kit-ready-potential-disasters/*.

2. *Dietary Reference Intakes for Water, Potassium, Sodium, Chloride, and Sulfate,* National Academies Press, 2005, *https://www.nap.edu/catalog/10925/ dietary-reference-intakes-for-water-potassium-sodium-chloride-and-sulfate/*.

3. "In Iraq, a Mighty Thirst," *Washington Post,* April 8, 2003, *https://www .washingtonpost.com/archive/lifestyle/wellness/2003/04/08/in-iraq-a-mighty -thirst/0fb42cf3-a463-41d4-93da-7eff54db4c1d/*.

4. "How Much Water Do I Use at Home Each Day?," US Geological Survey, *https://www.usgs.gov/special-topic/water-science-school/science/water-qa-how -much-water-do-i-use-home-each-day/*.

5. "Bottled Water Regulation and the FDA," *Food Safety Magazine,* August 1, 2002, *https://www.food-safety.com/articles/4373-bottled-water-regulation-and -the-fda/*.

6. "Make Water Safe," Centers for Disease Control and Prevention, *https:// www.cdc.gov/healthywater/pdf/emergency/09_202278-b_make_water_safe_flyer _508.pdf*.

Chapter 16

1. Steven K. Ritter, "The Haber-Bosch Reaction: An Early Chemical Impact On Sustainability," *Chemical & Engineering News,* August 18, 2008, *https://cen.acs.org/articles/86/i33/Haber-Bosch-Reaction-Early-Chemical.html*.

2. Vaclav Smil, "China's Great Famine: 40 Years Later," *BMJ* 319, no. 7225 (December 18, 1999): 1619–1621, *https://www.ncbi.nlm.nih.gov/pmc/articles/PMC1127087/*.

3. John Otis, "Venezuela's Food Chain Is Breaking, and Millions Go Hungry," *Wall Street Journal*, October 1, 2020, *https://www.wsj.com/articles/venezuelas-food-chain-is-breaking-and-millions-go-hungry-11601544601/*.

4. "Foods That Can Cause Food Poisoning," Centers for Disease Control and Prevention, *https://www.cdc.gov/foodsafety/foods-linked-illness.html*.

5. "Protect Yourself from Botulism," Centers for Disease Control and Prevention, June 6, 2019, *https://www.cdc.gov/botulism/consumer.html*.

6. Toby Amidor, "How Long Is Canned Food Good for After the Expiration Date?," Food Network, August 2019, *https://www.foodnetwork.com/healthyeats/healthy-tips/2019/08/how-long-is-canned-food-good-after-expiration-date/*.

7. Nell Greenfieldboyce, "A Disturbing Twinkie That Has, So Far, Defied Science," National Public Radio, October 15, 2020, *https://www.npr.org/2020/10/15/923411578/a-disturbing-twinkie-that-has-so-far-defied-science/*.

Chapter 17

1. Mark Cartwright, "Medieval Hygiene," World History Encyclopedia, December 7, 2018, *https://www.worldhistory.org/Medieval_Hygiene/*.

2. Bernadeta Dadonaite, Hannah Ritchie, and Max Roser, "Diarrheal Diseases," Our World in Data, November 2019, *https://ourworldindata.org/diarrheal-diseases/*.

3. Gholamreza S. Roodsari, Farhad Zahedi, and Shahriar Zehtabchi, "The Risk of Wound Infection After Simple Hand Laceration," *World Journal of Emerging Medicine* 6, no. 1 (2015): 44–47, *https://www.ncbi.nlm.nih.gov/pmc/articles/PMC4369530/*.

4. Carolyn Crist, "CPR Survival Rates Are Lower Than Most People Think," Reuters, February 23, 2018, *https://www.reuters.com/article/us-health-cpr-expectations/cpr-survival-rates-are-lower-than-most-people-think-idUSKCN1G72SW/*.

Chapter 19

1. "The Amazing Disappearing Spare Tire," AAA.com, *https://www.aaa.com/autorepair/articles/the-amazing-disappearing-spare-tire/*.

Chapter 20

1. "Number of Participants in Camping in the United States from 2006 to 2019," Statista, December 2020, *https://www.statista.com/statistics/191224/participants-in-camping-in-the-us-since-2006/*.

2. Andrea Schmitz and Benji Jones, "Where the 11 Deadliest Animals in the US Live," *Business Insider,* August 12, 2019, *https://www.businessinsider.com/deadliest-animals-us-dont-include-sharks-crocodiles-dogs-cows-2019-8/.*

3. Bryan Hill, "Bear Defense: Shocking Truth About Bear Spray & Guns," Pistol Wizard, July 10, 2021, *https://pistolwizard.com/studies/bears.*

Chapter 21

1. Jacqueline Howard, "Masks May Actually Increase Your Coronavirus Risk If Worn Improperly, Surgeon General Warns," CNN, March 2, 2020, *https://www.cnn.com/2020/03/02/health/surgeon-general-coronavirus-masks-risk-trnd/index.html.*

2. Abrar A. Chughtai, Holly Seale, and C. Raina Macintyre, "Effectiveness of Cloth Masks for Protection Against Severe Acute Respiratory Syndrome Coronavirus 2," *Emerging Infectious Diseases* 26, no. 10 (October 2020), *https://wwwnc.cdc.gov/eid/article/26/10/20-0948_article/.*

3. "Guidance for Private Gatherings," California Department of Public Health, October 9, 2020, *https://www.cdph.ca.gov/Programs/CID/DCDC/Pages/COVID-19/CDPH-Guidance-for-the-Prevention-of-COVID-19-Transmission-for-Gatherings-10-09.aspx.*

4. "Executive Order 2020-42," Michigan.gov, April 9, 2020, *https://www.michigan.gov/whitmer/0,9309,7-387-90499_90705-525182--,00.html.*

5. Laylan Connelly, "California Surfer in Handcuffs After Enjoying Empty, Epic Waves," *Mercury News,* April 3, 2020, *https://www.mercurynews.com/2020/04/03/malibu-sup-surfer-in-handcuffs-after-enjoying-empty-epic-waves/.*

6. Spencer Ackerman, "US Police Given Billions from Homeland Security for 'Tactical' Equipment," *The Guardian,* August 20, 2014, *https://www.theguardian.com/world/2014/aug/20/police-billions-homeland-security-military-equipment/.*

7. "Elimination of Malaria in the United States (1947–1951)," Centers for Disease Control and Prevention, July 23, 2018, *https://www.cdc.gov/malaria/about/history/elimination_us.html.*

8. "Factbox: How Much Radiation Is Dangerous?," Reuters, March 15, 2011, *https://www.reuters.com/article/us-japan-quake-radiation/factbox-how-much-radiation-is-dangerous-idUSTRE72E14R20110315/.*

9. "Lifetime Risk of Developing or Dying from Cancer," Cancer.org, January 13, 2020, *https://www.cancer.org/cancer/cancer-basics/lifetime-probability-of-developing-or-dying-from-cancer.html.*

10. Xiang-Hua Ziong et al., "Production and Radioprotective Effects of Pyrroloquinoline Quinone," *International Journal of Molecular Sciences* 12, no. 12 (December 5, 2011): 8913–8923, *https://pubmed.ncbi.nlm.nih.gov/22272111/.*

11. Can Demirel et al., "Effect of *N*-acetylcysteine on Radiation-Induced Genotoxicity and Cytotoxicity in Rat Bone Marrow," *Journal of Radiation Research* 50, no. 1 (January 2009): 43–50, *https://academic.oup.com/jrr/article/50/1/43/921111.*

12. Saijun Fan et al., "DIM (3,3'-diindolylmethane) Confers Protection Against Ionizing Radiation by a Unique Mechanism," *Proceedings of the National Academy of Sciences of the United States of America* 110, no. 46 (October 14, 2013): 18,650–18,655, *https://pubmed.ncbi.nlm.nih.gov/24127581/.*

13. V. R. Narra, R. W. Howell, K. S. Sastry, and D. V. Rao, "Vitamin C as a Radioprotector Against Iodine-131 In Vivo," *Journal of Nuclear Medicine* 34, no. 4 (April 1993): 637–640, *https://pubmed.ncbi.nlm.nih.gov/8455081/.*

14. Alireza Shirazi, Ghazaleh Ghobadi, and Mahmoud Ghazi-Khansari, "A Radiobiological Review of Melatonin: A Novel Radioprotector," *Journal of Radiation Research* 48, no. 4 (July 2007): 263–272, *https://pubmed.ncbi.nlm.nih.gov/17641465/.*

Chapter 24

1. @MayorofLondon, "No Excuses: There Is Never a Reason to Carry a Knife," Twitter, April 8, 2018, *https://twitter.com/mayoroflondon/status/982906526334668800/.*

2. Samantha Raphelson, "How Often Do People Use Guns in Self-Defense?," NPR, April 13, 2018, *https://www.npr.org/2018/04/13/602143823/how-often-do-people-use-guns-in-self-defense/.*

3. "Suicide and Self-Harm Injury," Centers for Disease Control and Prevention, March 1, 2021, *https://www.cdc.gov/nchs/fastats/suicide.htm.*

4. "Suicide Rates by Country, 1950 to 2005," Our World in Data, *https://ourworldindata.org/grapher/suicide-rates-by-country?country=USA~SWE ~GBR~ITA~FRA~DEU~BEL~NLD~NZL~PRT~DNK~FIN~ESP~CHE ~GRC~AUT~IRL/.*

5. Holly Hedegaard, Sally C. Curtin, and Margaret Warner, "Suicide Mortality in the United States, 1999–2017," Centers for Disease Control and Prevention, November 2018, *https://www.cdc.gov/nchs/products/databriefs/db330.htm.*

6. "Suicide Rates," Organisation for Economic Co-operation and Development, 2019, *https://data.oecd.org/healthstat/suicide-rates.htm.*

Chapter 25

1. "Criminal Law: Self Defense," University of Minnesota Libraries, *https://open.lib.umn.edu/criminallaw/chapter/5-2-self-defense/.*

Chapter 26

1. "Q589: Are There Any Legal Self-Defence Products That I Can Buy?," Police National Legal Database, *https://www.askthe.police.uk/content/Q589.htm*.

2. "Concealed Weapons Permit Scandal Grows; Grand Jury Indicts Santa Clara County Undersheriff, Sheriff's Captain, Apple Security Executive," KPIX 5, November 23, 2020, *https://sanfrancisco.cbslocal.com/2020/11/23/concealed-weapons-permit-scandal-grows-grand-jury-indicts-santa-clara-county-undersheriff-sheriffs-captain-apple-executive/*.

3. "Three Former Police Officers and Former Assistant District Attorney Arrested in Connection with Gun License Bribery Scheme," US Department of Justice, April 25, 2017, *https://www.justice.gov/usao-sdny/pr/three-former-police-officers-and-former-assistant-district-attorney-arrested-connecton/*.

4. Philip J. Cook et al., "Constant Lethality of Gunshot Injuries from Firearm Assault: United States, 2003–2012," *American Journal of Public Health*, July 12, 2017, *https://ajph.aphapublications.org/doi/10.2105/AJPH.2017.303837*.

Chapter 27

1. Christopher Ingraham, "There Are More Guns Than People in the United States, According to a New Study of Global Firearm Ownership," *Washington Post*, June 19, 2018, *https://www.washingtonpost.com/news/wonk/wp/2018/06/19/there-are-more-guns-than-people-in-the-united-states-according-to-a-new-study-of-global-firearm-ownership/*.

2. Christopher M. Donner and Nicole Popovich, "Hitting (or Missing) the Mark: An Examination of Police Shooting Accuracy in Officer-Involved Shooting Incidents," *Policing: An International Journal* 42, no. 3 (May 23, 2019), *https://www.emerald.com/insight/content/doi/10.1108/PIJPSM-05-2018-0060/full/html/*.

INDEX

employment, 91–93
encephalitis lethargica, 25
Energizer Ultimate batteries, 155
entertainment, 191–192
epinephrine inhalers, 150
Epsilon Data Management, 110
Equifax, 110
equities, 79–81
escheatment, 77
eugenics, 37
eugenol, 151
evacuation, 165–171
exercise, 117–118
expenses, 51–52
Experian, 110
Expose, 176
extinction, 34
extraterrestrial life, 43
extreme weather, 18, 156–158, 168

F

Facebook, 109, 110, 155
fall injuries, 98–99
false vacuum decay, 35
Family Radio Service (FRS), 186–187
farming, 137
Federal Emergency Management
        Agency (FEMA), 19, 132
fever, 150
fiat money, 64–65
fiction, 29–30
fighting, 113, 206
financial problems, 10–11
firearms, 196–197, 211–219
fires
        Butte fire complex, 18
        house fires, 11, 18, 103–104
        wildfires, 18, 44, 124
firewood, 158, 170
first aid, 149–152
fitness, 115–118
fixed-blade knives, 170
flashlights, 154–155
flat tires, 163
floods, 19, 147–148
floss, 151
flu, 25
fluticasone propionate, 150

FMJ (full metal jacket) bullets, 217
food-borne illness, 141–142
food preparation, 158
food security, 137–144
foraging, 168–169
foreclosures, 10–11
foreign currencies, 78–79
Forgey, William W., 152
Forster, E. M., 29–30
Fortune 500, 109
fractional-reserve banks, 64–65
fraud, 106–108
freeze-dried meals, 143–144
fridges, 152–153
FRS (Family Radio Service), 186–187
fuel, 156
Fukushima, 20
Fukuyama, Francis, 21
full metal jacket (FMJ) bullets, 217
funds, 49–55

G

games, 191–192
garden crops, 144
Garmin inReach, 183
gas masks, 177
gasoline, 156
Gattaca, 37
Geiger counters, 179
Generac generators, 156
General Data Protection Regulation
        (GDPR), 111
General Mobile Radio Service
        (GMRS), 187
generators, 155–156
geomagnetic poles, 35
Glock 43, 214
goodwill, 191–192
Google, 110
goTenna, 182
Graeber, David, 59
Graff, Garrett M., 40
Graham, Benjamin, 80
Great Depression, 22
Great Filter, 43
Gresham's law, 62
groceries, 51
gun regulations, 196, 206